A JUDGE IN MADRAS

CAROLINE KEEN

A Judge in Madras

Sir Sidney Wadsworth and the Indian Civil Service, 1913–1947

HURST & COMPANY, LONDON

First published in the United Kingdom in 2020 by
C. Hurst & Co. (Publishers) Ltd.,
41 Great Russell Street, London, WC1B 3PL

Printed in Great Britain by Bell and Bain Ltd, Glasgow

Distributed in the United States, Canada and Latin America by
Oxford University Press, 198 Madison Avenue, New York, NY 10016,
United States of America.

A Cataloguing-in-Publication data record for this book
is available from the British Library.

ISBN: 9781787383241

This book is printed using paper from registered sustainable
and managed sources.

www.hurstpublishers.com

CONTENTS

AUTHOR'S PREFACE

The core of the book is obviously the Wadsworth memoirs which, due to Sidney's ability to bring people and places to life, provided a fine base. I have added biographical details of some of the people with whom he worked in Madras and, as a backdrop to his career, included a broad sweep of the highly significant events which were occurring across India as a prologue to independence. I have also added excerpts from the private papers of other members of the Indian Civil Service based in Madras during the first half of the twentieth century to give some different perspectives on life in the province. All otherwise unattributed quotations are drawn from Sidney's memoirs.

It has been a great pleasure to follow Sidney's Indian progression. I was blessed with the most interesting and entertaining subject, and I am very grateful to Simon and Tim for giving me the opportunity to explore a major part of their grandfather's life.

Caroline Keen, *August 2019*

CENTRAL PROVINCES
N
0
75
miles
HYDERABAD
BOMBAY
PROVINCE
Godaveri
District
Rajamundry
Cocanada
Antarvedi
Eastern Ghats
Buckingham Canal
Gudur
Pulicat Lake
Venkatagiri
Sriharikota Island
South
Kanara
Madanapalle
Mysore
Chittoor
MADRAS
Bangalore
Vellore
Eastern Ghats
COORG
Mysore
Chingleput
Western Ghats
Ootacamund
Nilgiri
Hills
PUDUKKOTTAI
Kodaikanal
Indian Ocean
Cochin
Palni
Hills
Madura
Travancore
CEYLON
© S.Ballard (2019)

INTRODUCTION

In 1947, my grandfather Sir Sidney Wadsworth retired from his position as a High Court Judge in Madras, India. Along with many members of the former Indian Civil Service (ICS) who retired at or around Indian independence, he retired to the UK, and in his particular case, to the Isle of Man, where the parents of his wife Lady (Olive) Wadsworth had lived. During the first long winter he spent in retirement he hand-wrote his lengthy (375-page) memoirs of his time in India, and had them typed and annotated. He evidently decided that there was limited demand at that time for his memoirs in book form (there were obviously many retirees from the ICS who had similar ideas!). So at some point he consigned the manuscript to the bottom of the Library of the Centre of South Asian Studies at Cambridge University, his alma mater.

Fast-forward sixty-three years to 2009, and I was in the process of retiring from full-time employment. One day I idly Googled the name 'Sir Sidney Wadsworth', and much to my surprise up pops a record of the manuscript; I was able to obtain copies, and promptly sent them to his two daughters, to my mother (my father, Robert, was Sidney and Olive's only son and died in 1998), and to my brother Tim. Much to my surprise, none had any idea that my grandfather had written the manuscript.

Several years passed during which I showed the manuscript to acquaintances with academic backgrounds and with an interest in Indian history, and most found the manuscript to be fascinating. I also read it, but found that my lack of knowledge of Indian history made the manuscript seem to lack context. I believed that the manuscript could be brought to life by somebody who could provide the social, geographic, and political background of Sir Sidney's experiences in India.

In the meantime I wrote a book (on investing, with nothing to do with India or history!), and had it published. This experience led me to believe that it was a realistic objective to publish Sir Sidney's manuscript if it could be edited and put into its historical context. My work on my own book, various consulting projects and other assignments, together with an extensive travel schedule, kept me busy and so the manuscript continued to languish.

Taking up the project again in 2012, I made contact with Dr Caroline Keen. Dr Keen and her husband Nigel are some of the oldest friends of my wife and I, and we regularly keep in touch with them on our visits to the UK. As a result, I was familiar with Dr Keen's predominant field of study of Indian history during the British colonial period. Dr Keen was finishing work on two books, both now published, but took up the project to write what is effectively a history of Sir Sidney's career in the context of the Madras Presidency in the thirty-five years prior to Indian independence.

Sir Sidney Wadsworth

My grandfather Sidney Wadsworth was the eldest son of a Methodist minister, the Reverend Henry Wadsworth (1855–1939) of Loughborough (Leicestershire) and Sheffield (Yorkshire), England. Henry was the son of a silk manufacturer, John Wadsworth (1829–92), who was also Mayor of Macclesfield (Cheshire), and of Ann Wright (died 1903).

Rev. Henry and his wife Alice Nelstrop (died 1903) had two daughters (Mary and Elsie) and three sons (Sidney, Harry, and Frank). Sidney, who was born in 1888, went to Loughborough Grammar School. The school remains independent and was founded in 1495.

Sidney then went to the Sorbonne in Paris to learn French before going to Jesus College Cambridge in 1908 as the Loughborough Grammar School scholar, where he studied classics. Presumably he did well, as he was eligible to study for and sit for the Indian Civil Service

(ICS) exams, which he passed, and subsequently studied Tamil, before heading to Madras, India in 1913 to take up his position with the ICS in the administrative branch.

In 1916 he married Olive Florence Clegg (1895–1962); Olive was the daughter of Sir Robert and Lady Clegg, also of the ICS in Madras. We know that Sir Robert (1862–1925) was a Balliol (Oxford) scholar, who was knighted in 1917 (KCIE), and became First Member of the Board of Revenue of Madras and Additional Member of the Council of the Governor for Making Laws and Regulations. For health reasons, he retired early from the ICS and moved to the Isle of Man where he died at a relatively young age. It seems fairly evident that the match was a good one: Olive, the daughter of one of the leading lights of the Madras ICS, marrying Sidney, who had good prospects.

Dr Keen takes up the story of Sir Sidney's professional life in India beginning in 1913. In the mid-1920s Sidney decided that he would have better prospects of advancement if he transferred from the administrative branch of the ICS to the judicial branch. This required that he qualify as a lawyer in Britain (as a barrister in the British system), by being 'called to the bar', which he accomplished by 1931 after attending the requisite number of dinners at the Middle Temple, and after studying during his six-month leave in Britain in 1924. Despite not yet being technically qualified as a barrister he became a district court judge in 1926 and subsequently a high court judge in Madras.

On a personal level he had three children, my father Robert (1917–98), Elsie (b. 1919) and Margaret (1921–2016). As beset all European families of that time who could afford to make the choice, the question then arose of whether to educate the children in the UK (a month's sea journey away) or to educate them in India, and so in 1924 my grandmother began a two-centred life, spending six months of each year in India and the balance in England (and on the long sea voyage). The three children (aged 7, 5 and 3) came to England with her for Robert to attend prep school and then public school (Marlborough College), spending the vacations with an uncle and aunt in Sheffield, and the summers with his mother and grandmother in the Isle of Man. Robert graduated from Peterhouse, Cambridge in 1938, with a good degree in economics and the determination to spend his career in the UK so as not to separate his family. He saw his father only when he was on home leave from India (every few years), and so grew up barely knowing him.

My father and mother (Suzette Comport, 1921–2016) married in 1941, and lived in Birmingham, England. My father spent his entire working career at Cadbury's, becoming a board director, retiring in 1979, and interestingly, never returned to India.

My grandfather retired from the ICS in 1947 aged 58. He was knighted (Knight Bachelor) in the year before he retired. In the same year, my grandmother Olive was awarded the MBE for her work with injured service personnel in India during World War II. They retired to the Isle of Man, presumably because they (or at least my grandmother) had been used to spending time there and because of favourable personal tax rates.

As a boy (I was born in 1947, the year of my grandfather's retirement) I saw my grandparents relatively infrequently. As mentioned before, they and my father were not close, mainly due to the rare occasions on which they saw one another, and also because of the travel limitations in those days between Birmingham and the Isle of Man. I remember a visit in 1955, flying on a DC3 from Birmingham airport to the Isle of Man during the Isle of Man TT (motorbike) races. Both my grandparents were enthusiastic gardeners, and my grandfather (with his sharp mind and classical education) would complete the *Times* crossword puzzle in a few minutes daily. Meanwhile, in England, we were all busy living our lives, and ultimately my wife and I moved to the USA in 1971.

My father also had relatively little contact with his two sisters. They left England for India with my grandmother in the early days of the war, having an adventurous trip across Europe. The older, Elsie, married and lived in Cochin in India, and retired with her husband to live in Tunbridge Wells, England. In their retirement, my parents would occasionally visit her and her husband. My other aunt, Margaret, married a Canadian at the end of World War II and went to live near Vancouver, Canada, and subsequently moved to be near to her daughter in Melbourne, Australia.

My grandparents continued to live a relatively quiet life in the Isle of Man until my grandmother died in 1962, and my grandfather lived on alone, looked after by their housekeeper until she died. For a brief period he moved to live with my father's sister Elsie, and was able to attend the wedding of my wife and I in 1971 before he died in 1976.

My older brother Tim, his wife Wendy and their daughter Gemma travelled to South India in December 2004 and retraced some of my grandfather's steps. They had a most interesting time, seeing Sidney and Olive's 1916 marriage certificate in the Anglican Cathedral in Chennai (where one of the witnesses was Lord Willingdon, then the Governor of Madras). They also saw Sidney's official residence, which is now the British High Commission. My wife and I have not made the trip, and my interest was purely based on a curiosity about my grandfather's life after I happened upon the manuscript.

The story is an amazing snapshot of history and the daily life of administering the Indian Empire, and how my grandfather, who appears to have been an eminently sensible and moderate individual with a good sense of humour, was able to adapt to the changes rolling through the subcontinent. A reading of the manuscript gives the impression that he was trying to do his best for India, recognising the opportunities and shortcomings of the country, its people, and the system of that time. He seems to have personified the best of the ICS, emphasising that perhaps the reason that the Indian empire lasted as long as it did was due to people like him who did what they could to balance the requirements of their paymasters in London with the best interests of the Indian people.

Simon Wadsworth, Memphis, Tennessee, *August 2019*

SIR SIDNEY WADSWORTH TIMELINE

1888	Born 21 December, son of Rev. Henry Wadsworth, Methodist Minister of Loughborough and Sheffield
1899–1906 (Est)	Loughborough Grammar School
1907–8	Sorbonne, Paris
1908–11	Jesus College, Cambridge (Loughborough Grammar School Scholar)
1911–12	Study for Civil Service exams; accepted into Indian Civil Service
1912–13	Studies Tamil (in Cambridge)
1913	Indian Civil Service; arrives in Madras
1913–14	Sub-Collector, Vellore
1914–15	Assistant cable censor, Madras
1916	Marries Florence Olive Clegg, daughter of Sir Robert Clegg, ICS
1916–17	Sub-Collector, Gudur
1917	Robert born
1918–19	Undersecretary to Board of Revenue, Madras
1919	Elsie born
1920–1	Temporary assignments as assistant to the Governor of Madras and then to the Duke of Connaught
1921–4	Sub-Collector, Madanapalle
1921	Temporary assignment as Additional District Magistrate, Godaveri
1921	Margaret born

1924	Secretary, Board of Revenue, Madras
1924	Six months' leave to London; joins Middle Temple
1925	Registrar of the High Court, Madras
1926–8	District Judge, Chingleput
1929–33	District Judge, Madura
1934–5	District Judge, Chittoor and Bangalore
1935–47	High Court, Madras
1946	Knight Bachelor
1946	Olive awarded MBE
1947	Retires to Isle of Man, UK; writes his memoirs
1947	Indian independence
1962	Olive dies
1976	Dies 2 March, aged 87, at the home of his daughter Elsie

LIST OF ILLUSTRATIONS

1

THE HISTORY OF MADRAS

The city in which Sidney Wadsworth started and ended his Indian career is a place which marks the very earliest involvement of Britain in the subcontinent. About four hundred years ago Madras, under the name of Madraspatnam, was a tiny rural village on the Coromandel Coast, the southeastern coastal region of India which lies between the Eastern Ghats range and the Bay of Bengal.[1] The village was located in the region referred to by Europeans as the Carnatic. The town of Arcot was the capital of the area and its ruler, the Nawab of the Carnatic, was also referred to as the Nawab of Arcot. Scattered about in the neighbourhood of Madraspatnam were other villages, such as Egmore, Vepery and Triplicane, which were eventually to become the crowded districts of the great city of Madras. Apart from Arcot there was one other small town in the area, the Portuguese settlement of Mylapore, which had been established as the viceroyalty of São Tomé de Meliapore in 1523 and whose tall church façades provided a landmark for the Portuguese ships that occasionally cast anchor there.

By 1639 the Portuguese had been in India for nearly 150 years and their influence was waning with the arrival of the Dutch and, in 1600, the British employees of the East India Company. The first British settlement in India was established in 1611 at Masulipatam, about 300 miles to the north of Madraspatnam. Having set up a main agency which conducted a considerable amount of business, the East India

Company formed a fortified sub-agency at Armegon, near Nellore on the coast to the south of Masulipatam. The prime concern of the agencies was arriving at good bargains on the Company's behalf; getting the best prices for European broadcloths and brocades, and buying Indian muslins, calico and natural produce as cheaply as possible for export to London where they were sold at a large profit. However, local officials exacted ruinous payments from the British, and Francis Day, the Company's representative at Armegon, was instructed to find a suitable site for a new settlement.[2]

At that time the Coromandel Coast was under the control of the Raja of Chandragiri-Vellore. Under the raja, local chiefs or governors known as nayaks ruled over individual districts. Damarla Venkatadri Mayakudu, the Nayak of Wandiwash, who ruled the section of the region from Pulicat (thirty-seven miles north of Madraspatnam) to the Portuguese settlement of Mylapore, was persuaded in 1639 to lease a sandy strip of land lying between the Cooum and Egmore rivers to the East India Company. The raja was succeeded by his nephew in 1642, after which a new grant was issued. The grant affected the legal and civic development of the English settlement by allowing the British to administer English common law amongst the settlers and civil law between the settlers and the other European, Jewish, Armenian, Muslim and Hindu communities with whom the Company dealt. Furthermore, it expanded Company property by attaching an additional piece of land known as the Narimedu, or jackal ground, to the west of the village of Madraspatnam.

When the tract of land at Madraspatnam had been formally acquired in February 1640, the English colony at Armegon was shipped down the coast. With Andrew Cogan at the head, assisted by Day and another chief official, it included some three or four British 'writers', a gunner, a surgeon, a garrison of some twenty-five British soldiers under a lieutenant and a sergeant, a number of English carpenters, blacksmiths and coopers, and a small staff of English servants for kitchen and general work. In the course of a few months a number of buildings were fit for occupation. The main building in the middle of the fort was the 'factory' and it was here that the Company's chief officials, who were called 'factors' (agents), assisted by writers and apprentices, transacted the Company's business, and were also given accommodation. In the early days of Madras all the principal employees of the Company, from the governor to the most junior apprentice, lived together. Their bedrooms were in the same house and they had their meals at the same table. Included among the other buildings were warehouses for Company goods and also barrack-like residences for the Company's subordinate British employees, civil and military, according to their rank. From the beginning the settlement was called Fort St George, but it was several years before the buildings were surrounded by a high, fortified wall with cannons positioned on all sides of the bastioned rampart.[3]

At its start Fort St George was extremely small. Its external length parallel with the seashore was only 108 yards and its depth 100 yards, and due to the limitations a town soon sprang up outside the wall. The personal needs of the numerous settlers had to be supplied and purveyors, bazaar traders and workmen made themselves readily available. The requirements of the mercantile business were even greater. The Company's agents wanted not only native employees in their office (shroffs (cashiers), dubashes (interpreters), peons (orderlies), clerks and porters) but they also required wholesale buyers of the cloth and other articles that they imported from England and merchants who could supply them with large quantities of the Indian wares that the Company exported to England. Ten years after the acquisition of Madras the population of the external town was estimated at about 15,000. The Fort itself had to be enlarged since the growth of Company business demanded more factors and writers from England and more warehouses for the increasing amount of goods.

In time Indian and other immigrants flocked to settle down beneath the Company umbrella. The town that grew up was divided into two sections, 'the White Town' and 'the Black Town'. The inhabitants of White Town included any British settlers not in Company service of whose presence the Company approved, also all approved Portuguese and Eurasian immigrants from Mylapore and a certain number of Indian Christians. Black Town was the Asiatic settlement and the great majority of the original Indian settlers were not Tamils (comprising the majority of the population in the area) but Telegus, written down as 'Gentoos' in Company records.[4] The original Black Town covered the ground that was to become the site of the Law College and the High

Court and was at first without fortification, but to avoid the perils of adventurous marauders the town was enclosed by a mud wall, and in the reign of Queen Anne (1702–14) a masonry wall was erected. Meanwhile, numerous houses and streets had sprung up outside the wall on the site of the district of Georgetown which still existed in Sidney's day.[5]

The defences of the fort were put to the test some fifty years after its foundation when the stronghold was besieged for eight months by forces of the Sultan of Golconda. Later, a Dutch force, supported by Muslim cavalry, occupied Triplicane village in order to capture the French port of San Thome; however, the Dutch expressed little interest in Fort St George. During the reign of Queen Anne, Daud Khan, the Nawab of the Carnatic, marched upon Madras but was 'mollified with luxurious entertainment'. Inviting himself and his diwan (first minister) to dinner with the governor and councillors in the Fort, he was received with 'imposing honours' and was feasted in the Council Chamber at a magnificent banquet. The Company minutes related that after dinner he was 'diverted with the dancing wenches' and finally became 'very Drunk'. In his sober moments, however, he had been slyly measuring the Company's strength and six months later came back with a superior force and blockaded Madras for three months. The nawab plundered as much as was possible and on one occasion his spoil included '40 ox loads of the Company's cloth'. Company trade was entirely suspended and provisions in Madras were extremely scarce until the Council, fearing the wrath of the Directors in England at the loss of trade, came to terms.[6]

In 1746 Fort St George was under a considerably more powerful attack when, during the War of the Austrian Succession, a squadron of French ships blockaded the coast. At the end of an unhappy seven days the garrison capitulated, the French marched into the fort and all the English residents, both civil and military, including the Governor, Members of Council and Robert Clive,[7] who was then a young clerk, were sent to Pondicherry as prisoners of war. For nearly three years the French flag flew over the fort until, in accordance with the Treaty of Aix-la-Chapelle made between the combatants in Europe, Madras was restored to the Company. During their occupation the French made great changes, aware that a weak-walled native town lying against the northern wall of Fort St George was a serious danger. The houses offered convenient cover for enemies attacking the fort, and any disaffected townsman was in a position to give the assailants valuable help. The French governor, intent upon the deliberate destruction of Black Town, first destroyed the town wall and, for a distance of 400 yards from the northern wall of the fort, demolished every house. The area that in Sidney's day housed the Wireless Telegraph Station and the grounds of the High Court became an open space. When the English returned to the fort it was decided that the open space should remain and the development of a new Black Town began. It continued to be called Black Town until the visit of the Prince of Wales (later George V) to Madras in 1906, when it was formerly renamed Georgetown, ostensibly in the Prince's honour but in reality to meet the wishes of a number of the residents who considered the name of their locality to be objectionable.

In the light of the success of the French attack the defences of Fort St George were upgraded, proving invaluable when in 1758 a large French army under Count Lally besieged the Fort again, and after sixty-seven days of persistent effort was forced to beat a sudden retreat. However, although the directors of the Company sanctioned the construction of a wall around the new Black Town, the delay in putting the plans into action resulted in a humiliating confrontation between the Company and Tipu, the son of Haidar Ali, Sultan of Mysore, in 1769, when an imminent attack was only forestalled by a hurried treaty between the two parties, favouring the latter. In the aftermath a wall was deemed essential and within a year the work was almost finished. In 1780 Haidar Ali's cavalry raided San Thome and Triplicane, however, did not attempt to attack the newly fortified Black Town.[8]

On several occasions the representatives of various dynasties previously established in the Madras area made grants of additional land to the Company. Twenty years after the acquisition of Madras the village of Triplicane was granted by the representative of the Muslim Sultan of Golconda for an annual rent of Rs. 175, which ceased to be paid when in 1688 the state of Golconda was annexed by the Mughals and the sultan taken prisoner. Later, following a petition by the Governor of the Company, Elihu Yale,[9] to the Mughal Emperor, Aurangzeb, the Company received a free grant of Thandiarpet, Pursewaukam and

Egmore. In the reign of Aurangzeb's son, Bahadur Shah I, the village of Nungumbaukam (by Sidney's time the principal residential district of Europeans in Madras) was granted to the Company. The British were also intent upon acquiring the village of Vepery, which lay between Pursewaukam and Egmore, yet several attempts on the part of Governor Yale were unsuccessful and it was only in 1742 that Vepery was acquired from the ruler of Arcot, at the time a youth residing in one of the large houses of Black Town where he was feted by the British. The waning Portuguese settlement of São Tomé (now San Thome) was acquired in 1749 from Muhammed Ali Khan Wala-jah, the current Nawab of Arcot, in return for an undertaking to help him with men and money, and the nawab, who had many enemies in his capital in Arcot, sought and obtained permission from the governor of Madras to build a palace upon private land in an area of Madras named Chepauk.[10]

The career of Wala-jah's son and successor, Ghulam Hussaini Umdat-ul-Umara, was far from commendable and, after Tipu Sultan was killed by Company forces in defence of his capital at Mysore in 1799, it emerged that the nawab had been guilty of treasonable communication with the Mysore ruler. It was resolved that the Company should assume control of the Carnatic, and upon the death of Umdat-ul-Umara British troops were sent to occupy Chepauk Palace. In 1855 the last remaining nawab died without issue. The declared policy of Lord Dalhousie, Governor-General of India at the time, was that if the ruler of any native state died without heir, his dominions should formally lapse to the Company. Under this policy the Carnatic now became a formal part of British territory and the dynasty of the Nawabs of Arcot came to an end. Chepauk Palace was acquired by the Company and was eventually turned into government offices. However, after the 1857 Indian Mutiny the government of India, aware of the need to respect Muslim feeling, recognised the succession of the nearest relative of the late nawab and obtained for him the hereditary title of Amir-i-Arcot, or Prince of Arcot, a title higher than that of nawab.[11]

Madras remained wholly undisturbed by the Mutiny, partly due to the fact that the sepoys of the Madras Army were less attentive to their religious prejudices than their brothers in the upper Gangetic plains and central India.[12] However, the province, as it had become under the restructuring of William Pitt's India Act of 1784,[13] was undoubtedly affected by the aftermath of the uprising, during which Britain's relationship with the subcontinent was substantially restructured. The 1858 Government of India Act brought about the demise of the East India Company, moving its power into the hands of the Crown. The governor-general was given the title of viceroy by royal proclamation, but carried out the same duties as before. However, in order to stress the authority of the British government in London, a secretary of state for India was appointed and a council of fifteen provided to advise him.[14] Under the Indian Councils Act of 1861, legislative powers were given to the councils of Bombay and Madras, which, although promising little control at the start, allowed the councils to be used later as vehicles for democratic experiment and progress.

After the Mutiny the British in India began the construction of a complex, multi-layered but fundamentally conservative system of government, operating as an efficient and on the whole fair means of administering India. British rule appeared to be securely established during the latter part of Queen Victoria's reign, and the Indian Civil Service and the Indian Army the twin pillars which upheld its structure. At the pinnacle of the administrative system was the viceroy, who usually held office for four or five years. Under him were the governors of the different provinces, such as Madras, and under the governors were the civil servants, law officers, police chiefs and various other ranks. During British rule the key administrative unit was the district, and British India was divided into some 250 districts. The average size of a district was 4,430 square miles, however, in Madras the districts were larger. Several were more than 12,000 square miles in size (greater than Belgium) while the 17,000 square miles of Vizagapatam in the Eastern Ghats made it larger than Denmark and more than twice the size of Wales. The force which moulded the various districts into uniformity was the Secretariat, the central bureau of each province, which received the many reports from each area, recorded them for future reference and issued orders for the regulation of administrative details. Of the 1,000 odd top-level positions of the Indian Civil Service, almost all were held by the British, typically with an Oxbridge degree.

The great majority of these bright young men espoused the ideals of empire and service while displaying a strong commitment to India, its people and its progress. Collectively the ICS was conservative, mirroring in general its members' origins and backgrounds, even if individually those members remained strong-minded, producing rivalries, differences, arguments, envy and even hatred.[15]

At the head of each district was the collector and district magistrate whose duties were many and various. He was a magistrate, a judge in civil as well as criminal matters, a collector of revenues imperial and local, and charged with the management or supervision of jails, police, education, municipalities, roads, public buildings, sanitation and dispensaries, forests, canals and agriculture. The collector was to a great extent his own master, only answering to the appropriate department of the provincial Secretariat when obliged to do so, and free to initiate any reforms or improvements which he considered necessary. Under the collector were Indian Civil Service sub-collectors and magistrates and a small number of native deputy collectors from the Provincial Civil Service.[16] Beneath these officers in a large district was an extensive office divided into a dozen or so departments dealing with such matters as revenue, agriculture and education. These departments each had their head clerks and a bevy of record-keepers and other officials (by 1890 some 60,000 Indians had matriculated, chiefly in the liberal arts or law, and about a third entered public administration). At the bottom of the hierarchy were scores, sometimes hundreds, of messengers and orderlies, sweepers and water carriers.[17] The everyday preoccupation of the Raj was to enforce law and order, to attempt to improve public health and public education, to advance irrigation schemes, and to deal with huge problems such as famine control[18] and agricultural efficiency. The law administered by the British Indian courts, with which Sidney was to become intimately acquainted, consisted partly of statutes of the British Parliament, partly of laws of the Indian legislatures, partly of Hindu and Muslim domestic laws and laws of inheritance, and partly of customary law affecting particular castes and races. At the head of the administration of justice in Madras was the High Court, which was supreme both in civil and criminal business.

Recollecting his arrival in Madras in 1913 as a fledgling member of the Indian Civil Service, Sidney Wadsworth observed that the British Empire was 'still one of the immutable facts of life … untrammelled by the impact of world events, of orderly, unhurried progress and constitutional stability'. Nevertheless, in many areas the India which awaited him was undeniably flexing its muscles in an effort to loosen the ties of British imperial rule. By the early twentieth century organised political movements were challenging the smooth running of the administration and Madras could claim credit for a healthy number of the early proponents of nationalist activity. Of the 72 delegates who participated in the first session of the Indian National Congress at Bombay in 1885, twenty-two were from Madras. The third session of the Indian National Congress was held in Madras in 1889 and proved a huge success, attended by 362 delegates from the province. Subsequent sessions were held in Madras in 1894, 1898 and 1903. However, the Congress, founded in 1885, had after eighteen years outlived its original purpose as a platform for benign discussion, and the high-handed and abrasive nature of the viceroyalty of Lord Curzon, who resigned in 1905, helped to change it into a more radical and effective organisation. In particular, Curzon's abortive attempt to bring about the partition of the ancient province of Bengal aroused violent hostility, not only among the politically astute members of Bengali society, but also among nationalist leaders throughout the subcontinent. The foundation of the Muslim League in 1906 was another warning that the post-Mutiny policy, based upon administrative conservatism and minor concessions to Indian constitutional progress (such as the 1892 Indian Councils Act), had proved wanting.

The strength of Indian reaction to the 1905 partition of Bengal, and the split in 1908 between Congress 'moderates' and 'extremists', encouraged the Liberal government in Britain to introduce the Morley-Minto reforms of 1908–09 (named after John Morley, the Liberal Secretary of State for India and the Conservative Viceroy of India, the Earl of Minto). The resulting 1909 Indian Councils Act was an Act of Parliament of the United Kingdom that brought about a limited increase in the involvement of Indians in the governance of British India. It modestly extended the franchise, but quite substantially increased the numbers of elected and nominated Indians on the provincial and central legislative councils of the Raj. As a result, a diluted form of representative government was grafted on to the existing paternal bureaucracy, and observers were already seriously discussing the possibility that the British might leave India, although it was impossible to predict when or under what circumstances. Following the reforms, a number of terrorist outrages, an irresponsible and hostile popular press and the emergence of a body of nationalists who wished to wrest power violently from the British had by 1913 contributed to the impression that the Raj was more unsafe than at any time since the Mutiny. It is hard to know quite how widely this impression was circulated within Britain. Sidney does not appear to have harboured any apprehension at taking up his new post, although in the course of studying for the Indian Civil Service examination[19] he must have been exposed to details of current events in India. It is possible that as Madras was seen as something of a backwater he came to the conclusion that a potentially troublesome situation was unlikely to await him. However, by 1900 the Raj was less than fifty years from total disintegration and the India in which Sidney Wadsworth lived and worked was to prove a place of radical change.

2

MADRAS 1913

At the time of Sidney's arrival in Madras in 1913, the presidencies of British India had evolved into eight provinces that were administered either by a governor or a lieutenant-governor: Assam, Bengal, Bombay, Burma, Central Provinces, Madras, Punjab and United Provinces. For the annual recruits to the Indian Civil Service the most popular destinations were the northwest and the Punjab, with their frontier life and the paternalist policies of a government with grand schemes for building canals and improving agriculture. The least popular destination was Madras. W. O. Horne, later Chief Secretary, was allocated to Madras in 1882 because he was the second lowest candidate in the entire examination ranking list, having no choice in his posting.[1] However, at the end of the nineteenth century the regularity with which the southern presidency received the least promising candidates eventually persuaded the India Office to assign probationers at its discretion to ensure that Madras would obtain a few of the better entrants. It was not immediately clear why Madras had become so undesirable, although in its development it had been left behind by Calcutta and Bombay and was geographically far from both. The city itself boasted an attractive mixture of Greek Classical and Victorian Indo-Saracenic architecture,[2] the hill stations of Ootacamund and Kodaikanal were highly agreeable, and the landscape was an idyllic combination of lagoons, palms and paddy fields with red soil and white coasts. Moreover, the province could be administered in a leisurely manner without much difficulty and its people were less subversive than the Bengalis and less violent than the martial races of the northwest. However, Madras also had its disadvantages. The shooting was usually bad, the climate always enervating and the death rate for civilians was higher than average. For an ambitious official its chief drawback was its position as an administrative backwater from which he was unlikely to be plucked and awarded a post in the central government at Calcutta.

One of the governors of Madras admitted that the province had certain officials who were 'eccentrics' and 'bad bargains'. In addition, the Secretariat gained the reputation of being the most dilatory in India, and district officers were demonstrably less aware of what was going on in their districts than their colleagues further north.[3] In his study of the ICS, Philip Woodruff observed that 'To the last, the Government of Madras preserved a separatism of their own and were inclined to regard the Government of India as a rather vulgar late-18th century innovation'[4] to be treated with considerable suspicion. Contributing to this air of superiority was the fact that, due to its size, a Madras district demanded the same or greater responsibility than several divisions in a province like Bengal, needing 'a cross between the Governor of a medium-sized colony, and a senior Whitehall civil servant'.[5] Sir Christopher Hughes Masterman, a member of the Madras Civil Service from 1914 to 1947, agreed that the district collector in Madras wielded a remarkable amount of power as head of his allotted territory, responsible not only for the collection of land revenue and the duties of the chief magistrate, who 'though he may not try many cases himself, has to review the judgments and sentences of all the subordinate magistrates in the district, but is also head of all the other departments, i.e. the police, the Public Works Department, the Forest Department and the Excise Department.'[6] In the 1930s, a fellow Madras civilian Humphrey Trevelyan noted that Indians, 'brought up on liberal theories about the separation of powers', criticised the system, but it seemed to work well. Magistrates did not unduly favour the police, but they did not forget that they, with the police, were responsible for keeping the peace, and violence was seldom far below the surface in the Indian countryside with its endless civil disputes over family property and inheritance.[7]

Differing from his counterpart in the Gangetic plain or the Punjab, the Madras civil servant was not limited to cold weather touring, but obliged to tour every month of the year; for a minimum of thirteen days a month in the case of a sub-collector and ten days in the case of a collector. In addition, the Madras collector, uniquely in British India, reported directly to the government of Madras and not to a regional commissioner as was the case in other provinces.[8] The benefit was that he had direct access to government, thereby, in theory, streamlining decision-making. The disadvantage was that collectors often had an inflated idea of their own importance, provoking arguments with Secretariat superiors who were dismissed too easily as 'desk-wallahs.' In the late nineteenth century, the province's refusal to reorganise its districts in line with all-India changes had resulted in a situation where Madras developments and ideas were frequently ignored inside India and in the India Office, where it was automatically assumed that the south would oppose change.[9] However, the government of India was hardly in a position to criticise the autonomous stance of Madras in the light of its own dismissive attitude towards the British Government. A member of the Madras ICS in the 1930s observed that 'Dominion in India was established before the invention of the telegraph, and the tradition of independence was zealously maintained even by the aloof beings in Delhi'.[10]

In 1901 half of the British population of India consisted of the Army and its dependants.[11] Most of the other Anglo-Indians[12] lived in the major cities, with 4,000 in Madras (in 1900 among the largest of Asian cities, with a population of almost half a million people). Sidney commented that when he arrived in 1913, although Madras supported nearly twice as many European shops as later existed and although the clubs were always full, English society seemed much smaller than it was in later years, suggesting that 'the lines of demarcation were much more rigid and all sorts of people who now go everywhere were firmly relegated to the outer darkness.' The services and the old Madras firms constituted the 'aristocracy' and those 'outside this magic circle had to justify their existence'; Sidney recalled a women whose husband was a 'burra sahib' (big sir) of one of the old firms, who was heard to remark about an acquaintance, 'I think he's in some obscure firm like the Dunlop Rubber Company.' The established managing agency houses transacted much of the business which was later done by separate offices. Although by 1913 the Indian Civil Service was theoretically open to Indian competition, the fact that entrance examinations were held in the United Kingdom, combined with the weight of official disapproval at Indian advancement, ensured that only a handful of Indians had been appointed to the ICS. With no appreciable Indianisation of the service to swell the number of local civil servants, the central organisation was much simpler and there were many fewer headquarter appointments, so that the actual number of service men stationed in Madras at any time was comparatively small.

However, what the European community lacked in numbers, it made up in sociability and hospitality. People were affluent, prices were very low and pay went considerably further. Income tax was negligible and few saved money. As Sidney pointed out, 'Why should they, when they could look forward to a pension on which they could live at home in comfort and dignity?' European houses tended to be most imposing externally, with large compounds and a multitude of servants, although the interiors were somewhat grimly furnished. The occupants tended to hire their furniture from one of the small shops which existed for that purpose, with the result that the average drawing room looked rather like that of a 'third rate boarding house in Notting Hill Gate.' People slept on iron beds or camp cots, but their glass and china were of a high quality and 'at dinner parties made a great show against the gleaming silver on the long white table cloth.' At a dinner given by the Chief Justice, Sir John Wallis, in 1918 Sidney first saw the 'daring innovation' of place mats and an impressive guard of honour of white-robed chobdars, each holding a silver mace. On a more practical level, Arthur James Platt of the Madras ICS recalled that at a dinner party some years later every chair at the table had a folded white cloth on it, which transpired to be a pillowcase to protect one's legs from mosquitoes. Outside the city, long white canvas mosquito boots served the same purpose.[13]

'Calling upon' one's fellow Englishmen was a 'wearisome and rather expensive business' as it entailed long hours in a hired carriage traversing the many miles which separated the houses of the chief officials. Bachelors were expected to don blue suits (happily not frock coats and top hats as had been the case with their predecessors) and do their calling in the heat of the day. A later ICS entrant Geoffrey Lamarque recalled that outside each house was a box into which the newcomer could drop one card for the husband, two for the wife and one for any unmarried daughter. However, at least 'calling at houses in this way did not involve the tedium of meeting the occupants … as you were, as it were, introduced and it was up to the person called on to invite the newcomer to dinner, or to a drink, or to return the call.'[14] Eventually Sidney tired of this exercise, arguing to himself that it was a 'a pure waste of time and energy and all these good people would be retired long before I was likely to be stationed in Madras.' However, he was 'badly found out' as before the end of 1914 he had become a 'Mount Road civilian'[15] and was constantly meeting senior ladies who were unable recall his 'coming out.' Most significantly he had wilfully omitted to call on the parents of his future wife.

Despite its drawbacks, the process of 'calling' enabled the newcomer to explore the city of Madras, described by one of his fellow civilians, Hilton Brown, as 'A place of interminable and spacious vistas of open land, threaded here and there by lost and wandering roads to which fragmentary buildings clung desperately.'[16] To Sir Herbert Thompson, another contemporary, the city had much beauty:

> Strung out along ten miles of the Bay of Bengal, flanked by its famous surf and the sandy beach which divided it from the lovely Marina, Madras was naturally extensive. The nub … was the Fort presiding majestically over park-like spaces adorned by the dazzling white of the traditional-style administrative buildings with green-shaded Government House keeping a presidential eye on the whole. North of that was the harbour created by Victorian brains on an open coast, with inland of it the business centre of Georgetown … To the south of the Government House complex ran what in less glamorous areas might be called suburbia, the bungalows of official and non-official middle-class, all within their own huge gardens. These burgeoned into near parks when they surrounded the houses of the really great, Members of Council, High Court judges or the heads of the great firms who with their vast emoluments made the competitions of social life difficult. Finally at the southern fringes ran the River Adyar, flanked by still more gracious houses and its delightful Club with all forms of aquatic sport including sailing to add to its diversities.[17]

Sidney recalled his first drive down the main highway of the Mount Road:

> gazing open-mouthed at the unfamiliar sights on the road-side—the men who looked like women with their flowing garments and pendulous chignons, the coolies[18] straining and staggering as with bowed heads they slowly pushed along the heavily laden hand-carts, the jutkas packed with fat merchants ... the buffaloes looking like denizens of some infernal region, the goats calmly dining off old newspapers in the middle of the street, the shouting, chewing, spitting and wrangling crowds.

Years later he attempted to recall the streets without the many new buildings which were constructed during the first half of the twentieth century. He remembered the unfinished harbour, devoid of wharves and modern appliances, with a vast number of barges and few warehouses; the business premises of Georgetown (which people still tended to call Black Town), almost all of them two-storied buildings a century or two old; and Parry's corner looking like a Daniell print. The High Court existed with its 'barbarous jumble' of domes and minarets, but not the Small Cause Court, which later cowered in its shade 'like a poor relation.' Fort St George at a glance looked much as it did twenty years later, although it had no wireless station and the Secretariat was still a dignified and spacious building, free from annexes and undivided by internal partitions. As one approached the Island[19] the two oil companies' buildings (later known as the 'Haemorrhoid Palaces', being seated on piles) had not yet 'reared their pretentious heads' and there was, of course, no bus station, for the motor bus was still unknown. The Gymkhana Club was nothing but a football ground and rough golf course with a small changing pavilion, with no ballroom, billiard room, swimming pool, garden or lawn. There were no bridges over the railway and no electric trains. With very few motor cars and no taxis the horse was still 'the principal source of horse power', and senior officials and the burra sahibs of the firms drove down to the office in carriages and pairs. The juniors drove buggies or rode bicycles. The centre of the city had electric lights and fans, but in suburbs like Adyar and Kilpauk the punkah and the oil lamp still survived.

Moderately wealthy Indians, 'except for a few rajas and rich lawyers' still lived in the back streets of Georgetown and Triplicane. The thousands of villas on the outskirts of the city had yet to be built and the twenty-acre compounds of the old garden houses had not yet been cut up into quarter-acre lots. Madras, meandering across almost thirty square miles, consisted of two congested areas in the north and south, loosely connected by a belt of garden houses and villages on the outskirts, and where new villas and bungalows later sprang up there were strings of irrigation tanks[20] 'in the dry beds of which young men and maidens and others not so young were wont to exercise their jaded livers on horse-back before breakfast.' It took little time to find rural India on the very outskirts of the city. Just beyond the Marmalong Bridge, where a brand new statue of King Edward VII draped in a sheet was waiting for the unveiling ceremony, were brilliant green paddy fields, bullock carts with huge wheels, respectful villagers (who, as Sidney unashamedly reported, 'salaamed to me as a member of the ruling race'), hundreds of dhobis under the bridge beating wet clothes to a pulp, women with huge bundles on their heads and children on their hips, policemen in red pith turbans and leather belts which were 'always awry,' and 'the dark grey pigs rooting in the filth by the road, the children playing naked in the dust, the little shops crowded with betel, bananas, weird coloured drinks, packets of strange cheroots … everything was new and fascinating, full of colour and strange sounds and smells.'

The most impressive road in Madras was undoubtedly the Marina, the magnificent promenade beside the ocean where Sidney first saw the masulah boats in which his European predecessors had landed through the surf. There had been no pier until 1861 and before then steamships lay at anchor outside the surf, dispatching their passengers in the smaller boats that dumped them unceremoniously on the beach.[21] Later used for fishing, the masulah boats, which were light, open vessels whose flat bottoms and high sides enabled them to work well through continuous swell, were propelled by crews with curious oars consisting of long sticks with what resembled a black dinner plate on the end. Sidney also recalled scores of catamarans, 'as swift and graceful as the masulah boats were slow and awkward, skimming over the water at a good six miles an hour and handled with marvellous skill by their primitive looking crews.' In the evening a multitude of people descended upon the Marina from offices and shops, taking the air in jutkas and carriages, or walking along the broad walk with a variety of costumes and languages. In 1913 the Marina had not yet acquired many of its public buildings. The Senate House, the Chepauk Palace (the home of the Nawab of Arcot), the old Engineering College and the Presidency College were situated by the promenade, but further south there was nothing before San Thome but fishermen's huts and the elegant old Ice House which stored huge blocks of ice from the Great Lakes of North America 'in order that the Company's great men should not have to drink their brandy pawni [mixed with water] warm!'

It was on the Marina that Sidney first heard 'that strange macaronic language spoken by the educated citizens of South India in their moments of leisure—a language in which all the adjectives and most of the nouns are English, while the verbs and pronouns and the structure of the sentences are pure Tamil.' He recalled that later in his legal career when he observed an educated witness being examined in court, both witness and lawyer slipped unconsciously into this 'composite jargon', so that the unfortunate interpreter did not know whether to translate into English or Tamil and various parties had to be begged to talk in either language but not both at the same time. When Sidney first arrived in India, due to the fact that all of the colleges and most of the better schools had English, or more often Scottish, teachers on their staff, it was a relatively easy to understand the spoken English of educated Indians, despite the odd Aberdonian phrase which was interjected into the conversation from time to time. However, by the end of his time in the subcontinent, with the advent of Indian teachers of English, the Tamil pronunciation had made his own language a great deal less comprehensible. Sidney himself had spent a year at Cambridge attempting to learn Tamil under the tuition of an elderly retired missionary 'with a badly fitting set of dentures, which used to fall with a clatter when he attempted to put his tongue down the back of his throat in the approved Tamil fashion.' But the 'unending cataract of indistinct noises' with which he was assaulted upon his arrival appeared to defy comprehension and to include no words which he had previously encountered.

Not far from the Marina, just off Mount Road, the Madras Club was a daily haunt, and an absentee was always presumed to be ill. Dating from 1832, it had originally been a minor raja's palace and was noted for supposedly the longest bar in Asia, located in a large coach-house for the raja's rickshaws. It was the preserve predominantly of the ICS and the military, although in the late nineteenth century its membership expanded to include acceptable European members of 'civil society', particularly the city's commercial and professional elite. No women were admitted (except once in the bar after the armistice of World War I), strict behavioural codes prevailed, and seniority was prized and respected, although to a later young ICS entrant John Edward Maher such formality was anathema, making his first impressions of India 'of the utmost gloom ... probably due to the formalised Victorian social life and the European club, which though probably inevitable, I always regarded as the curse of the country.'[22] Geoffrey Lamarque, a contemporary of Maher, also deplored the depressing rigidity of the social system, observing that:

> the Members of the Indian Civil Service, the 'heaven-born', were regarded as being at the top of the social ladder, and therefore eligible for any club. Officers in the armed forces,[23] and in other Government services, came next, and then industry and commerce e.g. bankers, insurance men, shipping agents, oil-men, and the like. But, subtle though the distinction might be, woe betide you if you were not in commerce, but in 'trade', i.e. a retailer, or the like, for then the Madras Club at least would not accept you.[24]

Increasingly it became more of a sore point that Indians were neither allowed to become members nor to enter the premises, a ban most strenuously upheld by the business community or boxwallah[25] members who upheld the conviction that, being a residential club, separate facilities would have to be introduced to cater to caste Hindus.

The social life of the Madras community was taken with great seriousness just before the First World War (although it became far less conventional in the 1920s). When Sidney first arrived Indians were never present at dinner parties, even at Government House, for at that time the great majority of Indians 'of position' would only eat food cooked by Brahmins.[26] Senior officials would give huge dinner parties each week of twenty or more people, with champagne as the customary drink. Water was not considered safe, and abstemious Englishmen would drink soda water in the belief that the effervescence destroyed germs. At dinner parties a man would wear a swallow-tailed coat and white tie. There was no question of going on to a show afterwards, and the guests sat in the drawing room making polite conversation until a quarter to eleven when the senior female guest asked for her carriage. A bride was always in this role for six months after her marriage and no one was able to move until she departed, which could cause complications when 'a nervous young bride, fresh out from home, had not the least idea of her grave responsibilities and people sat and suppressed yawns until in desperation some bold person whispered to the defaulter that it was her business to make the move.' Sometimes the tedium of the evening would be relieved by games or a guest of 'known musical propensities' would reluctantly oblige by singing or playing. However, usually matters were reduced to conversation of a highly predictable nature.

Madras social life was well catalogued by the local press, also based in Mount Road. In 1913 newspapers were unashamedly local, containing paragraphs from 'our own correspondents' in Kumbakonam, Calicut, Coimbatore and a score of other places. Each correspondent was allowed a page to himself and saw to it that no public meeting, drama or cricket match went unnoticed. World news was of less importance and consisted of 'a serried mass of Reuter's cables, undistinguished by any attempt at arrangement or banner head-lines.' Literary contributions from amateur journalists were welcomed and sometimes even financially rewarded. There were two newspapers edited and owned by Europeans, *The Madras Mail* and *The Madras Times*. *The Mail* was a 'staid and rather stodgy journal', a solid supporter of the government and 'the mouthpiece of purely European opinion.' Its older rival, *The Times*, was already in decline and its editor, a retired ICS hand, 'Fuzzy' Graham, was aged with a long white beard and a reputation for eccentricity. *The Hindu* was the only Indian-owned paper of any standing, owned and edited by the 'extremely able' and wealthy S. Kasturi Ranga Iyengar from 1905 to 1923. Being the younger brother of a committed Anglophile, there was always a hope that at some point he might abandon his declared anti-British stance; however, in 1905 an editorial in *The Hindu* demanded total independence for India and offered its enthusiastic support to the Home Rule movement. All three papers were 'decidedly crude' in their make-up. Commercial advertising was in its infancy and most of the advertisements were from private individuals who had horses, tents or carriages for sale, or, in the case of *The Hindu*, daughters to marry. Weddings were written up at great length, with complete lists of guests and presents, while politics, as a feature of journalism, scarcely existed.

Among the tradesmen on the Mount Road there were a number of characters. E. D. Smith was a Eurasian who in his prime had been an extremely good tailor and 'a man of remarkable resource and ability' with 'the makings of a William Whitely in him.'[27] In his small one-floor shop there was nothing that he did not sell and, if not in stock, he would procure items in an hour or two. He knew the life histories of everybody who had been in Madras since the 1880s and had an embarrassing way of divulging the details of the most intimate purchases of his friends and acquaintances. His resourcefulness ultimately led to his downfall, as his shop backed on to the Army Clothing Factory, where, during the First World War, there had been 'serious leakages' of cloth. The police eventually discovered a bale of khaki drill of army pattern at the bottom of Smith's well and, in spite of efforts to persuade the court that an enemy had planted it there, Smith had to spend a year in the penitentiary. However, he came back in as cheerful a state as before, 'a charming old fellow and a very present help in time of trouble', continuing to be the general provider to half of Madras until old age and elephantiasis claimed him.

Another quaint old character was Voyvodech, the bicycle man, who also lived to a great age. As a young Czech sailor he had been wrecked in a sailing ship on the coast of Ceylon. He was employed as a diver on the construction of the Colombo harbour and afterwards worked in the same capacity under Sir Francis Spring, a British civil engineer who played a pioneering role in the development of the railways in East India and also served as chairman of the Madras Port Trust from 1904 to 1920.[28] In Madras, Voyvodech married a local woman and raised a family and, when too old to dive, set up as a bicycle repairer, soon to master the vagaries of the motorcycle when it first emerged. However, when the First World War broke out, despite not having been in Europe for forty years, he was in danger of being interned as a technical enemy; whereupon a considerable number of his allies composed a memorial to the government, which stressed the absurdity of locking up an innocent and industrious old man who was entirely pro-British in his sympathies. He was fortunately spared the disaster of imprisonment and continued to work and converse with his many friends in his 'strange jargon' until nearly eighty.

Upon his first visit to the Secretariat, Sidney was advised to step across to the Accountant-General's office for an advance of Rs 1,000, which he considered 'a very welcome suggestion, for I was almost penniless.' Part of the advance was to purchase suitable attire for the requirements of Madras life. The task of clothing the impecunious newly arrived members of European society was shared between two Muslim tailors. One was Sheik Buddoo, 'a tall, stately, dignified and rather mournful individual with a long black beard', who had a shop in General Patter's Road. The other was Sheik Muhidin, who lived in Thousand Lights[29] and was a complete contrast to his rival, 'being short, fat and perky ... like a well-fed cock robin.' He was said to be an opium addict, which possibly accounted for his occasional failure to deliver the goods on time, although his bright appearance made this an unlikely theory. He seemed to have a 'marvellous intelligence service' and, days before Sidney received his posting orders, was aware that the young recruit was to be dispatched to Vellore, a posting to the west of Madras. In 1913 the price for an office suit was about seven or eight rupees and something under two rupees for a pair of white drill trousers. In Sidney's opinion 'quite enough too when your net pay after all deductions was something like Rs 280 a month.'[30]

Sidney confessed that he was 'not much attracted' by Madras in the first few weeks he spent in the city. He intensely disliked the 'hot, sticky and oppressive' climate which reminded him of 'the inside of my father's greenhouse'. Moreover, he disliked living in a hotel which had become his lot after his first visit to the Chief Secretary, W. O. Horne, when he was congratulated upon his single status. It appeared that the Secretariat was inundated with married men and faced with a severe shortage of accommodation for the families of civil servants both within the city of Madras and up country. His bedroom in the first hotel in which he was housed, the third-best in Madras, resembled more an apartment in a zoo, with a large frog, a group of little grey squirrels 'chirruping as they chased each other along the verandah, lizards clinging motionless to the walls and, as dusk fell, a bevy of bats playing hide and seek under the rafters.' He was inclined to agree with Kipling's description of Madras as a 'withered beldame',[31] not yet aware of the great beauty of many parts of the fine, spacious old city, 'the almost rural atmosphere of the residential districts, the beauty of the sea front and the rivers, even including the odorous river Cooum, the lovely patches of coconut palms and paddy almost in the middle of town, the stately dignity of the old Madras Club' and the 'rustic charm' of the Adyar Club, with which he was to be closely identified. Moreover, Sidney was not attracted to many of the people he encountered, tending to write them off as 'empty-headed' due to his self-confessed inability to take an interest in the subjects on which most of them could converse well. Lonely, homesick, with much time on his hands, he was quite unable to imagine a time when Madras would be a place where he had 'a finger in every pie and an occupation for every minute of the day', developing a 'fierce local patriotism which would brook no criticism of the city which, with all its faults and all its smells, was our own home town.'

3

VELLORE 1913–14

Vellore, Sidney's first posting, about 78 miles west of Madras on the banks of the Palar river, was a good city in which to start life as a newly fledged member of the Indian Civil Service. Once a frontier station commanding the roads to the Mysore plateau, it boasted no fewer than three forts, two of which were in ruins on the rocky hill which looked down to the centre of the town, and the third almost in the middle of the bazaar. The last was still in good repair in 1913, despite dating from pre-British times, and decorated with the familiar 'grave-stone' type of battlements. In this fort the family of Tipu Sultan,[1] the ruler of the kingdom of Mysore and an implacable enemy of the East India Company, was interned after the conquest of Mysore in 1799, and was the site of the first rebellion against British rule (preceding the Mutiny) which erupted in 1806. The immediate causes of the revolt revolved mainly around resentment towards changes in the sepoy dress code, under which Hindus were prohibited from wearing religious marks on their foreheads, and Muslims were required to shave their beards, and both were ordered to wear a round hat associated with Europeans. The rebellion began with the massacre of British officers in church and was quelled by the prompt action of the officer commanding the cavalry at nearby Arcot, Colonel Rollo Gillespie, who galloped twenty miles to Vellore and charged the mutineers before they were able to consolidate their position.[2] No longer a garrison town in 1913, the buildings inside the fort were used to house the police school and various branches of the collector and district magistrate's office.

When Sidney arrived in Vellore, the collector and district magistrate was 'the great Marjy', who retired as Sir Norman Marjoribanks, KCSI, KCIE, acting Governor of Madras. Marjy was not only one of the ablest members of the Indian Civil Service, he was also a great character, known throughout the Madras Presidency long before he achieved official recognition. Born in India in 1872 into a large family, of which only two of the offspring were girls, his father was a member of the provincial civil service with a social position similar to that of a warrant officer in the army. In Marjy's childhood his father was treasury deputy collector of Chittoor, a town strategically located between Bangalore and Madras, on a salary too inadequate to pay for the higher education of all his family. However, there was one advantage in this upbringing; Chittoor happened to be situated on the border of Tamil and Telegu territory, and Marjy grew up speaking both difficult languages with great fluency. He had his early education at Bishop Cotton's School in Bangalore and, when the school ceased to be able to provide sufficient intellectual stimulation, his parents managed to scrape up the money for 'the cheapest university education which the British Isles could supply.' Marjy joined Queen's College, Belfast, which although admirable in many ways did not prove to be the best training ground for the rigorous competition to enter the Indian Civil Service. Nevertheless, he passed the ICS examinations in 1891 and was brought into the central bureau of Madras province, the Secretariat, where his fine analytical brain and 'remarkable memory for men and things' made him indispensable. So much so that towards the end of his time as under-secretary of the Revenue Department it was deemed unwise to issue a government order without Marjy's initials on it.

However, Marjy was 'no mere officewalla', being a fine sportsman and keen naturalist. He set to work to devise for himself a job which would provide congenial employment and at the same time allow full scope for the field sports which were his most absorbing interest, writing a series of powerful minutes in which he pointed out the need for a department of land records to overhaul the survey and registry of holdings during the thirty years' interval between revenue settlements.[3] In due course he was appointed director of the new department, giving him free rein to conduct the field work in which he had a particular interest while following the snipe and duck during the cold season and pursuing bigger game during the summer months. At the end of ten years he had 'an unrivalled knowledge of the Madras Presidency, its peoples and problems, its revenue technicalities and its official staff; while incidentally he had explored almost every bit of really shootable country from Ganjam to Cape Comorin, had fished most of the rivers and estuaries and had mixed with all sorts and conditions of men in the informal atmosphere of the country-side.'

In 1912 Marjy was sent to Vellore to organise the new North Arcot district, which had been carved out of three neighbouring areas and, as seemed to be usual practice, had been used as 'a dumping ground for the incompetents of all three districts.' Two years later Sidney had the good fortune to be sent to him as 'a learning boy'. Marjy was then in his early forties and frequently described himself as an 'ugly little blighter', being short, rather tubby, with close-cropped red hair and moustache, freckled skin and thick-lensed spectacles. He had 'a lurid vocabulary' which was culled largely from natural history; people he disliked were referred to as 'bog-stoats', stupid people as 'buffaloes', toadies as 'crow-catchers' and so on. Working under Marjy was a liberal education. He could in a remarkably short time absorb the contents of a huge file and regurgitate them in a note of three or four lines which 'left nothing more to be said on the matter.' He tended to be critical, but it was always felt that his criticism was just. Despite working at considerable speed he missed nothing ('a couple of words in the margin or a sly gibe when he next saw you, would make it clear that only the best was good enough'), and although he never praised his subordinates, he invariably backed them up if he thought they were right.

Sidney tells the story of one of Marjy's sub-collectors, given the pseudonym of Smith, who was tactless and very unpopular with the members of the local judiciary. Smith, when in camp in a remote area, tried and convicted a thirteen-year-old boy of theft and sentenced him, as was normal, to six strokes with a cane. The correct procedure in such cases was to send the offender to the nearest sub-jail, where the whipping would be administered by a head constable in the presence of the sub-magistrate and the local medical officer. In this particular case it involved marching the boy in police custody for about thirty miles to lie in jail for probably a day or two while the necessary formalities were concluded. Smith, having been a schoolmaster in a previous incarnation, knew much about caning boys and thought that it would be common sense to adopt the quickest course of action. He closed his court, 'that is to say, he got up from his seat under a tree in front of his tent', sent for a cane, and gave the boy 'six of the best', sending him away 'chastened, but with no sense of injustice.' However, he reckoned without the local judiciary who, 'Brahmins almost to a man and with a Brahmin's instinctive aversion from all forms of corporal punishment, considered it outrageous that a magistrate should play the part of executioner'. A memorial was sent to the government, letters were written to the press and questions were instigated in the legislature. The unfortunate sub-collector, who was in fact the mildest of men, was 'nicknamed "The Tiger", described as a sadist and a pervert, and represented to the public as a beast in human form who delighted in flogging innocent boys.'

Naturally the government could not ignore the outcry and Smith was asked for his explanation. With his customary lack of tact he composed a letter attacking his accusers and describing the charges as beneath contempt. Fortunately for Smith, the letter had to undergo the scrutiny of Marjy, who promptly tore it up and wrote a 'reasoned and moderate defence', setting out the facts and the special circumstances which had necessitated a departure from the usual procedure. Under pressure, Smith, 'who loved Marjy dearly', was persuaded to sign this document, which was forwarded under a covering letter from the collector in which he expressed the highest opinion of Smith's personal character. The result was that Smith was exonerated; however, as Sidney stressed, matters might have been very different under other collectors who operated in a manner less commendable than that of the 'shrewd and loyal' Marjy.

In the buildings housing the various branches of the collector's office Sidney was first introduced to office registers, 'those bugbears of an Indian official's life', and it was there that he made a rather half-hearted attempt at understanding the treasury accounts, aided by the old deputy collector, a Muslim theosophist[4] who, with his clean-shaven face and gold-rimmed spectacles, looked more like a Brahmin than a

Muslim, although he retained the 'courtly manners of his own community and had none of that combination of touchiness and arrogance which Brahmins occasionally display.' Also in the fort was the old munshi, who struggled daily with Sidney's inability to speak the Tamil language. On his retirement, many years later, Sidney expressed his gratitude for the constant support and help he received from Indian assistants and colleagues such as these two men when he was starting his career. A contemporary in the Madras ICS, Henry Julian Downing, also had great admiration for his Indian subordinates, remembering gratefully 'the patience and tact which these hard-worked and underpaid men exercised in showing the ropes to a young and inexperienced foreigner who had been sent to assume authority over them.' He realised too that as far as they were concerned, he was welcome 'not so much for any expertise I could contribute, for they knew much more than I did, but for the moral support my presence afforded them in carrying out their duties in the face of opposition.'[5]

In moments of relaxation the munshi pumped his superior for information on the early stages of the First World War. The excess of gloomy news from the front was hardly easy material to explain. The Indian asked whether it was:

> true that the government was about to evacuate Madras and take refuge in the Vellore fort as a result of the hostile movements of the Emden, a light cruiser of the Imperial German Navy which raided Allied shipping in the Indian Ocean early in the war. When asked what had prompted that idea, the old man replied that workmen who were patching up the gateway to the fort were said to be restoring the old drawbridge, so that the 'pundits of the secretariat' could write their office notes in safety. He went on to enquire whether it was true that the Emden was a ship that could fly in the air and travel under the sea and appeared not wholly convinced by Sidney's reply that such feats were impossible.

News of war had been greeted in India with a demonstration of enthusiastic support from the princely states, the Congress and the All India Muslim League. Recruitment exceeded all expectations and Indian troops sailed for diverse destinations such as Flanders, Gallipoli and Mesopotamia. In 1914 the Indian Ocean was frequently referred to as a 'British lake' due to British domination of the surrounding ports and the heavy traffic of British and Dominion merchant vessels in the shipping lanes. It was therefore a severe blow to British morale when on 14 September the *Emden* captured seventeen ships, all British except for two neutral Italian and Norwegian vessels which were duly released. Most of the captured British ships were quickly sunk, either by fire from the Emden's 10.5 cm guns, or by placing explosive charges deep in their hulls. However, the chivalry of her captain, Karl von Muller, during his command was to earn him the respect of both friend and enemy, and he was always most civil to the captains and passengers of the ships he captured. Several warships from the British, Australian and Far East squadrons, as well as a number of French, Japanese and Russian cruisers, were dispatched to hunt down the German vessel, but von Muller succeeded in eluding them all.

On the night of 22 September 1914 the Emden quietly approached the city of Madras. At 9.30 pm she opened fire at 3,000 yards on the several large tanks of the Burmah Oil Company within the harbour. These were set on fire with the first 30 rounds fired, and nearly 425,000 gallons of oil were lost in the attack. The largest number of casualties involved a merchant ship anchored in Madras harbour, injuring 26 members of the crew. Five civilian sailors were killed or died later of wounds. The action lasted about half an hour, by which time the shore batteries had started to reply; however, the Emden slipped away unscathed towards Pondicherry after firing 125 shells. Sidney himself was in Madras when the ship bombarded the city. He was playing billiards in the Madras Club at the time and knew nothing of the attack until reading the morning paper the following morning. The local populace was terror-stricken, despite the fact that little damage had occurred outside the precincts of the harbour, but nevertheless poured down to the beach from Georgetown and the suburbs in every possible form of transport to glean information. A huge exodus followed in case the ship targeted the city again. The railways and roads leading out of Madras were packed with hordes of refugees for days afterwards and there was no doubt that for many the subsequent destruction of the Emden was the turning point of the war.[6]

Prior to the start of the war and the dramatic local events, Sidney mixed with several notable residents of Vellore, and later declared that had he been asked in 1914 which of the inhabitants would be the first to reach the 'dazzling heights' of the Madras Executive Council he would not have had the slightest hesitation in voting for Marjy. However, the collector had to wait for many years before the course of official promotion brought him to the top, whereas another member of his small circle reached that 'lofty position' within six years. Mohammed Habibullah was a 'thin, hungry-looking, black bearded man of middle age, with courteous deferential manners and a complete absence of self-assertiveness.' With just enough education to become a small-town pleader he must have found it challenging to make a living at the bar and was happy to accept the post of paid municipal chairman on a salary less than that which Sidney received in his first year. Two or three years later Habibullah was elected by a Muslim constituency to the Madras legislature where he appeared to impress senior members with his 'modesty and common sense.' To much amazement in 1920 he was appointed to fill the vacancy for a non-official member of the governor's cabinet, a post which in the past had always been given to a 'person of great eminence and ability'. It appeared that the Secretary of State for India required a Muslim for political reasons and the field of choice was restricted.[7] Habibullah took office and on the whole did very well, without initiating major reforms. His public utterances were 'models of non-committal suavity' and on the files which came up to him for orders he evolved 'a series of masterly formulae for saying in different ways that he agreed with the last man who had noted and had nothing to add.' He eventually reached the heights of Sir Mohammed Habibullah, KCSI, KCIE, Diwan of Travancore,[8] but never became pompous or conceited and apparently never made a serious mistake.

Also featuring in the group of notable local residents of Vellore during Sidney's posting was Freddie Sayers, a junior acting District Superintendent of Police who not only distinguished himself by playing rugby for Madras until he was fifty and starring at tent-pegging,[9] but also was capable of conducting an argument of 'diabolical perversity' to keep the company amused. His appointment as Inspector-General of Police was inevitable and he achieved a well-earned KCIE, finishing off a brilliant career as a member of the Secretary of State's Council. Lesser lights of Vellore society included Cardozo, the Deputy Inspector General of Police, a mountain of a man who declared that he always slept outside, wet or fine, stating that his bed never got wet because he covered it so effectively. However, by far the most senior European resident was a little old lady of very small means who lived with her two nieces 'at the wrong end of the Officers' Lines'. Many years earlier she had come around the Cape in a sailing ship to keep house for her brother who was an officer in the Vellore garrison. After her brother died and the garrison was withdrawn she clung to her existence in India while her nieces rather pathetically spoke of England, a country they had never seen, as 'home'.

In Sidney's era Vellore was in the early stages of its development as the Indian home of medical education for women, due in particular to the work of Dr Ida Scudder, the most famous third-generation member of a large medical missionary family in India who devoted their lives to the work of the Reformed Church in America. Apparently as a young girl she rebelled against family tradition, determined to make a good marriage and enter high society in the USA. However, her intentions changed one evening in Madras when she was visited by both Hindu and Muslim men, begging her to treat their wives in childbirth as tradition would not allow a woman to be seen by a man outside the family, even a physician. Ida, with no medical background, pleaded with the men to let her father treat their wives, with no success. In the morning, three women had died and Ida, convinced that God had called her, resolved to become a medical missionary. In 1895 she entered the Women's Medical College in Philadelphia and graduated from Cornell Medical College, New York City, in 1899, as part of the first class at that school to accept women as medical students.[10]

Ida then headed back to India, fortified with a $10,000 grant from a Mr Schell, a Manhattan banker, in memory of his wife. With the money she started a tiny medical dispensary and clinic for women at Vellore, and in two years she treated 5,000 patients. Understanding the limitations of working alone to bring better health to the women of South India, Ida established a medical school for girls, the Christian Medical College and Hospital. Despite the comments of sceptical males she had 151 applicants in her first year (1918) and was forced to turn away many thereafter. At first the Reformed Church in America was the main backer of the Vellore school but, after Dr Scudder agreed to make it coeducational, it eventually gained the support of forty missions. In 1914 Dr Ida was still a comparatively young women, and Sidney knew her as a first-rate surgeon and 'a very charming person', always ready for a game of tennis at the club when she could escape from her work. Harry, her brother, who some years later was to baptise Sidney's younger daughter, also greatly enjoyed a battle on the court and was frequently late for his prayer meetings when his fellow players took a 'malicious' pleasure in enticing him into a new set.

However, the somewhat undemanding colonial existence of Vellore before the Great War was doomed and the next thirty years were to bring a huge change to the town, as to many other small upcountry Indian stations. For Sidney and his compatriots the ability to find fellow players of tennis, bridge or snooker at the club, or the opportunity to raise seven or eight guns for a station shoot, dwindled, as with the Indianisation of the services the European population faded away. Social relations between the two races were often uneasy during the first decades of the twentieth century, as the British continued to judge Indians by their own standards. When he first joined the Madras ICS John Edward Maher expressed the feelings of some other young Englishmen in experiencing an initial contempt for Indians with whom he came into contact, finding 'stupidity, corruption and nepotism' and believing that these were 'peculiarly Indian weaknesses', before appreciating the error of his youthful ignorance and the possibility that 'there was often more merit in the Hindu madness than in the English method.'[11] Although he never expressed such negative views, Sidney was realistic about the fact that, despite with the Indianisation of the services, there were 'many excellent Indians who took our places ... their outlook is different and their interests much less varied.' To him there was little doubt that 'it was a much pleasanter country for a European to live in when a man could be fairly sure of a cheery little circle of his own kind at the headquarters of every district.'

4

GUDUR 1916–17

In November 1914 Sidney was suddenly summoned to Madras, where he was handed over to the army for employment as an assistant cable censor, to spend 'eighteen idle and futile months sitting at a desk with little or nothing to do' but commiserate with his 'companion in distress', Michael Macgilligan, 'something of a Sinn Feiner, but a most entertaining fellow, who did much to save me from complete disintegration.' Fortunately there was one happy outcome from this otherwise fruitless existence, in that, with much spare time on his hands he was able to concentrate upon his future wife, Olive Florence, Sir Robert Clegg's daughter,[1] whom he married in 1916, soon after his 'internment' in the Cable Office had ceased. The possibility for marriage arose when Sidney was posted as sub-collector of Gudur, the second largest municipality in Nellore district (60 miles north of Madras), which included among its meagre attractions 'a habitable bungalow.' The description was somewhat misleading, as the teak beams which carried the heavy terraced roof turned out to consist of nothing but a thick coat of paint, and a large quantity of dust in the wake of an army of red ants.

A later sub-collector Henry Downing wrote some years later that, looking back, it was amazing that:

> one accepted so easily the primitive conditions in which one lived for so much of the time in the districts. As a young bachelor one could be

> expected to rough it to some extent but even the senior officials had to put up with lack of air-conditioning—ceiling fans if you were lucky, but many places still had no electricity—almost invariably no water-borne sanitation, hence 'thunder-boxes' and tin hip baths ... Yet [the conditions] did not strike one as intolerable at the time and there were, of course, compensations—the availability of servants, the fact that most of the buildings, even if somewhat primitive, were usually adapted to the climate with high ceilings and wide verandahs, and life, if simple in many ways, had a spacious quality which is seldom found anywhere today.[2]

Moreover, it was remarkably safe. Other Madras civil servants commented that they possessed little more than a light sporting rifle, and on tour frequently slept on the verandah of the rest house. At home, doors and windows were invariably open, no watchmen or police were required and no servants needed to be awake.

However, despite the relative safety of her situation, Olive, 'still an infant in the eyes of the law' and with no previous experience of the 'less civilized aspects of Indian life', was undoubtedly faced with a robust introduction to her new environment. At the Wadsworths' very first camp she observed a snake in the tent, and in hunting for it discovered a scorpion. This resulted in a 'complete spring-clean' of the tent in the course of which the servants killed twenty-three scorpions, a large centipede and the original snake. Gudur was certainly not much of a home for a town-reared bride. It was nothing more than 'a small railway junction, a miserable little village with a dirty little bazaar, two or three government offices and a subjail.' All the roads within a few miles of British headquarters were crossed by unbridged rivers, and the only other European within twenty miles was an unpleasant German missionary who was expecting on a daily basis to be interned due to the war. Eventually he departed and the Wadsworths were quite alone. To add to the disadvantages of Gudur, the work was highly demanding for a fairly inexperienced officer like Sidney and he was often forced to work from 7 am to 7 pm, leaving his wife entirely to her own devices. However, Olive not only survived the first year but 'managed to be happy'.

Compensations for the general discomfort included two horses and a motorbicycle with side-car which could be carried over the unbridged rivers. There were some attractive camps, as Sidney had within his beat the Pulicat Lake, the second largest brackish lagoon in India, and about fifty miles of coast. It proved possible to go by train to

Tada in the extreme south of his division, sail eighteen miles or so across the Pulicat Lake, enter the Buckingham Canal (running parallel to the coast and constructed by the British in the nineteenth century to connect most of the backwaters to the port of Madras) and be towed up the canal for about 40 miles through the island of Sriharikota to Dugarajapatam, where they could couple up the motorcycle and side-car and 'chug' in over a rough country road to Gudur.

In traversing the Pulicat Lake the Wadsworths were encountering an area of considerable historical importance. In the thirteenth century a party of Arabs had migrated to the shores of the lake in four boats after they were banished from Mecca for refusing to pay tributes to a new caliph. Adopting the Tamil language they became leading traders in the area, and from 1225 to 1275 Arab ships transporting tin from Malaya to Oman or Dhofar regularly stopped at the mouth of the lake at the town of Pulicat, possessing one of the few natural harbours on the coast of South India. In the fifteenth and early sixteenth century Pulicat rose to importance due to the stabilisation of the Vijayanagara empire and maintained strong links, including a road, to the great imperial city of Vijayanagara.[3] In this period Pulicat was the most important port in southeast India, with a population exceeding 50,000. The Coromandel Coast was a major producer of textiles and yarns for export to Malacca and Burma, and there was also a significant industry involving the cutting and polishing of precious stones such as diamonds, sapphires and rubies procured from the Deccan, Ceylon and Pegu. However, the decline of the Vijayanagara empire during the sixteenth century resulted in the increasing influence of Portuguese traders, who dominated the port until 1560, and in 1515 constructed the oldest church in the Madras-Mylapore Diocese, dedicated to Nossa Senhora dos Prazeres. These private merchants were beyond the control of the official Portuguese authorities in Goa and were in many cases viewed as renegades and pirates. In 1520 there were two to three hundred Portuguese inhabitants of Pulicat, and by 1545 six to seven hundred families; however, from 1565 the population began to diminish, and by 1600 there were fewer than 3,000 residents.

In 1606 a Dutch ship stopped on the shores of the Karimanal village, north of the mouth of the lake, requesting water. Local Muslims offered food and help to the sailors and a trade partnership was struck to procure and supply local merchandise to the Dutch to be traded in the East Indies. Fort Geldria at Pulicat was constructed as a defence from local kings and the Portuguese, and from the fort the Dutch soon monopolised the lucrative textile trade with the East Indies and other countries in the region. Under pressure from the Dutch, an English trading post established in 1619 was disbanded in 1622 and, following the repulse of several attacks by the Portuguese, Pulicat became the official headquarters of Coromandel (a governorate of the Dutch East India Company) until 1690. In 1615 the first Dutch East India mint in India was established in Fort Geldria, and in the 1620s the Dutch Company established a gunpowder factory in the town with such a substantial output that it was able to supply many of the major Dutch trading centres in the East Indies and homeward-bound fleets.[4] Although the Pulicat area was in 1760 ceded to the British, who finally captured the town in 1795, Dutch control lasted until the Anglo-Dutch Treaty of 1824. Thereafter its importance receded with the declining sea power of the Dutch and the increasing role of the Madras Presidency and the British port in Madras fifteen miles to the south. Pulicat then dwindled into a fishing village and British health resort with limited land access due to dense forest growth. Sidney and Olive would have seen evidence of the Dutch settlement in the ruined Fort Geldria dating back to 1609, consisting of a Dutch church and cemetery with twenty-two protected tombs dating from 1631 to 1655, and a further cemetery with seventy-six tombs and mausoleums.

The barrier island of Sriharikota[5] separated Pulicat Lake from the Bay of Bengal, and was divided from the mainland by a series of swamps and backwaters with an abundance of flamingos. When the Wadsworths visited it, the island was in parts malarial and was mostly covered by jungle. It contained the site of the first settlement established by the East India Company on the Coromandel Coast at Armegon, a place which, before the Buckingham Canal had been built, must have been 'one of the most inaccessible spots on the whole coast' according to Sidney. The sole virtue of the location was that there was a good anchorage off the coast, which later became the site for the Armegon lighthouse, an area which at the beginning of the twentieth century was so unhealthy that the staff of the lighthouse had to be changed every six months due to the high risk of malaria. It is possible that the climate was healthier three hundred years before Sidney's posting to Gudur, by which time malaria in the area had increased due to the shallow pits created to irrigate the casuarina plantations which were grown extensively to provide most of the Madras fuel supply. To Sidney there were 'few pleasanter sounds than that of a cool sea breeze sighing through the casuarinas in the middle of the hot weather.'[6]

In the 1920s it was possible to bathe off the coast of Madras without fear of encountering sharks, and indeed Sidney saw all the inquest reports from the fishing villages along fifty miles of coast for two and a half years and identified only one case of fatality due to a shark, despite the fact that the fishermen were constantly in and out of the water when launching their boats or hauling in their nets. However, later in the century a series of fatalities occurred. One theory pointed to the formation of a sandbank off the coast, due to the interruption of the coastal current by the Madras harbour, which forced sharks trapped inside the bank to seek food further inshore than was their normal habit. From Sidney's point of view the backwaters of the Nellore coast had much to recommend them, and there was fine fishing and good snipe and duck shooting in the country between the railway and the coast south of Gudur.

An administrative district in Madras was usually divided into four or five subdivisions, each headed by a sub-collector who ran his own division as best he could and was strongly discouraged from seeking advice from his superior, the collector and district magistrate, who had plenty of work of his own. Under the sub-collector were the Indian provincial services, consisting of sub-divisional magistrates, who could be moved between districts, and the members of the Revenue Department who always served in the same district. On the whole the standard of the provincial services was extremely high, and the employees, for whom an appointment carried much local prestige, tended to work 'outrageously long hours without overtime payment and it appeared to be a point of honour not to ask for extra staff'.[7] The sub-collector's role normally involved such duties as land assessment and acquisition, collection of land revenue and income tax, disaster management during natural calamities and, acting as magistrate, the maintenance of law and order and the supervision of the police and jails. Geoffrey Lamarque was of the opinion that the system was particularly efficient in the

Madras Presidency as 'the Madrassi was intelligent by nature, and took readily to education.' For this reason, and because of his long contact with the British, he spoke and wrote English 'beautifully', with the result that leading articles in *The Hindu*, the principal English-language newspaper in Madras, were indistinguishable from leading articles in *The Times*. When the intelligence of the Madrassi was linked to the administrative drive of the British, the fact that, astonishingly, 90 per cent of the land revenue (far and away the principal source of government revenue) was collected each year became more understandable but nevertheless a remarkable achievement. The land revenue system was undoubtedly more efficient in Madras than in other provinces due to the fact that village officers collected tax direct from the registered holder of land with 'no grasping middle man'.

Geoffrey Remarque noted how 'Every tiniest piece of land was carefully divided and sub-divided, marked with boundary stones, its precise dimensions, and the amount of land revenue at which it was assessed, all recorded in maps and plans and in registers kept in each village in the custody of the local headman and the accountant, and duplicated in the office of the tahsildar, the revenue officer in the nearest township.' Moreover, the trees were registered as well as the land. Because the green leaves in a 'land of pressures' were so precious for food or manure, every sizeable tree was marked with a number and had an owner duly registered in the karnam's village accountancy books.[8] However, in Sidney's day the main reason for maintaining an officer in a 'one-horse place' like Gudur was less to maintain the standards of revenue collection than to keep in touch with the Maharaja of Venkatagiri, Sir Raja Velugoti Gopala Krishna Yachendra, who owned about half of the land in the division and was one of the largest zamindars in South India, appointed as a member of the Madras Legislative Council in 1888.[9] Venkatagiri was a small town, abutting the mountains which separated the districts of Nellore and Chittoor and, according to Sidney, 'the place reeked of feudalism.' The palace was in the middle of the town, 'a huge barrack of a place', built around a large courtyard from which an archway opened into a public square where the maharaja's elephants paraded on ceremonial occasions. When Sidney first visited Venkatagiri in 1916 the old maharaja was still alive and a most imposing figure. Tall, erect and well built, he looked like an aged warrior and had 'the rare distinction of dignity without pompousness.' He spoke very little English and, as his prestige demanded that he used the language, conversation was somewhat stilted. He was highly conservative, managed his estate himself and declined to use a motorcar. His son, Sir Velugoti Govinda Krishna Yachendra, who succeeded him, was very different, being fat and flabby and 'rather thick in his speech.' He 'hankered after European ways', spending his time racing in Madras rather than attending to his estate, and certainly did little to enhance the status of his 'great house.'

Much mystery surrounded the death of the old maharaja in 1916. When it occurred Sidney was camping about fourteen miles away, but received no news of the event until after the inquest had been held and the body cremated. The story told at the inquest was that the maharaja, who was known to be a fine shot, killed a deer in the Venkatagiri forests. His shikari ran off to retrieve the animal and while he was away he heard another report, ran back and found the maharaja dead, shot through the head. The verdict of the inquest was that the maharaja had accidentally killed himself with his own gun. Sidney's suspicions were instantly aroused, since it was a well-known fact that there were two factions within the palace, one of which was 'virulently hostile' to the maharaja. It was also well known that the old gentleman had the reputation of being both expert and careful with his guns. The whole story rested upon the evidence of one witness, together with the medical evidence of the local doctor which could not be checked after the body had been burnt. Sidney also found it strange that, 'considering the eminence of the victim', as sub-collector he was not made aware of the essential facts until it was too late to verify them. This was undoubtedly a highly worrying situation for a young and inexperienced magistrate with no higher body to consult, since the district magistrate was a Brahmin who was not only very deaf, but tied to his office and unfamiliar with Venkatagiri politics. Eventually Sidney came to the conclusion that, were he to order a further enquiry, on the one hand he would receive little cooperation from the local police and on the other he would arouse the resentment of the new raja, achieving nothing. Years later he ruefully admitted, 'So I held my peace. But I still wonder who fired that shot.'

The succession of the new raja involved Sidney in numerous ceremonies, the first of which was the offering of condolences to the ruler upon his father's death, 'a task which was not rendered more attractive by my knowledge that the father and son had not been on speaking terms for years.' In morning coat and black tie Sidney was received by the raja, a man in his middle forties, in whom 'the protruding eyes of the Venkatagiri family were very noticeable.' Sidney recalled that he stood in 'a pose of tragic grief while I said my piece and listened to his expressions of filial sorrow.' Several weeks later it was necessary to make a formal call to congratulate the raja on his succession and to observe the pomp which was a necessary part of palace life. The Wadsworths were collected from the guesthouse in the state carriage with an escort of mounted sowars (cavalry), and a trumpeter standing on the back 'tootling away to his heart's content.' In the square in front of the palace the state elephants were drawn up in line to salute the party with more trumpeting, and Sidney was requested to inspect the 'ragged row of scallywags' who comprised the guard. With a struggle he assumed his most official demeanour and solemnly walked along the 'line of palace peons, in frayed Khaki uniforms, with belts tied up with bits of string and a wonderful collection of early Victorian firearms.' The English couple were then conducted into the durbar hall and seated on gilded chairs with red plush upholstery where their gravity was strained by the appearance of the raja's small Maltese terrier who 'in the excitement of his first visit to the durbar hall proceeded to cock up his leg at all the gilded chairs!'

However, by the time of the raja's installation the ruler had achieved much in smartening up his retinue and had appointed a 'very capable and energetic man' as his diwan, Balaji Rao Naidu, who had recently retired from government service and was to become one of Sidney's best friends. Several days before the ceremony, a messenger arrived from headquarters, bringing a copy of the government order of fifty years earlier which had laid down the procedure for the installation of the late maharaja, and Sidney was 'strictly enjoined to follow the same ceremonial.' He was informed that he would receive the government's letter of congratulation and a khilat,[10] consisting of two kinkobs, a karchobi (different types of gold-laced cloths) and a turban. He also discovered that Balaji Rao had arranged that the government's letter and present should be handed over immediately after the installation ceremony and before the giving of presents by the other guests and relatives. However, Sidney was adamant that the old procedure should be followed whereby a special durbar was held to which the raja would come in full attendance to receive the government's congratulations. Far from upsetting the palace schedule, this proved to be a great success, since the opportunity for another state procession delighted the raja.

The guests made up an entertaining party, living in tents pitched under the trees around the raja's Gymkhana Club. Most were district officials, apart from the collector, who avoided Venkatagiri, being uncertain of the precedence to be adopted vis-à-vis the raja. Among those who lived further afield was Julian James Cotton, an eccentric senior district judge who had followed his father, Sir Henry Cotton,[11] his grandfather and great grandfather in an unbroken line of Indian service. Cotton possessed 'a wonderful stammer and a talent for doing and saying the most unusual things', including the habit of administering justice clad only in a bath towel for which, in explanation, he submitted a medical certificate to the effect that he was suffering from severe prickly heat and was advised to wear only the lightest possible clothing. He arrived at Venkatagiri in the middle of the ceremony and mounted the dais 'clad in a crumpled old blue suit, in which he had obviously slept, his cheeks being adorned with two days' beard', declaring that he had never learnt to shave himself and, due to his arrival by a late train, had been unable to procure a barber.

The ceremony took place under a canopy in the middle of the palace courtyard and was 'a study in contrasts.' On the one hand there was the raja, 'gorgeous in a long white velvet, gold-embroidered coat and a gold turban, adorned with a pearl aigrette and an emerald as big as half-a-crown', together with a bodyguard of the princes in 'magnificent turquoise blue uniforms, white gauntlets and black riding boots.' On the other hand there were the Brahmin priests, 'naked from the waist upwards and heavily smeared with sacred ash, squatting on the floor', as they intoned Sanskrit prayers while all of the guests 'gossiped and giggled.' Most of the ritual had little significance to the onlookers, yet the symbolic acts of the raja's 'obeisance to a richly caparisoned elephant and a magnificent Arab horse', and the presentation of a sword of state to him by his uncle, the old Maharaja of Bobbili,[12] to martial strains from the band were reminders of the fact that the ruler was descended from a long line of warrior chieftains and justly proud of his hereditary title of 'Mansabdar of Ten Thousands'.[13] When the religious ceremony was over, the relatives and guests lined up to present their gifts, 'an occasion which at all Indian ceremonies is wisely attended with the utmost publicity.' After this the guests adjourned for refreshments in the palace and the women were taken into the zenana to be presented to the rani, who was kept in strict purdah. The seclusion of women was often associated with the rules of religion or caste, although this was not the case for the Venkatagiri rajas, who belonged to the Velama caste,[14] 'an agricultural and fighting community of good standing' which did not normally keep its women secluded. The practice was, however, adopted by those of the caste who belonged to the nobility in order to emphasise their superiority over other caste members and their equality with the Rajput rulers, for whom the seclusion of women was a matter of caste rule. To Sidney it was interesting to observe 'the curious phenomenon of social advancement bringing in its train a retrograde social practice.'

On the day of the state procession Sidney found himself perched on top of an elephant with Julian James Cotton as his 'companion in distress' who nervously regaled him with stories of unfortunate people who had been crushed to death when their runaway elephants charged through an archway with insufficient clearance.[15] Sure enough, when the raja climbed into the howdah of his huge state elephant and his subjects applauded, the Englishmen's beast headed off at 'a lumbering trot' straight through the archway, which happily had ample headroom, and into the middle of the dense crowd waiting outside. Fortunately, the mahout was able to stop him before damage was done, but for the rest of the evening the creature 'suffered from acute nerves' and Julian James was 'reduced to a state of gibbering incoherence.' The procession was, however:

> a fine show with eight or nine gaudily decked elephants, several gilded palanquins, the Rajah's gorgeous bodyguard mounted on beautiful grey Arabs, which they rode superbly, numerous carriages full of ladies and distinguished guests, a troop of mounted sowars, many musicians and drummers and a large body of uniformed retainers carrying torches.

Sidney recalled a moment when the procession stopped in front of the Vaishnavite temple and he was placed on a level with 'a most licentious sculptured frieze' which he hoped was situated too high to be observed by the ladies in the carriages. Following the state processions, the government durbar took place, at which Sidney read the official letter of congratulations and presented the kinkobs and karchobi, enlivened by a military display. The last day's show consisted of elephant races, which Sidney was forced to miss due to his workload, regretting that 'it would have been infinitely more entertaining than the trial of criminal cases, the hearing of rent suits and the perusal of the unending files which formed the daily round.'

Soon after the installation, Lord Pentland, Secretary for Scotland from 1905 to 1912 and Governor of Madras from 1912 to 1919, visited Venkatagiri and dined with the Wadsworths, having attended their wedding as a friend of Olive's father. During his tenure as Governor of Madras, Pentland became popular in India for his enthusiasm for the indigenous tradition and culture, and a deep interest in Hindu religion and philosophy. However, he was also remembered in a less sympathetic light for his crackdown on the theosophist lecturer Annie Besant and leaders of the Home Rule Movement. Despite his 'square-cut whiskers' which made him look somewhat grim and Victorian, Lord Pentland was 'a simple and charming man with delightful manners and the easiest person in the world to entertain.' Moreover, he had with him his private secretary, Tommy Moir, who was a friend of Sidney and Olive. Yet, although the Governor and his staff were beyond reproach, his servants at that time had achieved a reputation for stealing the silver from houses in which their master was entertained. Determined that none of their wedding presents would disappear, Sidney summoned the local head constable and warned him that all Government House servants were 'K.D.s (a familiar abbreviation for the "known depradators" of the Criminal Procedure Code)' and directed him to post his men at the entrances to the compound and admit no one without his orders. After the dinner Olive proceeded to dole out backsheesh to the servants who had worked hard to make it a success. Following the others, the Wadsworths' Yanadi[16] 'waterman-cum-gardener' came forward, declaring that he had been 'hiding all night in the tomato patch to prevent the Government House peons from stealing the fruit!'

When there were not such interesting diversions as a visit from a superior, the routine of court and office in Gudur involved Sidney to such an extent that little time could be spent on 'the more interesting and fruitful work of going round the villages and generally dealing with people rather than papers.' As a result, there were few opportunities to know the pursuits of the local inhabitants and 'to be able to visualise and humanise the many problems which come up for decision'. He did, however, witness a village ceremony which was becoming more rare, the festival of 'hook-swinging.' To carry out the ceremony, in the area in front of the temple of the village goddess a large upright post had been erected, considerably higher and thicker than a telegraph post. On top of the post was a swivel upon which a long horizontal pole turned, and to one end of the pole a long rope was attached so that the pole could be levered up or down, or swung around the heads of the crowd. From the other end a bright red canopy was hung and beneath it a 'nasty-looking' iron hook. The first step of the festival involved a preliminary sacrifice, and a goat was brought into the middle of the crowd where water was sprinkled onto its back. Everybody waited in silence until it shivered, whereupon one of the votaries chopped off its head with one blow of a sickle, and 'the chief worshippers were soon busy daubing themselves with the blood which spurted from the ghastly trunk.' When this had been done, a basket containing a coconut, some margosa (neem) leaves and a pestle was attached to the hook and lifted up high over the heads of the crowd, where it was taken slowly through the air in a clockwise direction for a complete revolution. It was then taken down and removed from the hook. The actual process of hooking and unhooking was hidden from view by a cloth which was held around the basket. Another goat was then brought forward and screened behind the cloth while the hook was inserted through the skin of its back. It was swung into the air with the levering device and made to revolve in a circle over the crowd, after which it was let down and allowed to run loose after the removal of the hook. The insertion of the hook had not drawn blood and during the whole proceedings the goat did not bleat or show any sign of pain.

After the swinging of the goat 'the Gollas, or shepherds, who appeared to be the principal people at this primitive festival, executed a weird sort of dance. The young men stood in rows opposite each other, every man holding in his hands a short rope of aloe fibre. The trumpets blared and the drums throbbed while they skipped about and pretended to strike each other with the ropes, advancing as they delivered the blow and crossing over, each to his opponent's place, and then beginning again', evidently miming a fight. Before colonial intervention outlawed such an activity, the next turn was frequently the swinging of a live man or woman, often dressed as a deity or depicted as a fighter and usually a member of one of the lower castes, such as Kallars or Pariahs, but in rare cases members of higher castes and even priests. The ritual was part of the annual temple festivals, which also featured other practices, such as walking over burning coals. As Brahmins of lower orders were sometimes involved in the cults of sakti (the personification of divine feminine creative power) and village deities, the festivals were mostly performed under their superintendence and the auspices of wealthier patrons.

Swinging festivals were intended to secure the wellbeing and prosperity of the entire community. By bringing together a large group of worshippers the goddess was likely to be pleased with the practice and angry if the custom were discontinued. However, the ritual was finally prohibited by law in 1894 in the Madras Presidency and, at the ceremony which Sidney witnessed in 1916, as a substitute for a live person a 'hideous wooden image was brought forward and carried three times around the temple in the hands of the young Gollas, who were evidently well primed with toddy and by this time wildly excited.' They carried the image with 'a mad rush, uttering a peculiar ululating cry as they ran.' After the third round, the swing was lowered and the dummy hooked on by the back, being shrouded carefully in the cloth the whole time. The cloth was then removed and the image hoisted up to revolve three times in the air. It was then taken down and the ceremony was over. After the ritual Sidney had a discussion with the old priest of the temple of the Balija caste, a mixed community of traders and cultivators spread mainly over the southern region of India. The old man told him about the last occasion some seventy years previously when a live man was swung, and he mentioned one year when as many as fourteen men took part and the performance was spread over several days. The hook was inserted 'through the skin of the victim's back and such was the power of the goddess that noone [sic] was any the worse.'[17]

In spite of the official ban on the swinging of men, it was clear to Sidney that the practice had continued in some places, as police officers informed him of the existence of scars of the hook on the backs of criminals whose identification marks were being examined. It was also fairly clear to him that the ritual must have resulted in fatalities, or it would not have been stamped out by the government. Records have certainly established that in the latter part of the nineteenth century hook-swinging was revived in parts of the Madras Presidency. Some colonial sources explained this resurgence as a reaction to economic and social suffering. Villagers claimed that since the ceremony had been banned rainfall had been deficient and crops scanty, cholera had been prevalent, and families with five or six children ten years earlier now had three or fewer. Even when the ritual was finally prohibited by law it did not fully disappear. Rather, its practice grew more varied, and instead of humans a wide variety of alternative objects was used in the swinging ceremonies as proxies; among them painted images, vegetables, and animals and puppets, as in the ceremony which Sidney observed.

Dealing with village settlements absorbed a considerable amount of Sidney's time during his posting to Gudur. Before his arrival there had been much interest in the subject of the '"semi-wild cattle of Sriharikota".' Sidney's attention was first drawn to it when he was appointed forest settlement officer to acquire all the private rights to land and trees on the island, so that the entire area could become reserved forest. A cursory inspection of the ground convinced him that this was going to be a 'very long and tedious job', since the few hundred inhabitants owned a very large number of fruit trees scattered through the jungle and he could see 'no earthly reason for turning them out' as there was very little valuable timber in the forest and to depopulate the island would be to deprive the forest department of its labour supply. Looking into the history of the government scheme, he discovered that the problem lay with 'the fertile brain' of Sidney's erstwhile friend, a deaf Brahmin collector, who had since moved on to another area. The collector had visited Sriharikota only once in his seven years of office and had 'evolved the theory that the forest was being ravaged by semi-wild cattle, the removal of which was essential in the interests of forest conservancy.' A suggestion was put forward that the government might institute regular kedda[18] operations on the lines of the large-scale trapping of wild elephants on the western hills. There was also a move to shoot the cattle—'a preposterous idea having regard to Hindu sentiment.' Thus the correspondence grew and the file became larger and larger until at last it was decided to remove the cattle by getting rid of the people who owned them, providing 'a typical example of the evils of paper administration.' Sidney pointed out, firstly, that the cattle were not semi-wild at all but decidedly domesticated; secondly, that the cattle did not belong to the people who lived on the island, but to the villagers who lived on the other side of the swamp who used to drive them across in the dry weather to graze; and thirdly, that the cattle were not harming the forest, which was in any case of little value. He therefore proposed that 'the whole scheme be scrapped' which, following a visit from the forest member of the Board of Revenue, M. E. Couchman, who proved to be infinitely more interested in poetry than the local livestock, successfully ended the matter.

Time and time again Sidney was struck by 'the readiness of the village people to accept an arbitrary decision from an impartial officer'. A good example of this was a dispute between two coastal villages concerning the fishery rights in a large backwater. The police had referred the dispute to the court because there was a grave danger of a breach of the peace. Both parties stated their case at some length but Sidney could find little in the form of reliable evidence to establish the true rights of the parties concerned. Eventually he asked them if they would abide by his decision if he inspected the place and arrived at the best possible boundary. He camped at Dugarajapatam, travelled by boat for about ten miles and, having inspected the disputed backwater, 'found what seemed to be a point equidistant from the two villages and planted a survey stone on each side of the backwater to serve as a fishing boundary.' The decision was 'greeted with acclamation' by both sides and the news spread along the coast, with the 'embarrassing result that I was overwhelmed with requests that I should go out and perform the same service for what seemed to be the majority of villages along the coast'. Such precise marking of territory was meticulously observed by British officers in general. According to Sir Herbert Thompson, a fellow Madras civil servant in the 1920s, 'In a properly administered Madras village every field had a boundary stone at every angle and these were related through more robust tri-junction points to the official Bench Marks built somewhere in the vicinity.' In settlement training ICS officers learnt by use of chain and cross-staff to conduct elementary exercises in geometry on the ground and replace any stones or numbers of stones which might have been moved.[19]

In addition to the threat of potential disputes associated with land demarcation, Gudur suffered from the more devastating consequences of constant epidemics of smallpox and cholera. The distress caused by these diseases was illustrated when, while walking along the railway line beside a large tank, Sidney and his wife saw a poor woman, 'clad in scanty rags' and sitting upon the line. When some railway employees were asked to explain her behaviour they stated that she had smallpox and had tried to throw herself under the previous train, had been prevented and was now awaiting the next one. Thereupon Sidney left his wife on guard, hurried into the village and 'borrowed' two constables from the police station, ordering them to take the would-be suicide away and lock her up in safety. It was bizarre to see the two constables attempting to remove the poor woman without physical contact; 'they stood near her gesticulating and shooing, for all the word as if she was a refractory goat, while she kept turning on them, jabbering and weeping.' Eventually they moved her in the right direction and she was locked up for the night and then released; however, there was no information as to what became of her.

Sidney received weekly epidemic statements from all the villages under his control and was able to study the way in which cholera worked its way down the various rivers and streams, carried by the water which the people used both for bathing and drinking. One village in particular, some miles from the nearest road, was returning the most alarming cholera figures, and in order to encourage the local doctor to visit the site, Sidney decided to go there himself, sending his horse ahead and arranging for a guide to be at the roadside where he left the motorcycle. The guide took him to within a couple of miles of the infected village and refused to go further, merely pointing in the right direction. Sidney rode on and his horse became badly bogged down in a swamp before he was able to access some solid ground and pull out the creature. The village, when he arrived, was 'a gruesome sight.' More than half the population was dead and by that stage of the epidemic the corpses were 'just flung down on some waste land and left to the jackals and vultures for disposal.' The survivors were 'sunk in a state of complete apathy.' Sidney managed to find the village magistrate and from him ascertained that the doctor, hearing of his proposed visit, had come to the village the previous day. He seemed to have come to the conclusion that the source of the infection was the village tank and, upon learning that there was a submerged well in the bed of the tank, suggested that the water should be let out so that the well could be disinfected and the village provided with a safe water supply.

However, Sidney discovered that the destination of the cholera-laden water which emerged from the tank was a string of tanks lower down the hillside, spreading the disease far and wide. He at once countermanded the doctor's directions and substituted 'a drastic campaign' for boiling the drinking water. Many more deaths occurred in the village, but the epidemic did not spread.

When the Wadsworths had been in Gudur for nearly two years, Sidney was given a short spell of special duty in the Secretariat at Madras, which coincided with the birth of their first child, Robert, on 25 September 1917. Despite the fact that the baby was seen as 'very interesting', he proved to be a great complication when the couple returned to the relatively primitive conditions of Gudur. They attempted to take him with them in camp but 'the problems relating to milk and water, flies and mosquitoes, laundry and regular hours seemed well nigh insuperable.' On the other hand, if Sidney left Olive behind she was quite alone, without friends or neighbours, and with no doctor or nurse on whom to fall back. Therefore when the jamabundi (annual settlement of land revenue) season involved him in almost continual touring, his wife joined her parents in Ootacamund (in the Nilgiri Hills three hundred miles west of Madras) with the baby, and during the following two months Sidney saw a white face once, and then only for a few minutes, resulting in 'a lonely life, but too busy to be positively unhappy.' He found time to spend a few weeks on the coast for some enjoyable fishing and in the process acquired 'a very unpleasant dose of malaria.' Without the help of a fully qualified doctor in Gudur he was forced to spend 'a miserable fortnight trying magisterial cases while riddled with fever, seated in an easy chair on my verandah, in a misguided attempt to empty the local jail before I left for Ooty (Ootacamund) on a month's leave.' He admitted later that it would have saved him much future trouble if he had downed tools at once and found proper treatment. In Ooty he was put to bed and given substantial doses of quinine, which left him 'deaf, dyspeptic and disgruntled.' He survived, but unfortunately so did the malaria.

Remembering his time in Gudur, Sidney was repeatedly struck by the changes which had taken place in the area since he was first posted there. Upon his arrival the main roads were 'execrable and almost entirely unbridged' and there were no village roads at all. He travelled in the first motorbus which was introduced at the end of his time there, in 1917 or 1918. However, by the time he left India there were 'tolerable' roads throughout Madras Presidency and unbridged rivers and streams were exceedingly rare, while motorbuses served nearly every village, profoundly affecting the life of the local inhabitants. With no ice-boxes or refrigerator the Wadsworths had been forced to live 'on the country'. There was 'no bacon (unless we were extravagant enough to buy it in tins), no butter except the rancid, adulterated stuff sold by the Bombay dairies, which could only be made edible by washing it in milk. We lived on the local chicken, goat mutton, rice and eggs, except at Christmas time, when we used to indulge in a Nilgiri ham and had to eat it at every meal to get it finished before it went bad.' For lights there were ordinary oil lamps and lanterns, as no petrol lamps had yet come into use and there was no electricity outside Madras city. Their furniture was 'the plainest utilitarian stuff, mostly collapsible, so that it could be taken into camp when necessary.' Not possessing a thermometer they never knew the height of the fierce temperatures in which they were living, 'But it was mighty hot at times and it was something of a relief to be able to retire for a short period of time to the relative civilisation of Madras.'

5

THE SECRETARIAT 1918–19

Madras ICS officers had two main worksites. The Secretariat occupied Fort St George, handling high-level policy issues and decisions. The Board of Revenue ran day-to-day matters and resided in Chepauk Palace, former home of the nawabs of Arcot. The Board directed the collection of provincial taxes and was headed by four then eventually three members in charge of specific areas.[1] Board members resembled ministers, and in the Secretariat ICS members of the Governor's Council fulfilled a similar role. Powerful secretaries (four in the Secretariat and two in the Board) reported to those senior men. Reporting to the secretaries were the undersecretaries, whose ranks Sidney joined, and beneath them literally hundreds of clerks and other officials, comprising a vast, complex bureaucracy that over many decades had developed its own ways of conducting the business of receiving the multifarious reports from each area of the province, recording them for future reference and issuing orders for the regulation of all details of administration. Geoffrey Lamarque some years later noted the impressive way in which every problem was examined by an army of clerks:

> its past history scrutinised, precedents analysed ... and the whole submitted to the decision-making authority through a chain of officers of various grades. The most junior officers would be presented with a long typed note, written in impeccable English and copiously referenced in the margin, with a stack of supporting files bedecked with 'flags' and

other reference points. Each officer, if he was conscientious, as most of us were, would add his own comments, and finally, on the top, if the papers were going for a decision by a Minister or the Governor or Viceroy, there would be a succinct summary of the whole. Faced with a vast file of this kind, Lord Curzon recorded his reaction in a vivid phrase: 'I drove my pen like a stiletto into its bosom'.[2]

Sidney's duty call at the Secretariat occurred at a most opportune time, when Lionel Davidson, the Chief Secretary, had just been given approval for a new department to deal with matters arising from the First World War (such as the supply of food) and thus needed an under-secretary with some urgency. It appeared that such a post would solve many of the Wadsworths' more pressing problems in that the couple would no longer be separated and there would be fewer difficulties as far as the baby's dietary and medical needs were concerned. Moreover, Olive would be with her parents during the last six months of their time in India, while Sidney had his foot 'firmly planted on the bottom rung of the ladder of promotion.' However, such an ideal situation had its drawbacks. In Gudur, with no shops, clubs or social life, it was possible to live on Sidney's salary with ease. In Madras it was impossible to avoid entirely the 'gaieties' of the city, still less the social requirements of Ootacamund, deep in the Nilgiri hills, which served as the summer capital of the Madras Presidency, accommodating the Madras government and its officials from April to October of each year during the hot season. The governor's residence, Government House, was the focus of activity, and there was a splendid Club House with a fine golf course, polo, swimming and tennis. Ooty also sported a cricket ground with regular matches played between teams from the Army, the Indian Civil Service and the business sector, and riding stables and kennels from which the Ootacamund Hounds hunted across the surrounding countryside. Maharajas, the business fraternity and senior civil servants all had summer cottages and, although senior officials were most generous in issuing invitations without expecting to be entertained in return, the social life inevitably entailed more expenditure on clothes, transport and clubs, while the half-yearly move of the Secretariat staff from Madras to Ooty and back again made it 'fatally easy' to spend far too much on house rent.

In Ooty, Sidney was first introduced to the Toda people, described in some detail by Yvonne Fitzroy,[3] private secretary to the Vicereine of

India, Alice, Marchioness of Reading, while on tour in 1926. According to Yvonne, the Toda traditionally lived in settlements called mund, consisting of three to seven small thatched houses, constructed in the shape of half-barrels. These houses were:

> perhaps five feet high … the doors are not more than two feet square. Here the Toda live summer and winter, rain and fine. They pasture their herds of cattle and water buffalo on the downs and sell the milk and ghee (clarified butter). They never till the soil, though they levy a tribute in agricultural produce from the cultivator, a mysterious tradition having made them in some sense the overlord. They have their own language and customs, though as a race (they number about 700 all told) and in spite of strenuous missionary efforts, they are dying out. Disease is winning the day and the monsoon months deal harshly with them. Their single hygienic instinct seems to be to crawl out onto the downs to die, but that, after all, they share with the animals. They are savages, but very gentle savages.[4]

Although the interesting features of the Nilgiris were much appreciated by those who visited the area, such as the Readings, the 'Exodus' to Ooty was 'extremely unpopular with everyone except those who benefited by it.' The European merchants in particular bitterly complained, especially during the worst of the hot weather when, abandoned in Madras with 'their livers perhaps not unaffected by the necessity for repeatedly quenching a raging thirst', they experienced the sweltering heat of Georgetown in September and 'thought with ever-increasing bitterness of the idlers in the secretariat, taking the afternoon off to watch the point-to-point on the Wenlock Downs.'[5] This feeling came to a head in August 1914 when Lord Pentland and his government took the decision not to move down to Madras on the outbreak of war, causing outrage among those marooned in the city. Sidney tended to sympathise with their point of view, pointing out that a case could certainly be made of the fact that 'a government working 7,000 feet above the sea level is apt to acquire an excessive degree of detachment from mundane affairs, to become too Olympian and to lose touch with mere mortals toiling in the scorching plains.' Intellect might function better in a good climate than a bad one, but truly effective government was impossible without 'continual and personal contact with the governed.'

In an early posting to the hills, the twenty-four-year-old ICS novice Humphrey Trevelyan undoubtedly enjoyed the 'progression from the suburbs to the shires, to the meets of the Ooty hounds and the society of intelligent Indians in the Madras Government.' His task was to decipher telegrams from the government of India which came in at great speed during the civil disobedience movement. Many 'immediate' telegrams arrived in the middle of the night but, learning from experience that they were of little urgency, Trevelyan became expert at signing for them in his sleep and in the morning observed with curiosity the number which displayed his signature. In doing so, he learnt 'one of the basic facts of Indian life, "Delhi is far away"' and saw how 'those exceedingly competent men who were the Government of Madras looked with an indulgent or irritated sense of superiority on the antics of the men at the centre who busied themselves sending unnecessary immediate telegrams and did not understand the south.'[6]

The Madras government in the second decade of the twentieth century consisted of the governor, who did a considerable amount of touring and interviewing, an Executive Council of two ICS officials who normally had many years of district experience and an Indian member who was usually a distinguished lawyer. This small cabinet controlled policy and administration and was at that time little influenced by the views of the legislature. It was, however, considerably influenced by the views of its secretaries and even at times by the opinions of 'those insignificant juveniles', the undersecretaries. Both secretaries and undersecretaries were not supposed to hold their appointments for more than three years, after which they normally returned to district life. Therefore the Secretariat was 'no Whitehall', but was 'effectively controlled by men who had recent district service and could from personal experience visualise the practical effect of the measures they were recommending or criticising.' In addition, they could, from personal knowledge of the needs of the people, initiate measures which they knew to be necessary in the interests of 'the inarticulate villager.' B. W. Day, a Madras sub-collector in the 1930s, added that the practice of switching officers between district and Secretariat also had the effect of 'making us regard rules as our servants and not our masters'. When it was understood how easily rules could be changed, 'Most of us … started by deciding what would be the just solution to some problem, and then seeing if there was a rule which could be stretched to cover it'.[7]

Sidney was firmly of the view that government should not be run for profit as was the case in a private enterprise. Misguided attempts to apply a standard of profit and loss to government assessments was 'largely responsible for the shelving of many excellent irrigation projects in India, greatly to the detriment of the food supply.' Moreover, government in India consisted of a large number of huge departments, some of which had conflicting interests. It was financed mainly by a compulsory levy in the form of taxation which required sanctions and treasury control, thereby limiting its spending power. Government was also an organisation whose operation involved 'the most drastic interference' by its officers in the affairs and finances of private individuals and, in order to prevent 'arbitrariness' on one hand, or on the other hand constant referrals to headquarters for orders, it was necessary that the officers concerned should be guided and controlled by rules. In addition, government had to 'contend with a body of shareholders who are far more numerous, more vocal and more interested than those of most commercial firms.'

Accordingly, when a new proposal was sent to the central offices of government it had to be scrutinised from many different points of view: how much it would cost, how it would be financed and what would be the profit or loss. Furthermore, it had to be decided whether new legislation or rules would be required, how it would affect other departments, whether the reactions of the legislature, the press and the taxpaying public would be favourable to it, or whether it might create an 'awkward precedent' or 'offend against declared policy'. It was essential that the different departments should be coordinated, the available funds fairly distributed and all possible objections met before going to the secretary of state for India for sanction, or to the legislature for statutory power. Matters were complicated by the fact that there was a constant change in the superior personnel of government offices as a result of the system of frequent transfers of men between districts and periodic absences on home leave, making it necessary to maintain more elaborate records not only of decisions, but the reasoning behind them.

A good example of the Secretariat system was the scheme for the Cochin harbour, with which Sidney was closely involved and which had a long history going back for fifty years, during which several previous schemes had been 'propounded, reported on and for one reason or another abandoned.'[8] The scheme emerged as a proposal from the Marine Department before being handled by the Revenue (Special) Department of the Secretariat where clerks had to search the indexes, collect the old files, prepare an abstract of previous proposals and determine how the new contender differed from its predecessors. It was apparent that previous schemes had been wrecked mainly by political difficulties and customs disputes. There was a 'doubtful boundary' between Cochin state and British Cochin which ran through the middle of the proposed harbour, while Travancore state was also vitally interested in the customs revenue. A suggestion was put forward that the harbour should be built and worked by a joint port trust deriving its powers from two identical acts, one passed by the Madras legislature and the other by the government of Cochin state. Sidney represented Madras at a conference with the diwan (or prime minister) of Cochin where the solution was tentatively accepted and the difficult boundary dispute shelved for the time being. The proposal for the joint port trust and the customs agreement then had to go up to the government of India for orders and the necessary letters were drafted in consultation with the Public Works and Revenue Departments. Meanwhile, the engineering aspects of the scheme were referred to the Public Works Department, who arranged for a referral to a firm of consulting engineers in Westminster to consider the technical challenges, to draw up preliminary plans and estimates, and specifications for the dredger. The Finance Department had to approach the government of India concerning the provision of the initial capital with which the new port trust could finance the work, and the Revenue Department had to acquire the necessary land. Finally, the Home Department had to be 'moved' to take legal opinion over the form and substance of the new Port Trust Bill, which also had to go up to the government of India, whose business it was to obtain the sanction of the secretary of state for the scheme as a whole.[9]

To deal with the intricacies of inter-departmental dealings such as those involved in the Cochin port project, Sidney was fortunate in possessing a staff of able, hard-working and experienced clerks; however, they were mainly Brahmins with little experience of the world outside the Secretariat other than the reading matter of the office files. They were 'experts on rules, entirely reliable where there was an established precedent and the best of them had a marvellous command of official English.' But when faced with a new challenge with no precedents and uncovered by existing rules, they were usually 'out of their depth' and it was the undersecretary who was forced to do the original thinking. In the Revenue (Special) Department there were endless problems arising from enemy aliens and their properties. One particularly complex case was that of the Basel Mission Industrial Company, which before the First World War was a prosperous, well-organised weaving concern, the surplus profits of which went to support various German mission activities. Having been sequestrated as an enemy business, it was to be vested in trustees who were to hand it over to a new trust company to run it for the benefit of the trustees controlling enemy missions during the war. In confusing two lots of trustees with the trust company much difficulty arose in defining the nature of the transfers to be made, and Sidney was forced to resort to subterfuge to get the necessary files past his superiors, whose over-conscientiousness threatened to delay matters indefinitely.

For most of Sidney's time in the Secretariat the other undersecretaries were men of his own year, all great friends who 'made merry over the defects of our superiors and vied with one another in drafting saucy replies to legislative council questions.' It appears that the 1913 intake of Madras civilians was unusually diverse and interesting, including the undersecretary of the Home Department, Charles Hilton Brown, best known for his biographies of Kipling and Robert Burns. Brown was also a novelist and travel writer as well as a regular contributor of light verse to *Punch*, writing without interruption into the 1950s. Another civilian of Sidney's year was Sir Benegal Rama Rau, who had been his sole companion in the Tamil class at Cambridge and pursued a very distinguished career with the government of India, serving eventually as deputy high commissioner in London and ambassador in Japan and the United States. When, due to his superior's absence on home leave, Sidney was allowed to assume charge of the department for a short period, he also encountered Sir Frederick Nicholson, who had retired from the ICS long before his own birth and had subsequently been involved on a regular basis with the development of Madras industry and fisheries, as well as being deeply involved in the origins of the cooperative movement in India. Sidney was full of admiration 'for the grave courtesy and official decorum with which he treated me, for he must have thought of me as a babe in arms' and the 'vigour and mental fertility' of the old man which enabled him with 'his customary thoroughness' to convince the government to sanction the opening of a small government jam factory in the Nilgiri Hills in the First World War to supply a deficiency in current food stocks.

As far as Sidney and Olive were concerned, the more pleasurable aspects of the Nilgiris and Ootacamund tended to elude them, due to a lack of money for the hunting and fishing which 'give one a real knowledge of that wonderful country.' By the end of their second Ooty season, the financial depression was becoming acute. The post-war inflation made the position of a married undersecretary very hard and with a fixed salary Sidney was eventually getting less pay in the Secretariat than he could earn as a sub-collector. Moreover, 'the allurements of headquarters society were beginning to pall and we began to think more kindly of the simple joys of district life.' As a result, Sidney applied for a transfer and, as Olive's health was not good, the government was accommodating enough to agree to send them to Madanapalle, 'a station with a really good climate and an excellent mission hospital' about 170 miles to the northwest of Madras in Chittoor district. However, before settling down in Madanapalle, Sidney was recalled to Madras for two short interludes—at a time when the political situation in India was dramatically changing.

6

TWO INTERLUDES 1920–21

From 1920 to 1922 India was convulsed by a display of mass non-cooperation and organised protest. From South Africa by way of Britain and a failed attempt to enlist in the ambulance corps, Mohandas Karamchand Gandhi, aged forty-six, had arrived back in India in 1915 where he continued to support the war effort and encourage enlistment, retaining a strong belief in British justice. While living in Natal, to deal with the racial challenges of South Africa he had developed a form of protest called satyagraha, or 'truth-force', consisting of passive civil disobedience and non-violent confrontation. In India satyagraha, practised on a nationwide scale, had the ability to involve millions of citizens in a series of peaceful demonstrations to undermine the authority of the Raj and, due to its simplicity and quasi-religious features, the movement became a mass exercise, not the preserve of an Indian western-educated elite.

Following the First World War, Gandhi became the dominant figure in the Congress and at his instigation the organisation was transformed into a more permanent, representative and effective institution. Protest focused upon the repeal of the Rowlatt Acts of 1919 by which the government opted for stricter control of the press, arrests without warrant, indefinite detention without trial and juryless in camera trials for proscribed political acts. The acts were met by widespread anger and discontent among Indians, notably in the Punjab region, and in early April 1919 Gandhi called for a one-day general strike (hartal) throughout the country. In Amritsar on 10 April the news that prominent Indian leaders had been arrested and banished from the city sparked violent protests in which soldiers fired upon civilians, buildings were looted and burned and angry mobs killed several foreign nationals. A force of several dozen troops commanded by Brigadier General Reginald Dyer was given the task of restoring order, and among the measures taken was a ban on public gatherings.

On the afternoon of 13 April, a crowd of at least 10,000 men, women and children (many of whom had come to the city to celebrate Baisakhi, a spring festival) gathered in a space known as the Jallianwalla Bagh, with only one exit, which was sealed off by Dyer and his troops. Without warning, the troops opened fire on the crowd, reportedly shooting hundreds of rounds until they ran out of ammunition. According to one official report, an estimated 379 people were killed and about 1,200 were wounded (although other estimates were considerably higher). The shooting was followed by the proclamation of martial law in the Punjab, including public floggings and other humiliations. Indian outrage grew as news of the shooting and subsequent British actions spread throughout the subcontinent. The massacre marked a turning point in India's modern history. It left a permanent scar on Indo-British relations and was the prelude to Gandhi's full commitment to the cause of Indian nationalism and independence from Britain.

Gandhi, initially hesitant to act, began organising his first large-scale and sustained non-violent protest, the non-cooperation movement of 1920, which was quickly taken up by the Congress whose members, already in an uproar over the Punjab atrocities, were examining the implications of the long-delayed Montagu-Chelmsford reforms of 1918–19 (taking their name from Samuel Montagu, Liberal Secretary of State for India during the latter part of World War I, and Lord Chelmsford, Conservative Viceroy of India between 1916 and 1921). On the surface, the concessions appeared substantial: three out of the seven ministers on the viceroy's executive council were now Indian; the 1919 Government of India Act considerably enlarged the Indian electorate, creating Indian majorities in the great provincial councils; and in the provincial governments (administrations ruling huge regions such as Bengal, the United Provinces and Madras) a system of dyarchy was introduced whereby Indian and British ministers shared ministerial office. However, under this system, Indian ministers were only given 'safe' portfolios such as education, public health, agriculture and irrigation, whereas British minsters held key offices necessary for the control of the state, such as justice, police and revenue. Moreover, the viceroy could veto legislation passed in the provincial legislatures, suspend provincial councils and, if necessary, rule as an autocrat with the backing of the armed services, a situation which remained the case until independence in 1947.

It was arguable that the steady devolution of power, both at central and provincial government level, was essentially a British device to bind even greater numbers of India's elite and educated groups to the status quo. It also seemed to offer the British a further advantage in that the responsibilities and opportunities to which Indians could now aspire, in local as well as central government, enhanced the chances of communal, provincial and ethnic rivalry. Hindus and Muslims had achieved a surprising level of cooperation in their campaign against the Raj following the political accord established by the Lucknow Pact of 1916, in which the Congress and its Muslim counterpart, the Muslim League, agreed to give Muslims separate electorates in all provincial legislatures and to allow them special weighting in Hindu-majority provinces. However, with the defeat of Turkey in the First World War, increasing numbers of Muslims began to fear for the independence of the Ottoman sultan, whose position as khalifa (caliph) of Islam in their eyes was vital to the maintenance of the law and faith of Muslims everywhere.

The Khilafat agitation, with its distinctive organisation, helped to define the emerging identity of Indian Muslims. Although 1916 to 1922 was a period of communal harmony, in the following years the organisation of parallel, yet separate, activities by the Congress and the Khilafatists gradually intensified, and Hindu and Muslim leaders turned to mobilising followers by the use of each religion's distinctive symbols. The result was an explosive era of rioting and recrimination to which Madras was not immune. In April 1919 the Marquess of Willingdon[1] was appointed as the Governor of Madras, shortly after the Montagu-Chelmsford reforms of 1919 were formalised by the

Government of India Act. In 1921 he was forced to deal with a series of communal riots that broke out in August in the Malabar District, declaring martial law just before the government of India sent in a large force to quell the riots.[2] At around the same time, a general strike associated with Gandhi's non-cooperation movement involved over 10,000 workers in the Buckingham and Carnatic Mills of Madras city.

When A. C. Duff, private secretary to Lord Willingdon, took a month's absence from Madras in 1920 in order to be married, Sidney was called in to act for him. Fortunately he and Duff were of a similar size and he was able to borrow the requisite uniforms: a yellow-faced dress coat worn by all the staff in the evenings, and the political uniforms worn by the private secretary on state occasions. Sidney was only forced to wear the latter once, when the governor paid a state visit to the maharaja of Cochin in October 1920, and although his body was of much the same dimensions as that of Duff, his head was about three sizes larger, 'with the result that his brass-spiked helmet wobbled about on the top of my head in a manner which upset His Excellency's gravity to a most undesirable extent. However matters were arranged by my carrying the diminutive hat in my hand and honour was saved.'

Government House, where Sidney carried out his duties, was originally the property of the wealthy Luis and Antonia de Madeiros. Antonia sold the property to the East India Company in 1753 and it became home to the governors of Madras until Indian independence in 1947. It was considerably remodelled around 1800 under the patronage of Lord Edward Clive, when John Goldingham, an astronomer and engineer with the Company, was commissioned to build an adjoining banqueting hall to commemorate the Company's victory over Tipu Sultan in the Fourth Anglo-Mysore War. The hall was built in the form of a Greek temple with Doric columns, believed to have been modelled after the Parthenon in Athens, and was enclosed by a gallery with portraits of Anglo-Indian administrators and British monarchs. This edifice was later described as resembling 'a Heroum, a neo-classical temple for hero worship', which seemed appropriate bearing in mind the general adulation given to the Governors of Madras.[3]

The job of private secretary was not the 'gilded sinecure' that Sidney had anticipated, and the routine varied little. Punctually at 9.30 am he would go to his excellency's study with the day's files (perhaps a dozen or so), of which three or four would be 'big contentious matters' and the rest of a more formal nature. Sidney's job was to brief the governor thoroughly, summarise the minutes, call attention to possible problems and suggest various ways of dealing with them. This duty had to be finished within about three quarters of an hour for the governor to be in his room at the Secretariat in time for the day's interviews, involving a great deal of 'midnight oil' for Sidney. However, since many of the larger files emanated from his own department, they were already familiar to him. During the interviews, which normally were carried on without respite until lunchtime, Sidney would be in the adjoining room to the governor's office at the Secretariat, through which the passing traffic allowed him little time for his own work. His 'paramount duty' was to get his excellency back to Government House in time for luncheon, at which meal there would normally be guests. Along with the rest of the staff, Sidney had to be on hand to look after the assembled company and to make sure that the governor, who enjoyed conversing with his guests, did not linger and disrupt his timetable. Also present at lunch was Lady Willingdon, who was in Sidney's view 'quite the most remarkable woman I have ever met.[4] She misses nothing, ignores nothing and forgets nothing.' When a matter arose in conversation which needed attention she would pass him her pad so that he could make a note of a letter to be written, or telephone call to be made and followed up, and 'woe betide me if I left that note in my waistcoat pocket! Her Excellency would be sure to ask me a day or two later what I had done about the matter and she had no sort of use for the inefficient.'

After lunch Sidney would return to his office and attempt to deal with the work left unattended from the morning: the dictation of numerous letters, the arrangement of the governor's timetable, the preparatory work for the next tour, the copy in his own hand of the private correspondence between governor and secretary of state, and many other miscellaneous duties. After tea he was free to have a game of tennis or a swim unless needed to help the staff by accompanying either Lord Willingdon or his wife to some function or other. In the evening, the next day's files would arrive, and either before or after dinner he had to find time to study them, memorise their principal contents and be prepared to take the governor through them in the morning. As Sidney maintained, 'It was certainly a very full day's work and one had the rather oppressive feeling of never being finished.'

The business of 'devilling up' a future tour was particularly testing. The Secretariat received copies of the various addresses which were to be presented to the governor and prepared minutes on the numerous requests which they contained. Sidney drew up a list of the speeches which would be required, principally dealing with replies to addresses, and marking inaugural functions such as the laying of foundation stones. Lord Willingdon then indicated which speeches he would handle and which Sidney needed to draft. The governor was a good extempore speaker and 'his practice was to speak on the spur of the moment on all occasions which did not involve statements of policy or commitments of the government.' Such sensitive issues he would give to his private secretary who, with the help of a Secretariat note, would produce 'well-rounded-paragraphs promising nothing more than "the earnest consideration of my government"' to the relevant requests, 'most of which were hardy annuals which had already had all the consideration they deserved.' With each version of such paragraphs Sidney admitted that he found it progressively difficult to embody the same 'vague promises' in different words, since 'all these uninspired effusions would be reported verbatim in the local press and studied with meticulous attention by the people concerned'.

As Sir Herbert Thompson, a Madras Indian Civil Servant from 1923 to 1926, pointed out, both Willingdons 'set their stamp on all things Madrassi, partly because of a weakness for permitting their names to be used as a label not only on the usual new creations, roads, hospitals and schools, but also renaming well-known landmarks whose vernacular names enjoyed the sanction of the Presidency's long history.'[5] Furthering the couple's exploration of the area, towards the end of his acting period Sidney had a narrow logistical escape. One Monday at the lunch table Lady Willingdon decided that a picnic should take place the following Saturday at the Seven Pagodas, 'a group of most interesting and very ancient monolith temples' situated at Mahabalipuram, on the coast fifty miles south of Madras.[6] Sidney was asked to make the necessary arrangements and at once wrote a personal letter to the collector of Chingleput district (even in Sidney's day more of a Madras suburb than a district) asking him to arrange for the local tahsildar (district officer) to provide boats to take the party across the backwater with the lunch baskets. Upon arrival on the Saturday morning it was evident that the tahsildar had produced 'a most superlative bundobust' (feat of organisation), with many boats and coolies, a series of flagged posts marking the course across the shallow backwater and a rickshaw to carry her excellency over the sandy tracks. Meanwhile, the local zamindar with the village officer and the temple priests were waiting on the bank to welcome the distinguished visitors and 'the little rest-house was so clean that it positively shone.' Sidney took an early opportunity to thank the tahsildar for his outstanding work and was 'distinctly shaken when he whispered to me that he only received news of our visit at 2 am that very morning when in camp ten miles away.' It appeared that the collector had gone on leave to Ooty a few days before the letter arrived; however, when it was forwarded to him he wired the tahsildar immediately with only just enough time to achieve such spectacular results. For a long afterwards Sidney confessed that he had a 'sinking feeling' when visualising the scenario of arriving at the backwater with no boats, no coolies and no tahsildar. Despite having a 'heart of gold', Lady Willingdon's tolerance of carelessness was low in the extreme.

Poor Duff had 'a tragic end'. He finished his time as private secretary and was sent as collector of Vizagapatam, the site of a minor naval engagement in the Bay of Bengal in 1804 during the Napoleonic Wars. He was in camp with a young assistant who was very anxious to shoot a tiger and was sent out alone with a shikari. When the tiger duly appeared, the boy shot it but the creature was only wounded. Duff felt it was his duty to see that the tiger was not left to prey on the villagers and took on the very dangerous task of finishing it off. During the course of this foray the tiger attacked him and 'mauled him terribly'. As he was being carried in, he was met by the local tahsildar to whom he dictated his will and he was forced to sign it with his toe print, as both his hands were useless. He died very shortly afterwards.

The second brief interlude in Madras occurred shortly after Sidney's spell as private secretary. The Duke of Connaught[7] was to visit Madras in January 1921 and his secretary, John Maffey, later Governor-General of the Sudan, had asked for a local man to be attached to him as 'a sort of liaison officer and general handyman.' Sidney had to board the cruiser which brought the duke and his staff into the harbour, introduce himself to Maffey and take his orders. In fact there was little for him to do other than deal with a number of letters penned by locals to the duke, 'almost all of them written by obvious lunatics or eccentrics', which required an acknowledgment. Sidney was then asked to 'devil up' a speech for the 'grand reconciliation function', at which the duke was to give his blessing to the union of the two rival scouting organisations: on the one hand the 'orthodox' Baden-Powell scouts, started by British scouting enthusiasts, and on the other the 'more politically-minded body' organised by Mrs Annie Besant as part of her 'Home Rule for India' campaign. Sidney produced what he considered to be 'an elegant little speech' calculated to last about ten minutes. However, it transpired that only about four sentences of his draft were actually used, which proved to be the closest he came to personal contact with his royal highness, although he was to be deeply involved with the Scout Movement at a later stage.

7

MADANAPALLE 1921–24

Leaving the rapid pace of Government House, Sidney happily embarked on his next posting up country. To reach Madanapalle by road (and apparently it was 'sheer lunacy' to attempt the journey by train) one left Madras by the main Bangalore route and travelled due west for about 130 miles, where the road suddenly rose dramatically before reaching the town of Palmaner in 'a radically different climate', more than 2,000 feet above sea level. Turning northwards through rocky, scrub-covered country, the hills became more thickly wooded and the valleys more fertile. Sidney describes on the road the 'bands of picturesque Sugali women, carrying huge head-loads of fuel to market—handsome creatures of gipsy origin with wonderful figures, clad in tight-fitting jumpers and gaudy kilt-like skirts which swing gracefully to the rhythm of their stride.' 160 miles from Madras there was a narrow pass between two sizeable hills, one 'a mass of tumbled boulders' and the other covered with forest. On the far side of these hills was the little town of Madanapalle, which was to be the home of the Wadsworths for the next three years and 'our spiritual home for many years more.'

The station had great appeal with an excellent climate, cool or almost cold for nine months of the year and not unbearably hot for the other three. The surrounding country was attractive with 'none of the dirty, squalid towns which deface so many parts of India.' It was 'a land of picturesque villages, many of them roughly walled and protected by a ruined fort, nestling in fertile valleys between well-wooded hills.' To get from one village to the next it was necessary to scramble on horseback over a rocky pass, yet the main roads were excellent, so that it was possible to undertake interesting round trips by combining the use of motorbicycle and horse. However, the chief charm of Madanapalle was its people who were 'kindly, friendly, and … unsophisticated' and, having surveyed the Wadsworths at a distance for several months and found them acceptable, the local population readily adopted 'the whole lot of us and especially the children in whom their interest was unfailing.' Sidney felt that they began to look upon him not simply as a mere tax-gatherer and magistrate, but as a sort of elder brother: 'They consulted me about everything, deferred to my views and bore no malice if the decision was against them.' Nor was this friendliness 'a mere courting of the man in power.' When in 1934 (twelve years after his departure from the area) Sidney had to return on inspection duty, the whole town turned out to greet the couple, complete with brass bands and rose garlands. In 1942, when Madras was facing a Japanese invasion and the High Court was evacuated, Sidney and Olive spent a week on Horsleykonda, a hill 4,500 feet high twelve miles above Madanapalle, remembered by a fellow Madras civil servant, Hadden Hamilton Carleston, as 'a delightful place' possessing an ideal climate all year with no mosquitoes and consequently no fever.[1] Most touchingly, while there the Wadsworths received a number of visits from the sons of old friends who had died, who trudged three miles up a steep bridle path 'just to show friendliness to their fathers' friends and to see if there was anything they could do to help.'

Possibly the secret of the 'happy relations' during his stay in the area lay in the fact that Sidney was no longer tied to a desk. The amount of paperwork and court business was not excessive, and there was time for meeting people in villages and fields rather than passing orders on reports from tahsildars[2] and revenue inspectors, which inevitably occurred in 'heavier' districts. Sir Christopher Masterman, an ICS contemporary of Sidney, agreed that district touring was particularly pleasurable in Madras, possibly because it was predominantly an agricultural province with few industries outside Madras city, and there were consequently no particularly influential industrialists or merchants in the districts. In Masterman's opinion the British ICS officer 'got on well with cultivators and the poorer classes, and at the other end with the land-owning aristocracy, the polo players and the race goers etc., but disliked the middle class Indian—the shopkeepers, the money-lenders, the smaller landlords, who exploited the poor … and never had any real contact with them.'[3]

As Alan Westlake (also in the Madras ICS in the first decades of the twentieth century) described it, a South Indian village was an organised community with a headman (the village munsiff) responsible to the government for the collection of revenue and the peace of the village. He was assisted by the village constable (talayari). The village accountant (karnam) had copies of large-scale maps which showed the position and boundaries of every field in the village, and kept the land revenue accounts. He also had a henchman (toti). In addition there were a number of village servants who had originally been remunerated by grants of land but were later supported by 'customary gifts' from the villagers. Most important among them were the carpenter (much in demand to mend carts and ploughs), the laundryman and the barber, who often combined massage, minor surgery and music-making with shaving. A temple priest might also be employed (although the temple dancing girl had ceased to have official recognition) and there was a fund used mainly for religious buildings and festivals.[4]

In Sidney's view the people of India responded best to 'personal rule'. He was firmly of the opinion that 'If only the man in charge will come and see for himself, an adverse order will be accepted with cheerful resignation; whereas the same order passed on a tahsildar's report will be fiercely resented and ascribed to favouritism or malice.' The process of visiting villages was undeniably time-consuming, often involving twenty or thirty miles by road and ten miles or more across country and, upon reaching a village, the tank or channel to be inspected could be another three or four miles. However, by camping in a central position and collecting all the matters which needed attention within a radius of about eight miles it was possible to deal with the remoter villages without a great sacrifice of time. In Sidney's words:

> what fun it was riding across country in brilliant sunshine, fanned by a cooling breeze, with wooded hills on either side of the track and always something interesting to look at—the duck on the tanks, the green

> pigeons in the lofty ippa trees, the tall waving crops of millet, the bright green patches of paddy and sugarcane, the women gossiping round the well with their water-pots balanced on their hips, the jungly Yanadis robbing the wild bees of their honey, perched on crazy slings of bamboo and creepers, on which they dangled precariously against the face of a cliff. Journey's end would be a group of village elders squatting under a banyan tree, who would cluster round with fruits and fresh coconut milk for my refreshment and grass for my horse, before we started on the business of the day.

Nancy Dearmer, the wife of a Church of England missionary, in a letter to her mother in 1916, described living conditions in a typical South Indian village. She recalled when entering a house, 'we had to bend double to get inside. The walls were mud, the floor was mud and the roof was palm leave [sic] ... there was a tiny space of courtyard inside and the roof, seen from outside, only covers a small space around the courtyard ... divided into tiny "rooms"'. The rent for such a house was not excessive; fuel was only used for cooking and consisted of dung mixed with some other substance, such as coconut fibre. Rice or millet formed the basic diet and both were cheap. Clothes were scanty and the children wore none for the first year or two. A few earthenware and brass vessels and a curry stone were all that was required for cooking, and baskets, buckets and the children's slates for schools were all made out of the useful palm leaf.[5]

As Sidney became more familiar with village life, he became increasingly interested in the 'complexities' of the caste system, under which, based on the social groupings of jati (birth groups) and varna (literally colour, outward appearance), Indians were classified into four classes: Brahmins (priests), Kshatriyas (rulers, administrators and warriors), Vaishyas (artisans, merchants, tradesmen and farmers) and Shudras (labouring classes). This categorisation had implicitly a fifth element which consisted of those people deemed to be outside its bounds, such as tribal members, and the Dalits, or untouchables, who provided the farmer's reserve of casual labour. Alan Westlake observed that the south of India had been highly Brahminised and in places Brahmins had been so much admired that they were induced to settle down with large grants of prosperous wet land. In general it could be said that the population of South India was formed of a vast middle class, varying from poor to quite rich, with an intellectual aristocracy of Brahmins and at the base a large population of untouchables. Administrative jobs and senior appointments were granted only to the upper castes.[6]

Sidney's interest in caste helped to brighten up those 'otherwise dreary hours' spent in the trial of criminal cases, as the witnesses provided a good cross-section of the population and 'the stories they told shed much incidental light on their customs and manner of life.' In the course of his work Sidney began to learn some of the 'minute differences which distinguish one caste from another—not merely differences of clothing and customs, but differences of character and outlook. Thus one caste would be noted for foxiness, another for cowardice and a tendency to try and please both sides; yet another community had a reputation for lechery, while a closely connected caste was renowned for its piety and simplicity.' Many of these communal characteristics were embodied in local habits which came to the surface under the stress of events which were described in the witness box. Sidney was delighted when, 'in the course of an otherwise tedious stealing and receiving case', he discovered how a Sugali woman's kilt was made by 'sewing together long horizontal strips cut from different coloured cloths, each strip ... representing a different item of stolen property.'

The sub-collector's house at Madanapalle was 'a fine old building', despite being badly in need of repair. The landlord was the keeper of the local beer shop and could only be moved to attend to the maintenance of the property after hints from Sidney that his liquor licence was in danger. The house consisted of a central area of 'more or less conventional' bungalow design, with a large main hall and two smaller rooms on either side. At each end of this main block there was a separate wing. One consisted of a dining room which had to be locked up as its roof appeared to be 'totally without support, all the rafters having been eaten by white ants'. Indeed, a year later it did collapse one night in the middle of a storm so noisy that the crash went unnoticed, and the room was finally repaired. The garden was attractive, the dominant feature being an enormous banyan tree 'so big that it was frequently borrowed for public meetings and functions.' There was also a good tennis court and a large kitchen garden which produced fresh vegetables for almost all the year.

Among those people with whom the Wadsworths were in contact on an almost daily basis were the doctors and nurses of the Arcot mission, who 'exercised a very humanising influence over thousands of people who had not the slightest intention of becoming professed Christians.' Dr Louisa H. Hart, who came from Nova Scotia, had received a handsome donation of $10,000 from the Women's Board in America to start a hospital in memory of an American social worker, Mary Lott Lyles, and was the first physician-in-charge of the new establishment in 1911. According to Sidney, with 'white hair, rosy cheeks, the bluest of blue eyes and a sunny smile which lit up her whole countenance ... one was not surprised to learn that one of her chief attributes was to keep the men away from her hospital.' With the able assistance of two Dutch sisters, Josephine and Sarella Te Winkel, a number of barely educated Indian Christian girls were turned into highly competent nurses and work of a more evangelistic nature was carried out in the women's quarters of local houses.

In addition to the women's hospital, four miles from Madanapalle was a United Mission Tuberculosis Sanitorium, built in 1912 and inaugurated in 1915 by Lord Pentland. Its first medical superintendent was a Dane, Dr Frimodt-Moller, who ran the sanatorium on behalf of a joint committee of Protestant missions and played a major role in India's fight against tuberculosis through the training of specialist workers, the conducting of surveys and the introduction of BCG vaccines in 1948. Sidney remembered that Fridmodt-Moller 'struggled unceasingly to prevent his limited accommodation from being clogged with advanced cases for which little could be done; and it must have been very distressing to have to turn away the worst cases in order to have room for those who had a fair chance of recovery.' The situation was exacerbated by the popular belief that the Madanapalle climate was good for tuberculosis, with the result that many consumptives took up residence in the town, attracting a number of quacks who professed to cure even the most hopeless patients.

The Wadsworths, with the family of the executive engineer, E. P. Walsh, spent the hot weather at Horsleykonda and the men travelled up and down the hill for their respective jobs. There was a good road for the first twelve miles from the valley whereas the three final miles of the ascent were somewhat steep. However, one could arrange for chairs to carry up the women and children while the men rode. With no stables and a number of bears at the highest point it was impossible to keep horses at the top of the hill, and Sidney usually walked down in the cool of the morning and rode up in the evening 'when the forest resounded with the call of jungle-fowl, spur-fowl and peacock.' The lower slopes were thick with bamboo, but near the top the forest department had planted sandalwood, 'a small and unimposing tree, but extremely valuable'. The Wadsworths had a great deal of sandalwood in their garden at Madanapalle planted by their landlord, 'an old rogue', to provide cover for 'his activities as a receiver of illicitly felled sandalwood belonging to the forest department.'

In addition to the Walshes and the mission workers whom Sidney and Olive met on a daily basis, there was a European household with whom they had no contact. Dr and Mrs James Cousins were in charge of a half-finished and 'rather moribund' theosophical college. This was at a time when Annie Besant, head of the theosophical organisation which had its headquarters in Madras, and hardly a favourite of Sidney and the British establishment in general, was 'endeavouring to ingratiate herself with the local intelligentsia by becoming the leader of extreme Indian nationalism and publishing violent anti-British articles in her newspaper, New India.' Geoffrey Lamarque was very aware in South India of the 'torrent of words poured out every day in the newspapers, and from the lips of politicians, attacking British "imperialism" and British things generally.' He recalled that:

> if those who uttered this kind of stuff really meant what they said, or if they represented Indian feeling generally, then clearly … the days of the British were numbered, and indeed the sooner we went the better. But I discovered that neither of these hypotheses was correct … I was invariably treated with a courtesy and respect beyond my deserts, from Ministers down to the humblest villagers. Animosity, and it could be real enough, was not between Indian and British, but between Indian and Indian, Brahmin v. non-Brahmin in the south, and Hindu v. Muslim in the north. British rule depended on the good will and cooperation of countless Indians at every level of society, and continued to get it throughout its life. Political speeches and newspaper articles attacking the British made no impact outside a restricted circle in the big cities and even there were treated with cynical indifference.[7]

Sidney, as he writes in the last chapter of his memoirs, undoubtedly agreed that the inflammatory nature of nationalist propaganda did not affect relations between the great majority of Indians and the British, and was happy not to fraternise with any perpetrator of such material. He was therefore relieved to discover that James Henry Cousins (an Irishman) who espoused the same 'political line' as Annie Besant, could not under the circumstances mix freely with the local representative of the British Raj, and he himself made no advances to Cousins, considering the man to be 'an oddity—fluent, visionary and inclined to be fanatical.' Cousins had been Professor of English Literature at Keio University in Tokyo for a year and established the Tokyo Lodge of the Theosophical Society in February 1920. From May 1919 to March 1920 he contributed several articles to the *Asian Review*, the English journal of the Black Dragon Society, a Pan-Asian association which allegedly harboured Indian revolutionaries. He was therefore marked by British and Indian agents due to his potential threat to the Anglo-Japanese alliance and British India.[8] As well as publishing several books of 'rather modern' poetry, Cousins also wrote with some authority on Indian art, intimating that 'all things Indian are perfect and full of inner meanings'. Sadly he failed to convince Sidney that there were enough 'inner meanings to make me admire some of the gross sculptures I have seen on Vaishnavite temples.'[9]

To complete the picture of the religious community around Madanapalle there was a French Catholic priest and, at the criminal settlement at Bhumanagadda, seven miles away, Captain and Mrs Green of the Salvation Army. Captain Green was 'a handsome, well-built man' who had been in turn a miner, a prize-fighter, and a keeper of a fish stall in Cardiff market. The Greens' flock consisted of about 150 families of Kathiras, 'a community of drunken, degraded, physically degenerate folk, who, when left to themselves, followed the hereditary callings of thieving and prostitution, the women acting as spies for the burglarious activities of the men and the men acting as pimps for the women.' Registered under the Criminal Tribes Act, the Kathiras were required by law to stay in the settlement unless given a pass, and the Greens had been given the task of teaching them to earn an honest living by cultivating the rather unprofitable surrounding land. Most members of the community were 'physically incapable of sustained manual labour and all their natural inclinations were in favour of a wandering life of comparative sloth.' Constantly absconding, they were rounded up by the police and placed before Sidney to be given a jail term. However, they were 'passionately attached' to their children, and attempts to remove their offspring to separate schools where they might have a chance to learn better ways were nearly always defeated when the children ran away to re-join their 'deplorable' parents.

Despite the fact that to an outsider the work seemed hopeless and highly depressing, the Greens 'stuck to it loyally, managing to keep cheerful and live decently on the miserable pittance which the Army allowed them.' The seven years which they served between one furlough and the next must have seemed interminable, but 'their devotion knew no bounds.' In 1918 the settlement was struck by the influenza pandemic, which was accompanied by an outbreak of cholera in its most virulent form. The inmates 'died like flies' but the Greens were steadfast in nursing the sick and comforting the dying, although they were under much pressure to leave. At a later date a small girl was badly burned and needed a graft of healthy skin to heal her injuries. None of her relatives was prepared to help so Captain Green himself offered to undergo the operation for the graft, suffering a great deal of pain and a number of septic wounds.

The Indian residents of Madanapalle included people of 'education and refinement' and many of the leading farmers and merchants sent their sons to college. However, such an education failed to prevent family altercations concerning the division of what was frequently a considerable family property. The joint family system inevitably seemed to involve a complicated partition in every generation, and the partition generally went to the courts if the property was substantial, each branch of the family asserting that the other was suppressing family assets in order to get an undue share. By its very nature the case would raise issues on which only the members of the family, all of whom were partisans, knew the truth, and a legal decision on each of the issues was therefore something of a gamble. Such a suit involved accounting, inventories, commissions to divide land, receiverships and so on, which brought more fees to the lawyers, who were unsurprisingly interested in 'elaborating the procedure and postponing the decision.'

No doubt honourable lawyers existed who attempted to save their clients from futile litigation, yet there were some who regarded their clients as 'cows to be milked' and others who even employed agents in the villages to 'foment strife and to bring the resultant litigation to their principals' offices.' In Sidney's view 'It has always seemed to me the greatest reproach to our rule in India that we have delivered the country over to a devastating legalism which gives justice to the man with the longest purse.' Henry Downing, of a later Madras ICS intake, agreed that 'the British administration may well have been responsible for the excessive volume of litigation by imposing an educational system which produced a surplus of people with a literary education who had a vested interest in encouraging their clients to resort to the law', but he suspected that the phenomenon was not uncommon in any traditional agrarian society where 'matters of land and water are vital to people's livelihood and disagreements can set family against family.'[10] Moreover, the Indian villager loved litigation, and it was said that 'the proudest moment of his life was when he walked into the court behind his Vakil [advocate] carrying his load of law books.'[11]

Away from the more affluent sector of Madanapalle, Sidney was in close touch with the local peasantry, seeing matters 'to some extent through their eyes.' In the process of jamabundi he would make a detailed inspection of village accounts and pass final orders on matters such as penalties for encroachments, water charges, remissions for crop failures and other issues emerging from village administration. He would also looked at registers of births and deaths, vaccinations and other miscellaneous items. Following such extensive scrutiny, he was in a position to commend, reprove or even fine village officers for their work. A fellow Madras civil servant, Sidney Dunlop, recalled in more detail how in a temperature of 105°F, he processed to the fields to conduct his own jamabundi:

> preceded by two talayaris with their long poles of office, my peon with his sash and badge behind me, the village headman (who spoke no English but always smiled) just a little in the rear, and three or four village menials further behind … [I] stalked most self consciously through the village while a concourse of children followed and stared and every house seemed to have its quota of men and women with nothing to do but watch us go by. I used to sit under a pandal (awning) outside the taluk office,[12] passing accounts, checking water rates, receiving petitions, around me a sweating, malodorous crowd pressing in on every side excluding air, from 7.30 am to about 3.00 or even 4.00 pm without rest. After that Court work, and after that judgments had to be written, ordinary revenue work, village officers' enquiries,

> files, etc. had to be attended to. I snatched a quarter of an hour for tea—rose from Court at about 7.00 pm and sometimes even 9.00 pm—dined hurriedly and then back to the desk again until midnight. It was regularly a 16 to 18 hour day.[13]

Among his own many administrative tasks, on the subject of irrigation Sidney represented local opinion when approaching higher authorities. The Madanapalle area was irrigated mainly by chains of small tanks, officially described as 'precarious sources', governed by special rules, and with which the Public Works Department had no dealings. Repairs were carried out by overseers working under revenue officers, and there was a rough scale of amounts which could be spent on this work, dependent upon the government's income from the source. As a result, if a tank was breached or seriously damaged, there was a grave danger that it would be abandoned. However, a few hundred rupees could mend such a tank, which would not only irrigate six or seven areas of paddy but would also keep up the subsoil water level on which many wells irrigating other crops depended, and would serve as a supply of drinking water for men and cattle in an area very liable to drought. Sidney would therefore battle with the government and often succeed in procuring half or two thirds of the cost of the unprofitable work if he could raise the rest in the village in question. He would visit the village, 'assemble all the people concerned under a convenient tree, explain to them exactly what would happen if this tank was abandoned, how their wells would go dry, their trees would wither, their cattle would die for want of water'. He would then move to the matter of the local balance required to complete the repairs, worked out in terms of rupees per acre, before appealing to the cultivators to pay this small sum and to arrange for one of them to take up the contract to make sure that the work was well done within the estimate.

When travelling within the countryside, the comfort of the sub-collector would depend greatly upon the efficiency of the peons (called chuprassis in the north of India) who were 'personal orderlies' and whose usefulness appeared to vary 'in inverse ratio to the importance of the officer to whom they are attached.' Since a sub-collector, however great his local influence, was 'really a very junior and unimportant person', he tended to have an excellent team, whereas the peons of a High Court judge were 'always lazy and frequently dishonest'. In Madanapalle,

Sidney had five peons allotted to him and they proved to be 'an uncommonly useful and loyal team.' The duffadar (police officer) was a steady-going, elderly man whose duties kept him mainly in the office. With him at headquarters was Chentsayya, a dhoby by caste, who, to the benefit of all parties, returned to his 'ancestral calling' when not fulfilling his official duties, upholding his 'well-established right to wash the clothes of the sub-collector's children in return for a monthly payment', whether or not the government would have approved of this arrangement. The three 'camping peons', Abdul Khadir, Gangoji and Ramayya, were all characters. Abdul Khadir was 'a big, boisterous, blustering ruffian, with a great gruff voice … thick lips, half hidden by a black beard and blood-shot eyes which would now and then twinkle with unexpected humour.' He wore 'a white turban, a long smock hanging down to the knees and beneath it a pair of battered old jodhpurs' and had the grave fault of snoring 'horribly, persistently, raucously' which eventually forced Sidney to travel with an extra tent.

To atone for the sin of snoring, Abdul Khadir had 'great virtues'. He could shoe a horse without laming it and always had tools and a stock of shoes in his roll of bedding. To Sidney, who had experienced 'a ten mile tramp in the hot sun' as a result of a horse casting a shoe, 'a competent farrier was 'a pearl without price.' Moreover, Abdul Khadir was a born shikari with a fine collection of 'apocryphal stories of the prowess of sahibs of old, who never missed a sitting shot and slew tigers of portentous dimensions', giving Sidney hope that even though his shooting could be far from impressive, he would go down in history 'with a halo of ever-increasing magnitude'. As a cooly-driver Abdul Khadir had few equals and was in his element when moving camp. Taking up a commanding position he would pour forth 'a polyglot mixture of instructions and objurgations, rarely using ten consecutive words in one language, but apparently achieving the same electric effect, whatever the medium'. On the domestic front he was unable to read or write but was able to recognise most of Sidney's reference books by their size and colour; moreover, he proved to be 'the gentlest of nursemaids' and touchingly fond of the Wadsworth children.

Gangoli was totally different. A Maratha Hindu, he was 'small, lean, hungry-looking and terribly zealous.' When asked to complete duties for Sidney he always wanted to do more, frequently with disastrous results. Set to pull the punkah, he would 'rouse a gale which would sweep all the papers off the table', and when Sidney was writing at his desk would stand over him with a blotter 'in a threatening attitude', waiting for the moment when he could bang it down just in time to catch the tip of his retreating pen and 'scatter the ink far and wide.' Ramayyana was probably the best of the three, 'young, tall and erect, with a pleasant, open face and a cheery smile' he was both willing and competent, and brave in sorting out physical disputes which arose among the carters employed to move camp. He was also a good handyman, and when Sidney's family outgrew the motorbicycle and side-car and they acquired a 'Tin Lizzie', Ramayyana was taught to drive and look after it. When the Wadsworths left Madanapalle he took long leave and worked as their driver in Madras until the old duffadar at Madanapalle retired and Ramayyana went back to take his place, 'eager for the dignity of a silver chevron on his belt and an ornamental dagger stuck into his girdle.'

There was evidence throughout the countryside of the 'troubled times' which existed 150 years before Sidney's posting in the area, when the Madanapalle terrain must have been 'very much a no-man's-land'. He described that:

> Everywhere there were ruined forts; some, like that at Gurramkonda,[14] were elaborate structures with bastions and redoubts which could have stood up to any attack not backed by regular siege artillery; while others were little more than village watch towers. Countless armies must have marched along the once rough roads and many traces of their passage could be seen in the local population. There were Muslims who must have come in with the armies of Tippu or the Mughal governors, Mahrathas whose advent can be ascribed to the marauding trips of Shivaji and his followers, Poligars by the dozen, descended from the local war-lords who used to sell their swords to the highest bidder.

However, in Sidney's opinion the most interesting relics of past armies were the Sugalis, a gipsy community which originally provided the drivers of the pack animals used by invaders. These people lived 'as a race apart, speaking their own language which was akin to Mahrathi, wearing a distinctive dress and occupying isolated hamlets known as tandas. The men are stalwart and somewhat Jewish in appearance.' Their ostensible occupation was that of graziers, however, in fact they tended to be professional cattle and sheep thieves, operating as a rule many miles from home, 'creeping stealthily up to the flock by night and carrying a sheep bodily away' or entering a village in the darkness and stealing a bull from a stall, being twenty miles away with their booty by daybreak. In the rare cases where they were arrested and brought before a court, all the women from the tanda would invariably appear to display their babies before the magistrate and, despite being vigorously deterred by the orderly, would begin 'a pantomime of supplication'.

On a certain day of the year all the Sugali women put on new clothes and danced in front of whatever audience they could find. The women had good features and the young girls were often exceedingly pretty, 'clad in their gaudy kilts and jumpers, with bare back, arms and legs laden with bone bangles, hair hanging down in long strands, heavily ornamental with cowries, and their fingers, toes, nostrils and ears loaded to capacity with heavy brass jewelry.' With much whispering and giggling they assembled for the dance, standing in a ring facing inwards and hands clasped above their heads. As the circle began to revolve slowly there was an accompaniment of 'a strange, plaintive melody … unlike any South Indian music, a song of weird beauty, resembling some Hungarian folk-song with its sad minors and sudden ecstasies.' As the pace quickened the song grew louder, almost rising to a shout, and the dancers swayed towards the centre 'with a swirl and clash of sound'. Then the music died away, the circle ceased to revolve and 'the stately ballet is transformed into a crowd of chattering, jostling shrews, who discuss loudly the colossal amount of baksheesh they hope to get.'

No less unscrupulous in their occupation than the Sugalis, although of a distinctly higher status, were the Poligars, warrior chieftains who were often little better than robbers, historically terrorising the countryside with their ill-disciplined armed bands. When at the beginning of the nineteenth century 'that greatest of revenue officers', Sir Thomas Munro,[15] was carrying out the land settlement of the Ceded Districts (the area in the Deccan[16] which was 'ceded' to the British India Company by the Nizam of Hyderabad in 1800), it was one of his chief objectives to disempower the Poligars. Most of them were pensioned off, 'distinguished from their neighbours by a gold-embroidered head-dress and an allowance just sufficient to prevent them from doing any useful work.' The Raja of Punganur was evidently too important a man for Munro to tackle, and in Sidney's day he still retained an estate which formed about a third of the area of the Madanapalle division. The greater part of the estate was poor, barren land and the line of Punganur rulers had been impoverished by continuous litigation. However, although the days of lavish entertainment were over, the current raja was anxious to maintain the outward appearances of hospitality, and Sidney had to stay at least once in his dilapidated guesthouse 'where the process of decay revealed the fact that the balusters of its ornate terrace were made of beer bottles covered over with plaster'.

In Sidney's view the most interesting aspect of Punganur was neither the palace nor the fort, but the raja's visitors' book, which provided a record of a hundred and twenty years, without a break, of every traveller who had partaken of the raja's hospitality. In the middle of the nineteenth century, with no railways, Punganur was a regular halting place for troops and travellers journeying between Madras and the Deccan, and there were interesting examples of the hardships of travel on the 'barely passable' roads of the region, 'strewn with graves of travellers of former days.' The earlier pages of the book were full of records of marching regiments whose officers were 'royally feasted at the palace' and turned out the guard to honour the raja with a salute. An entry of August 1852 recorded the 1st Madras Fusiliers marching from the military station of Bellary in the Ceded Districts on their way to field service in the Second Burmese War. However, the 1857 Indian Mutiny received no mention, providing proof of the 'profound quiet which prevailed in most of South India during that great upheaval'. The year 1877 contained many references to the severe famine which was particularly devastating in the Punganur neighbourhood and in particular the entry of a special correspondent of *The Statesman* who was touring the area to chronicle the horrors of the situation.

Sidney was 'unable to resist a pressing invitation to dine at the palace' and was quite relieved to find that his own cook was permitted to take his food to the palace where he ate with the raja (a young man, but 'a physical wreck', who died soon afterwards) with his uncle, the kumararaja ('a cheery, robust old boy') in attendance, with 'scores of unseen eyes peeping at me through the lattice screen behind which were the ladies of the zenana.' In future visits Sidney stayed in an unoccupied mission bungalow where, in the coach house, he discovered an old car built in about 1900. In appearance it was a high wagonette and was powered by steam, with the boiler under the front seat, until the missionary to whom it belonged forgot to fill the boiler and burnt it out. Nevertheless, the vehicle was still brought out whenever there was a wedding among the local Christians, who put the bride and groom on the high front seat and, using a yoke of oxen, dragged them 'in slow and dignified procession' around the streets.

In Sidney's opinion Indian Christians displayed a remarkable ability to achieve social mobility. Most were recruited from the 'untouchable' castes and prior to conversion had been living in extreme poverty and total illiteracy. However, it was not unusual to find the children of converts taking university degrees and arriving at positions of considerable responsibility. In Telegu country there was much 'mass conversion', a process whereby the leading members of a small community or hamlet came under Christian influence and persuaded the total populace (men, women and children) to be catechised and baptised. For the second generation this process was extraordinarily effective, as exemplified by a couple known to Sidney. An entire hamlet near Madanapalle was baptised and among the converts was Ramayya, a labourer 'who could just read and write his own language with extreme difficulty'. His wife was a grass-cutter and 'quite illiterate'. Upon his baptism Ramayya took the name of Jacob and became a waterman in the house of one of the local Europeans. In the course of time Jacob's wife became an ayah (nanny) in the same house, where she was trained and 'from this start both husband and wife progressed, learnt English and improved themselves socially and economically, until Jacob became the butler and his wife made herself quite indispensable.' They had one son, Paul, who was sent to the local mission school and eventually became a spare-time employee of his father's master, earning enough to enrol in the Madras Christian College and to graduate. He entered government service as a clerk and, when war broke out in 1914, was given a temporary commission as a second lieutenant in the Indian Army. He went through the Arakan campaign,[17] was found to be an efficient and reliable officer, and at the end of the war was a captain on the staff 'with almost unlimited possibilities ahead of him.'

Although such cases were quite common and illustrated the way in which conversion to Christianity had the ability to 'take the low caste man out of his dreadfully narrow groove', the difficulties for the individuals concerned tended to be considerable, in that people of the higher castes were inclined to resent the rise of these 'upstarts', who often had a great deal of trouble before their new status was recognised, particularly in the villages. Sidney cites the case of a probationary revenue inspector called P. Abraham, who was 'small, spectacled and very black and his appearance at once proclaimed his humble origin'. Being conscious of this, he had apparently developed a severe inferiority complex which led him to behave 'in a bumptious and self-assertive manner', giving orders to village officers and local dignitaries 'before whom Abraham's father would have cringed in abject humility.' As a result, the elders devised a plan to remove him.

On one particular occasion during the course of jamabundi Sidney was dealing with petitioners from the village and inspecting the work of the revenue inspector, the Abraham in question. At the end of the session, an influential member of the Reddy caste,[18] who was headman of a large and inaccessible village on the Mysore border, presented to Sidney 'a detailed and circumstantial accusation against the objectionable Abraham', alleging that he had raped a low-caste girl who supplied him with milk when he was camping in the village. Presuming that the Englishman would be glad, like the fellow members of their own community, either to have Abraham transferred or his case referred to the police, the revenue inspector's enemies were surprised when Sidney, aware that 'the protection of one's subordinates is a paramount duty', demanded an immediate personal investigation. After a convoluted exercise (during which, in order to obtain the truth, Sidney was forced to frame a formal charge against the accountant of the village concerned for failing to report the felling of government trees) it became obvious that the accusations of the Reddy were totally false. In the ensuing trial to prosecute the headman, following the delivery of Sidney's evidence the Reddy declared his wish to compound the offence and Sidney agreed to withdraw the prosecution if the Reddy paid a substantial amount of the compensation to his wife's pet charity and gave Abraham enough to cover his costs 'handsomely'. Although supporting his subordinate, Sidney obviously had some sympathy with his persecutors, declaring that, 'There one has the mentality of the average respectable Indian villager in a nutshell. He can see nothing wrong in fabricating a false case to secure the punishment of a man whom he knows to be a menace to the community.'

8

POLITICAL WARFARE

GODAVERI 1921

The 'rustic peace' of the Wadsworths' life at Madanapalle was shattered by a telegram ordering Sidney to act as additional district magistrate in the district of East Godaveri which, physically larger than Wales, was one of the major districts of the presidency, situated about 300 miles north of Madras city. From September 1920 to February 1922 the non-violent non-cooperation movement, backed by the Indian National Congress at Calcutta in September 1920 and launched that December under the organisation of Mohandas Gandhi, attempted to urge the British to grant self-government, or *swaraj*, to India. Indians were encouraged to sever all ties with the Raj, resulting in the resignation of titles; the boycott of government educational institutions, the courts, government service, foreign goods and elections; and the eventual refusal to pay taxes.[1] The campaign was successful in certain areas for a brief time, and in the Madras Presidency the 'storm centre' was along the east coast within the Northern Circars, comprising the districts of Godaveri, Kistna and Guntur.[2] In these districts 'a situation had arisen which needed very firm handling if there was not to be a complete breakdown of law and order' and it was therefore decided to allot to each area an additional district magistrate with full powers. As a result, there would always be one magistrate at headquarters while the other toured and dealt with the disaffected areas.

Sidney's role as the upholder of law and order was to deal with the proposed action of the non-cooperation movement to counter the 'emotions of loyalty' which the visit of the Prince of Wales in November 1921 was expected to arouse in India.[3] Such action was to be non-violent, although, as Sidney declared, 'one never knew how long non-violence would last when the demonstrations were backed by regiments of congress volunteers, armed with formidable brass-bound staves or lathis.' As he was an additional member of the ICS drafted in to cover the district, there was no accommodation available and it was decided to leave Olive and the children at Madanapalle where they had many friends and a comfortable house. In April 1921 Sidney, having little to pack other than 'ordinary camp stuff', set off immediately on the long train journey, crossing on the second day 'the majestic bridge which spans the broad waters of the Godaveri river' (after the Ganges the second longest river in India, rising in Maharastra and flowing for 910 miles into the Bay of Bengal).[4] At Rajamundry,[5] one of the principal towns of the district situated on the banks of the Godaveri, he was met by the sub-collector, Eric Wood, who brought instructions from the current collector of East Godaveri, G. T. H. Bracken,[6] to the effect that Sidney should leave the train to travel by boat to the mouth of the river, where he was to take charge of a potentially dangerous festival at the coastal village of Antarvedi.

Settling down for the day in a room at the small Rajamundry Club on the bank of the river, Sidney surveyed the town, which, despite appearing impressive from the bridge, did not improve on closer acquaintance. It proved to be 'a large, congested place, seething with Brahmin lawyers and students of very advanced political views.' The more affluent inhabitants of the district consisted mainly of the merchant class of Komatis, and the agricultural community of Kammas who, like the Reddys, were politically and economically dominant in the area. For some reason the Komatis and Kammas had been 'induced to make common cause with the Brahmins, whom they had hitherto regarded with hostility and distrust.' Apparently the Komatis were swayed by the fact that Gandhi also belonged to a Hindu merchant caste and they had been promised that *swaraj* would result in the abolition of the income tax which they detested. In the case of the Kammas, the 'popular theory' was that some of their women had formed liaisons with Brahmins and in this way Brahmin influence had been brought to bear on the entire group. It was clear that the three communities operating together had in many areas almost paralysed the machinery of government and it was Sidney's responsibility to get it working again. The seriousness of the position was demonstrated by the stationing of an officer from the Leinster Regiment at Rajamundry in case it was necessary to summon British troops from Madras.

The journey to the coast was entirely by water as there were very few roads within the Godaveri delta but, as the network of irrigation canals covered the region, there were few villages of importance which could not be reached by boat. Sidney was provided with 'a comfortable house-boat' which was towed by a launch to the great barrage at Dowleishwaram,[7] below which he travelled along one of the major canals, where the boat was towed to avoid the wash of launches. This stretch was somewhat monotonous as the high banks obscured the view of the countryside; however, eventually the boat left the canal and entered the broad tidal waters of one of the main branches of the river. About twenty-four hours after leaving Rajamundry he tied up at Antarvedi, 'a biggish village with a large and very sacred temple,[8] situated between the sea and a small backwater.' The huge crowds attending the festival were already beginning to gather and Sidney made contact with Walter Wright, the district superintendent of police, who had a force of forty men from the armed reserve to deal with possible violence. The press estimated the number of people at roughly 100,000 which was possibly an exaggeration, although there were undoubtedly many thousands and a large bazaar had been set up to supply their needs. To provide for the festival, boatloads of unripe bananas had been dumped on the bank of the river, which the merchants ripened 'by the simple process of lightly baking them in large earthen ovens'. Sanitary arrangements were 'completely inadequate' and the vast area of sand surrounding the village was 'rapidly being transformed into an evil-smelling latrine.' The habits of the local inhabitants had been greatly influenced by their contact with the thousands of unskilled Burmese labourers who travelled every year to work in the fields and mills, with the result that 'opium-eating was almost universal, while men, women and children smoked cheroots', supposedly to ward off fevers caused by high temperatures and humidity. Sidney quotes the example of 'an old, old woman with a "whacking great cheroot" giving a light to an eight-year-old boy who was similarly equipped.'

During the most significant day of the festival the British were instructed to prevent the celebrations from deteriorating into a political demonstration. In particular, to make certain that a photograph of Gandhi was not placed beside the image of the goddess Lakshmi on the great temple car which was dragged around the streets by the local fishermen. Early in the proceedings, hundreds of Congress volunteers armed with lathis were in evidence and it was clear that, were a fight to break out, it might well degenerate into a massacre. To deal with this eventuality, before daybreak a police guard was placed around the temple car, with orders that temple officials and priests would be made to give their assurance that only the customary images and decorations were placed upon it. When Sidney walked into the village after breakfast the temple car was already in position, 'towering high above the roofs of the houses, with the half-naked priests standing round the idol, which was almost buried under its load of gold-embroidered robes, rich jewels and garlands of flowers.' The great ropes with which the car was to be pulled were lying along the street in preparation for the fifty or sixty men who comprised the crew, and the streets were 'packed with a huge but very orderly throng', marshalled by a large force of Congress volunteers. However, somewhat ominously, there was not a single woman in the crowd, 'a most unusual circumstance at a religious festival', which convinced Sidney that people were anticipating trouble.

Wright had stationed his armed men up a side street outside the crowd, where they could be brought up quickly if needed. Within the crowd were only a few local constables, stationed near the car. Sidney approached the leader of the Congress volunteers—'a small, be-spectacled [sic], fanatical-looking man'—and asked him if he could line the street with his men to prevent the pressure of the crowd from forcing people under the wheels of the car, 'a very real peril, for these massive cars weigh many tons and have nothing in the way of brakes.' The Congressman willingly agreed to cooperate and the volunteers proved quite useful. Moreover, 'it kept them in a good temper and it prevented them from concentrating in dangerous numbers.'

However, when the car seemed ready to start, nothing happened. Sidney was at first unperturbed, 'punctuality not being the most noticeable of India's virtues', but soon realised that the delay had been caused by something other than unpunctuality. Upon making enquiries he learnt that the temple car had been instructed not to start until Gandhi's photograph had been placed upon it. Being of the opinion that 'Passive resistance is a game that two can play', he procured a chair from the village school, had it placed in the middle of the street where he sat down and lit his pipe and 'there I sat through the whole of that incredibly long day, smoking pipe after pipe and doing precisely nothing else.' Having had no lunch, as the festival was expected to be over in two or three hours, he found himself in a 'confined area, jammed with unwashed humanity, with no shade from the merciless sun' until sundown when, with no lighting arrangements in place, he ordered the priests to put the goddess to bed. At that precise moment he was hit in the eye by a banana and suspected that the situation was becoming heated. However, the missile was merely an offering to the goddess, hurled from too far a distance to reach the car.

The net result of 'this tedious business' was a victory for law and order with 'no deification of Gandhi' and no violence. In addition, the public blamed the Congress for stopping the procession. Sidney and Wright were quite pleased with the day's work, since they were outnumbered by 'something like a thousand to one and were twenty-four hours from reinforcements.' Their orders had been carried out and there was no subsequent trouble. After this experience Sidney felt better equipped to deal with the next festival, which was at the other end of the district. Arrangements were made for police pickets to disarm all the volunteers as they arrived in threes and fours at the outskirts of the village, where they hoped to stage a demonstration. Once disarmed, the volunteers became mere members of the crowd, which could be controlled with the greatest of ease. Sidney recalled that years later he still owned 'a trophy in the shape of a magnificent congress flag, removed from one of these men and never reclaimed.'

Although his nominal base during this period was Cocanada, the headquarters of the East Godaveri district, Sidney spent little time in the town, which did not appear to have been a great loss. Once a seaport with considerable trade, it had become less important due to silting, which forced ships to anchor some five miles out where they discharged their cargo. The view from the port was therefore monopolised by 'a fleet of barges and a great expanse of muddy shoal water shimmering in the heat of the sun.' The town was connected by two canals to the massive waterways threading through the area, but there was little real industry other than a light steelworks, three rice mills and five printing works. According to Arthur Galletti, an earlier member of the Madras ICS whose first posting was in Godaveri, members of the local population were highly superstitious and heavy smokers and, excluding the Brahmins who tended to dominate local life, there was a passion for cockfighting. Women played board games, boys flew kites, and puppet shows provided one of the principal forms of entertainment.[9]

A number of Europeans were based in Cocanada. In addition to the district officials, there was quite a large commercial contingent, including twenty or so merchants and bankers. However, notwithstanding the European presence, the Cocanada club, although impressive in its facilities, was somehow 'dead' despite local efforts to organise cricket and golf. It is possible that the social 'stickiness' of the station was due to the rather mixed nature of the population. Several miles from the city there was a small French settlement, Yanan, which seemed to have been a 'breeding place' for a large number of French Eurasians, many of whom came to live in a suburb of Cocanada called Jagganaikpur and were known as 'the Jagganaikpur county families'. Several of the women of these families had married members of the Cocanada firms and had helped to create an 'atmosphere of touchy conventionalism'. Indeed, at the start of the twentieth century, Galletti (a great advocate of Indian political reform) had complained vociferously that the Cocanada club happily included French Eurasians and others 'uncountenanced in Madras', but refused entry to Indians.[10] In Sidney's view it appeared that many of the people in the club were 'on their dignity, looking out for slights and lacking in friendliness' and he found it a relief to escape to the 'freer atmosphere of the smaller, but more homogeneous station, Rajamundry.'

Although Geoffrey Bracken was Sidney's host as well as his boss, their paths seldom crossed as their timetables were so different. However, in Sidney's opinion Bracken was 'a first class man' under whom to work, with 'a complete grasp of the situation' and the ability to take strong measures to deal with it. Much of the work consisted of not only 'showing the flag', but also taking the opportunity of demonstrating that 'the government intended to govern and that those who wanted the help of the authorities must come out into the open as loyalists.' Showing little sympathy with the nationalist cause, Sidney agreed with Bracken in expressing the widely held opinion of the British in India in the 1920s that, 'Far too many people were sitting on the fence and it was politically desirable to get as many as possible to come down on our side of it.'

Between 1920 and 1922, strong protest centres emerged in the Godaveri and Guntur districts, where local Congress leaders linked a no-tax payment campaign to Gandhi's non-cooperation movement.[11] The huge mid-nineteenth century Krishna-Godaveri rivers irrigation scheme had markedly improved agricultural production in the area, and a canal system was created which connected the region directly with the Madras city markets. The new commercial opportunities boosted an already highly profitable natural productivity and substantially increased landholder prosperity with the introduction of silk and cotton weavers, sugar and tobacco producers, and several rice and oil mills. As landowning families in the area grew wealthier by growing grain and cash crops, they dominated local political associations from the mid-nineteenth century onwards, and after 1885 also controlled local branches of the Indian National Congress. When late in the nineteenth century the government of Madras proposed an increase in revenue by raising land and water taxes, the local population objected and a string of new political organisations emerged to contest the proposals. Anti-tax leaders aligned themselves increasingly with the Congress, and activity to undercut government authority simmered into the twentieth century. In the early 1920s it was apparent to Lord Willingdon that the campaign against tax payment had taken a firm hold, exacerbated by government of India inaction. As a consequence, with a Rs 65 lakh[12] shortfall, the government of Madras faced a financial crisis which, if it continued, would necessitate a loan from the government of India.

When towards the end of January 1921 the water level of the river Godaveri fell rapidly, it became necessary to drastically reduce the area of second crop irrigation. In selecting the villages which should receive the water, Bracken gave preference to those areas which had not joined the non-cooperation movement, 'thereby demonstrating in the most convincing fashion that it paid to be loyal.' He also took action against those tracts which had come out in 'open rebellion', issuing notifications under the Police Act that special police would be required for the maintenance of law and order in those areas. Moreover, the cost of the extra security would be recovered from those whose misconduct had made it necessary. Sidney was to visit the rebellious villages to make arrangements for the imposition and collection of the new tax to cover the surveillance. This was hardly an easy task since all the village officers and servants in those areas were on strike and he would clearly have no help of any kind from the local people.[13] Having been given a free hand by Bracken, Sidney's only instructions were to exempt the low-caste people from the assessment, as they had taken little part in the trouble, and to see that the tax fell heavily on the rich villagers who were largely responsible for the unrest. Unable to determine how long the extra police recruits would be required, he was forced to guess the total amount to be raised by the punitive tax.

The most challenging area was a group of eight large villages, of which the largest was Sitanagaram, situated on the banks of the Godaveri twenty-one miles above Rajamundry. As Sidney was to live on a house-boat, Olive came up from Madanapalle to join him for the 'very pleasant sail up the river, which was alive with country sailing boats and timber rafts'. Unfortunately, they had no time to explore the spectacular gorge twenty or so miles further upstream where the Godaveri cuts though a deep cleft in the wooded Papi Hills of the Eastern Ghats, creating a series of beautiful lakes reminiscent of Scottish lochs. There was 'serious work to be done and sight-seeing was out of the question.' Tying up at Sitanagaram with all necessary supplies on board, Sidney met his staff, consisting of two young Indian probationers fresh from college and thirteen men from the armed reserve police. No help was forthcoming from the neighbourhood, as suspected, and when he conducted a preliminary survey of the affected villages, the inhabitants shut themselves inside their houses and the streets were deserted.

To deal with the challenge of assessing a new tax without village accounts, registers or the names of the villagers, it was necessary to tax the houses, which still carried the numbers painted upon the doors at the recent census. It was then necessary to arrange the tax so that the rich paid the most and the poor went free. Upon examining the police it was found that seven out of the thirteen armed reserve members could read and write 'tolerably' in Telegu. These seven were appointed temporary accountants for seven of the eight villages, the largest of which was given to the junior of the two probationers. The other probationer was made a supervisor. Lists were prepared of all the houses, 'classifying them into huts worth less than Rs 50, second class houses worth from Rs 50 to Rs 500 and first class houses over Rs 500.'

Sidney then posted a proclamation stating that the levy would take the form of a house tax for the present, that the houses would be classified as indicated, and the poorest houses would be exempted altogether. Any villager who wished to appeal against his liability on the grounds that he had 'openly disassociated himself from the non-cooperation movement' was give three days in which to do so. A further proclamation was subsequently posted, stating the amount of the tax and announcing that any taxpayer whose name was not handed in to the temporary accountant within twenty-four hours would automatically have his tax doubled. By the end of the week a complete demand statement had been sent into the taluk office and all the village officers and servants of the eight villages had submitted petitions 'praying to be excused for their sins and withdrawing their resignations.' The process was repeated by the two probationers in the next group of disaffected villages and, when Sidney went inland to join them, the Congress flags had been hauled down and Union Jacks hoisted in their place. He was met by a large deputation of the leading citizens 'ready to swear eternal loyalty to the government whose powers of taxation had been so effectively demonstrated' and the village officers had all returned to duty. Having quelled the rebellion, with a sign of relief he 'shook the dust of the Godaveri district off my feet and returned to my beloved Madanapalle.'

9

THE BOARD 1924

Sidney had not been back in Madanapalle for long before he received an offer of the post of secretary of the Board of Revenue, which had administrative, advisory and appellate functions. The greater part of the Board's work was carried on by correspondence, partly with district collector-magistrates and their assistants, and partly with government. In its administrative capacity it prepared and submitted to government an annual report on each principal subject under its control, such as land revenue, excise, customs, salt, opium, licence tax, stamps, stationery, shipping and whatever other miscellaneous subject was deemed worthy of an annual report. In essence the Board's reports swallowed up the work of all its subordinates and reproduced it for the edification of government. Every official throughout the province contributed his quota. When the report had been through the hands of the drafting clerk and the secretary it was submitted to a member of the Board who read and revised it before it was sent to government. It was then carefully analysed by a Secretariat clerk who prepared the draft of a resolution upon it for submission for the approval of the governor. If approved, the government resolution was then communicated to the Board which passed it back with a copy of their report to the subordinates, who were anxiously waiting for it in the hope of official praise or in dread of some inconvenient censure. In the Board's other role as a form of appellate court, it tended to deal with serous disputes regarding land where a case had usually been investigated by a deputy collector, then reinvestigated and decided by a district collector, before the final appeal arrived before the Board.[1] However, in general collectors were not supervised by the Board other than through an amendment of orders or in exceptional cases.

Possibly deterred by the intense amount of bureaucracy associated with the Board and enjoying a peaceful and happy family life in the hills, Sidney made a speedy and somewhat 'short-sighted' decision to turn down the appointment which would have been undoubtedly good for his future prospects. Yet his refusal fell on stony ground and before long an order arrived directing him to join the Board the following week with 'no arguing about it.' Sidney was forced to finish those cases which he could, rush to Madras, take over the new office and start hunting for accommodation, while Olive organised the packing and transport of the family belongings from Madanapalle; hardly an easy task as they were eight miles from the railway by bullock cart. The staff house allotted to the Wadsworths was ideal, standing alone in the middle of Guindy Park[2] where the governor had his country house, about six miles from the centre of Madras. The park, 'an extensive stretch of grass and jungle', was traversed by pleasant sandy rides where Sidney could exercise his horse in the early mornings, and there were shady trees under which the children could play 'in complete privacy.' Providing great excitement for the family were the black buck which fought under the windows and the jackals which howled around the house at night.

The Chepauk Palace, which housed the Board of Revenue, with its 'graceful minarets and lofty central dome', was considered to be a fine specimen of Muslim architecture, 'magnificently placed on the sea front about a mile south of Fort St George.'[3] Sidney had a large room looking out to sea, from which in the hot weather he could hear the heavy surf begin to break every afternoon at about 3 pm, 'a sign that the sea breeze had come and that the heat of the day was over.' The work was heavy but there were compensations. He had by then acquired 'a fairly good practical knowledge of the intricacies of the Madras land revenue system' and was therefore dealing with matters in which he was able to take a professional interest. Moreover, he was fortunate in having admirable 'masters'. There were three members of the Board at that time and they were all 'men of first rate ability and personally most congenial.'

The first member, who had the greatest involvement with Sidney's land revenue work, was M. E. Couchman, whom he had first encountered during the episode of the semi-wild cattle of Sriharikota. Couchman was in poor health, with constant eye problems which forced him to spend an hour every afternoon with his eyes shut, and it was Sidney's business to spare his eyes as much as possible. Noting was reduced to a minimum and Sidney was given a 'very free hand' to deal with all the unimportant matters. In spite of his physical infirmities, Couchman was 'always bright and cheerful and never failed to see the funny side of anything which had one.' As a result, in Sidney's view it was 'pure joy' working for him. Couchman had done most of his service in South Kanara[4] and Coorg[5] and was apparently an 'expert in the peculiar tenures of those abnormal tracts', about which Sidney knew nothing. The second member, Neil Macmichael, was in charge of the specialised subjects of survey and settlement, and was 'a canny Scot with a pawky sense of humour and a caustic wit.' His departments were at that time 'very slack' and he had remarkably little work, enabling him to keep 'a novel in the top right hand drawer of his desk and a large file in front of him. When anyone called, he was busy with the file; as soon as the caller left, he was deep in the novel.' However, he knew his job well and performed it very thoroughly. The third member was Sidney's old boss from Vellore, Marjy, who controlled 'separate revenue', including such 'repulsive subjects' as stamps and excise which Sidney was fortunate enough to pass on to a fellow secretary. Later, when Couchman took leave, Marjy came over to land revenue and 'old relations were resumed.' By a stroke of good fortune there was a vacancy in the office and it was possible to bring in A. Appadurai Pillai who had been the sheristadar (or court administrative officer) in Vellore in 1914, so there was 'a complete revival of the old firm.' Appadurai was a prominent Methodist and had trained in the Secretariat. As a result, he was extremely competent when it came to office work and was also 'an extremely likeable little man, modest and unobtrusive but always ready with an intelligent suggestion when one was needed.'[6]

The Board's tiffin (luncheon) table was in Sidney's room, and there the members and their two secretaries gathered daily for 'bodily and mental refreshment.' They ate at an old round table which had a central well surmounted by a small revolving platform. According to Sidney, in the days when the Board held formal meetings and passed its resolutions after oral discussion, 'the papers for consideration used to lie on the central platform while those that had been considered were hurled into the well beneath.' However, in Sidney's time the Board never congregated around the table except for tiffin, when the main subjects for discussion were usually 'the stupidity of the local government, the fatuity of its legislature and the misdeeds of the Board's two secretaries who had to submit cheerfully to the witticisms of a very witty Full Board.'

Sidney's work was 'arduous, but very varied', consisting of keeping up to date the 'revenue officer's bible—the Standing Orders of the Board of Revenue', a large code of detailed instructions, many having the force of law. This covered the whole range of revenue work: grants of land, encroachments, irrigation, village officers, land acquisition, remissions of revenue and many other subjects which affected the welfare of millions of people. The system was constantly undergoing revision and each proposed change was the subject of reports from collectors which were consolidated and examined in his office, after which the proposal was either rejected or made the subject of an amendment to the standing orders. As all new legislation and statutory rules affecting the land had to be carefully examined and sometimes actually drafted, his office was forced to deal with a 'mass' of government litigation, to pass pleadings and to correspond with the law officers. Arthur Galletti recalled that as early as 1902 he had instigated a campaign to abolish the Board, arguing that, while the institution had been invaluable during the mid-nineteenth century, it was now costly and unnecessary in that the district collector was capable of dealing directly with ryots and collecting their taxes. In his view, Board members were highly paid but unproductive, filling time by altering orders unnecessarily and complicating work for field officers. Several layers of bureaucracy within the government of Madras could be removed to create better stability and cost-efficiency, and money saved through reform could fund personal assistants to overworked collectors in the huge Madras districts.[7]

Attending to standing orders, although extremely time-consuming, was not the only task facing Sidney. The Board was also responsible for the administration of the Famine Code, and as two 'small' famines occurred during Sidney's time, this proved to take up a considerable part of the day's work. In addition, the Board of Revenue was the Court of Wards, of which Sidney was the secretary, providing him with many interesting and difficult cases. When a large landholder died leaving an heir who was 'either a minor or a lunatic or for some other reason incapable of managing the property', the Court of Wards, acting through the local collector, stepped in to take charge of the estate. Some of the estates were so large that an officer of the ICS had to be put in charge of their management; others consisted of only half a dozen villages. However, in Sidney's view, 'Each one of them, big or small, could be relied upon to produce a packet of trouble.' Most were usually semi-insolvent when taken over and British officers were forced to 'wrestle with the importunate demands of a host of relatives, all of whom expected to be maintained in idleness and affluence, whatever the state of the finances. Often the affairs were in hopeless confusion—boxes of unlisted jewels, rooms full of unsorted records, villages unlawfully alienated to concubines, irrigation works in ruins, trust funds misappropriated'. As a result, Sidney found himself:

> corresponding with jewellers over the value of gold and precious stones, dealing with tradesmen who put in enormous bills for the late zemindar's [sic] extravagances, arranging for the survey of lands which were often found to be 25 per cent more extensive than the areas shown in the rent rolls, arranging for the education of minors and even for their marriages, scrutinising budgets, supervising litigation, auctioning temple offerings and so on.

Marriage arrangements were usually based on questions of finance. The family of the minor would demand 'an enormous sum as the lowest expenditure consistent with the status of the family', fixing the amount without any consideration of the ability of the estate to find the funds. The Court of Wards then had the 'distasteful task' of whittling down their demands to a reasonable figure. He recalled one case where the minor zamindar was a Maravar, of a community which favoured what were known as 'cross-cousin' marriages, in which a man married his father's sister's daughter or his mother's brother's daughter. The 'proper' bride according to caste usage was a child of five or six, and the family argued, not unreasonably, that if the young man had to wait for eight or nine years for his wife to 'come of age', he was likely to get into bad ways. However, this was not considered a reason for abandoning the customary marriage and an 'ingenious plan' was devised whereby the youth married two wives simultaneously; one whom it was his duty to marry, and the other a 'lusty' girl of almost his own age but of slightly lower status, 'who would be guaranteed to keep him out of mischief until her co-wife was old enough to perform her wifely duties.' In Sidney's view, this arrangement, 'so foreign to our ideas, but so eminently practical', was duly approved and appeared to work admirably.

Marjy, who was 'no respecter of persons or institutions', used to refer to the Secretariat as the 'Monkey House' and the Board of Revenue as the 'Pinjrapole'. The latter term referred to an institution in Madras supported by pious Hindus, wherein 'old, worn-out and useless' cattle were kept in 'well-fed idleness' until they died of old age. There may have been a time when the Board deserved this term of opprobrium, but when Marjy was the 'moving spirit' of the organisation the Board not only developed into 'a vigorous and well-informed critic of the government's more questionable measures', but also became the real initiator of change in revenue administration. This inevitably resulted in a series of official battles on questions of policy, but such was the combined force of the wisdom and experience of the three members that the outcome was rarely disputed.

An unusual side-line into which Sidney was diverted during his time with the Board involved the complications which arose from the closing down of enemy missions during the First World War. Even by 1923 these complications had not been satisfactorily resolved and he was appointed as the representative of the government on the board of trustees which controlled the finances of the defunct missions. During this task he forged a friendship with the chairman, the Reverend J. S. Hooper, 'a gentle, quiet fellow, with a twinkle in his eye and a modest manner' which masked a firm will and a powerful political brain, and it was due largely to Hooper's 'ability, tact and persistence' that the idea of church union in South India became a reality.[8] Sidney and Hooper's work focused principally upon the administration of provident funds run by the Basel Mission for the benefit of its teachers, catechists and others. Unfortunately, these funds had been started without actuarial investigation and they promised benefits which could not be given out in full from the accumulated subscriptions as the funds matured. There appeared to be a presumption that any deficiency would be made up out of the profits of the Basel Mission Industrials firm, but under its post-war organisation the company showed no immediate sign of making a profit. The two men were therefore in the undesirable position of paying out benefits to retired subscribers out of current subscriptions, well aware of the fact that the funds were like to become insolvent before the current subscribers retired and claimed their benefits. They were at the same time constantly beset by 'hard-luck stories' (all too familiar in Indian climatic conditions) involving subscribers who, owing to illness, had defaulted for a few months and asked to be readmitted to the fund, or for reasons of health had been compelled to retire from service shortly before they had qualified for benefits.

Hooper and Sidney were forced to maintain that, in view of the probable insolvency of the funds, the only course which they could 'honestly pursue' as trustees was to adhere rigidly to the rules of the funds and allow no exceptions, 'however deserving of pity they might be.' However, the other trustees were Indian Christians of good standing, in Sidney's view all worthy men but with 'the defects of their qualities' in that educated Indians tended to be 'full of sympathy for the man who is down on his luck, whether he be the prisoner in the dock or a poor man pleading for charity'. Moreover, it was only human nature that they displayed even more charity when dealing with trust funds rather than their own money. As a result, Hooper and Sidney had the greatest difficulty in persuading the 'sympathetic majority' to subscribe to the views of the apparently hard-hearted two Englishmen, but with Hooper's tact and ability he was always able to persuade the trustees to accept the uncharitable solution without losing their respect and friendship.

Before leaving the Board's office, there was a 'sudden boom' in manganese ore which created some excitement. Mining was part of Sidney's portfolio and a subject with which he was familiar following his experience in Gudur (the main centre of the mica mining industry). The manganese deposits were situated in several districts and, when prices rose, competition for mining and prospecting licences increased dramatically, including some competitors who were 'not too scrupulous in their methods.' In particular there was a European merchant from Bombay who had sold forward a large quantity of ore in the hope of being able to buy at a favourable price. When the market went up his only solution lay in finding a deposit of ore to work himself until he had satisfied his customer. He therefore applied for the mining lease of a plot in the Bellary district;[9] however, a member of the Kamma Naidu community had already taken out a prospecting licence for the same land and under the rules was entitled to the highly desirable lease. Therefore, in spite of the protestations of the Bombay merchant, the Board stood by the rules and gave the lease to the Naidu. The merchant appealed to the government and through the intervention of a relative he was able to approach the Governor of Madras, Lord Willingdon.

Sidney was then summoned to a meeting between the governor and the Raja of Kollengode,[10] 'a very nice little man and an old friend ... but not a person of any great ability or strength of character', in whose hands lay the particular mining portfolio. The hope was that Sidney could find a flaw in the Board's order which might justify a reversal of events. It appeared that to Lord Willingdon the matter was merely 'a question of business—whether a little man of no capital or standing ought to have a valuable concession in competition with a representative of big business, especially when the latter was a personal friend of the governor.' The Raja of Kollengode was evidently in a quandary; on the one hand he did not wish to offend the governor, but on the other he wished to maintain good relations with the Board, for whose members he had 'a wholesome respect.' Quite possibly he was also aware that they would be in office, perhaps high office, long after the governor's term had expired. Sidney's position was 'very unpleasant', but he insisted that were the Board's order to be upset, the result would be a suit by the Naidu against which the Madras government would have no defence, incurring heavy damages. In spite of this warning, the lease was given to the Bombay merchant but fortunately, instead of filing a suit, the Naidu appealed successfully to the government of India and the original order of the Board was restored 'without the expense of a disastrous litigation.'

Before leaving the Board an event occurred which determined Sidney's future career. A long time previously he had decided (very much against his wife's wishes) that he would remain with the executive side of the Indian Civil Service. Not only did the work interest him and provided scope for his abilities but, like most magistrates, he had become extremely tired of the monotony of trying criminal cases and the prospect of two months' leave did not seem to him to be adequate compensation for ten months of 'almost unrelieved drudgery as a district judge.' However, he happened to play golf one day with Mr Justice Edward Wallace, a 'charming fellow' with an attractive dry Scottish humour when he overcame his shyness, who lived largely for his books and his painting. This encounter led to further weekly fixtures, during the course of which Wallace was to counsel Sidney. He pointed out that if the process of constitutional reform continued as planned, the prospects of becoming an executive councillor were extremely limited and his advice was to study the civil list in order to work out how Sidney's chances of becoming a member of the Board compared with his chances of succeeding as a judge on the High Court. Upon investigation, Sidney discovered that whereas he was 'hopelessly blocked' for promotion on the executive side, there seemed to be a real chance of a 'big clearance' on the judicial side which would give him a straight run to the top. Moreover, judicial life would be 'free from the petty annoyances which were likely to make life difficult on the executive side when once the politicians were in full control.' As a result he made the life-changing decision to write to the government asking to be transferred from one branch of the service to the other.

As it happened, this decision coincided with a change of policy at government level. The First World War had had a dramatic effect upon the Indian Civil Service, like other British institutions. As the war dragged on, making increasing demands on manpower, vacancies mounted and by 1918 the service was 200 men short. After the war it was difficult to interest young men in a career in India, and the India Office was forced to abandon its set ratio of European to Indian candidates. Moreover, members of the ICS found it increasingly difficult financially to make ends meet in the 1920s. The old nineteenth-century joke that an Indian Civil Servant was a good bet on the marriage market (worth £300 dead or alive and assured of an increasing income, culminating in an annual pension of £1,000) turned sour when the bottom fell out of the rupee market. ICS salaries and conditions of service no longer compared well with those offered by business houses, and many European officers began to question whether they should stay in India. Moreover, the mounting scale of Gandhi's non-cooperation movement and the vacillation of the government of India in dealing with the problem served to deepen the self-doubt of members of the service.[11]

To deal with the shortfall in European candidates and as a gesture toward Indian nationalism, the Raj committed itself early in the 1920s to a policy of Indianisation for the civil service, the police and the Indian Army, which could be interpreted as a sign of good intent. The rate of progress for these reforms was slow: the 1924 Royal Commission on Indianisation recommended that the Indian Civil Service should be half Indian within fifteen years and that the police force should become half Indian within twenty-five years. The Indianisation of the army was a far more contentious issue, for obvious reasons, but an eventual compromise was reached by 1926 when it was agreed that the Indian Army would be half-Indianised by 1952. These proposals were unlikely to satisfy Indian nationalists and certainly had the effect of frightening off British recruits. The freshly graduated products of Oxbridge and the British public school system indicated plainly that they believed India held no long-term career prospects for them.

10

BELOW THE LIGHTHOUSE 1925

As a result of his transfer to the judicial branch of the service, Sidney took long leave in 1924 and joined the Middle Temple. It took six months to complete all the bar examinations and he was able to obtain an exemption from four terms' dinners, but the eating of the remaining eight terms' dinners was spread over seven years, and he was not called to the bar until 1931, when he had already been a district judge for nearly five years. Fortunately, the dinners, in which one made up a 'mess' of four perfect strangers from all over the world, were enjoyable. Surprisingly, few of the students had any intention of practising at the English bar, which in Sidney's opinion was 'just as well, as most of them would have starved.' In the Middle Temple there was by convention a fairly rigid colour bar for dinner, with Indians, Africans and West Indians sitting on one side of the hall while white men sat on the other. The intake was undoubtedly diverse; in one 'mess' Sidney was grouped with a soldier from Aden, an official from the League of Nations Secretariat and a civil servant from West Africa; and another mess included an American international lawyer practising in Paris, a doctor who intended to become a coroner and an undecided undergraduate from Cambridge.

When his long leave was over, Sidney returned to India and took up the appointment of Registrar at the High Court, a post which he had refused five years earlier when he had had no intention of becoming a judge. However, it was necessary to learn how the judicial machine worked, although he was by that stage too senior to remain in the appointment for long, and he was housed beneath the lighthouse which surmounted the great dome of the 'huge, ill-planned, ostentatious building' which since 1892 had contained the High Court of Madras.[1] Despite the fact that many people admired this 'monstrous structure', Sidney was of the opinion that it merited the description given to it as 'a huge edifice in the P.W.D.–Byzantine-lavatory style of architecture.'

The registrar was the secretary of the High Court, which controlled the judicial department throughout the presidency. He was also secretary to the chief justice, who was personally in sole control of the very large staff of the High Court office. In his capacity as secretary of the High Court, the registrar's duties were mainly administrative and supervisory, and consisted of scrutinising the files on all administrative matters. He worked under whichever judge was looking after a particular subject, but mostly under the senior Indian Civil Service judge who was by convention in charge of the most important administrative duties. The 'portfolio judge', as he was called, was for the majority of Sidney's time Sir Charles Spencer,[2] said to be a cousin of Sir Winston Churchill but of a very different ilk, being 'reserved, hesitant of speech and rather frigid of manner', although not a man under whom it was difficult to work. However, Sidney's most significant work was for the Chief Justice, Sir Murray Coutts Trotter. Coutts, as he was always called behind his back, was an excellent classical scholar and a lecturer in classics at Liverpool University, when he took a ticket in the Derby sweepstake and drew a horse which was considered a rank outsider. Coutts, knowing nothing about racing, consulted a friend as to whether he should sell his ticket and was advised not only to keep the ticket but also to place a further five pounds upon the horse, which subsequently won. On the proceeds he was able to leave teaching and make a start at the bar, building up a good practice on the northeastern circuit until the arrival of the war. With little financial acumen and an expensive family to educate, he then accepted the offer of a seat on the bench in Madras where he was soon known as 'a judge of outstanding ability and a most entertaining talker'. When the current Chief Justice, Sir Walter Schwabe, resigned unexpectedly, Coutts was appointed in his place.

Despite his brilliance, Coutts was not a great success in the role. Being by nature a 'friendly, convivial soul' he proved to be quite incapable of 'that aloof dignity which, however unattractive it may be, is a necessary incident of the great position of the head of the judiciary.' He was in his element in the bar of the Madras Club where he was 'a wonderful raconteur and his Yorkshire dialect stories were quite irresistible … but altogether too hail-fellow-well-met for the Chief Justice.' His convivial habits led him 'to smoke far too many cigarettes and to consume much more whisky than was good for him and his health began to suffer.' His amazingly quick brain became less and less capable of sustained effort, and when a complicated case reared its head he searched for 'short cuts to its disposal'. If none were forthcoming, he would often remit the case to the lower court for some inadequate reason. As an aspiring musician, Coutts played the cello 'tolerably' and at one time conducted for the Madras Musical Society, where certain people took 'a malicious pleasure' in describing how he would lose his place in the score and 'be beaten at the post by the orchestra!'

Like many able lawyers, Coutts had no interest in administrative work and largely left it to his registrar. In Sidney's view this resulted in 'the registrar exercising far more power than was desirable' and he found himself 'almost an autocrat' in the huge office of the High Court where even the composition of the benches and the posting of the work to the judges was left in his hands. Unfortunately, the judges at the time included several 'very cantankerous individuals who … were rather apt to give vent to their personal feelings by acid criticisms of one another's judgments' which would subsequently be made the foundation of legal arguments, wasting the time of the court which became clogged with arrears. A stronger man than Coutts would have pulled the team together, but as it was 'they sometimes behaved like a lot of bickering schoolboys and judges' meetings were occasionally chaotic.'

This lack of harmony was extremely difficult for Sidney, who constantly found himself confronted with situations requiring 'an excessive display of tact.' The very constitution of an Indian High Court made for divergences of opinion, as the judges were recruited from three radically different environments. By statute one third of the judges (including the Chief Justice) was recruited from barristers ('a term which was always read as meaning practising barristers'), one third from district judges who were members of the Indian Civil Service, and one third from vakils (lawyers). Each of these three classes of men was 'the product of a very distinctive and different type of training which profoundly affected their habits of thought.' The judges were also divided racially and the Indian judges were divided by caste. When a number of 'personal antipathies' were added to these inevitable divisions it was apparent that the job of registrar was not a happy task. On the plus side was Sidney's excellent relationship with his boss, who always treated him with 'the utmost friendliness and consideration.' Coutts was 'the most charming and interesting of men' and his lack of interest in administrative affairs made the relationship even easier. However, it was apparent that, despite being 'a scholar, a gentleman and a brilliant lawyer with a magnificent command of concise and powerful English', he was 'too kind-hearted and too loyal to his friends to run a big administrative organisation.'

On one occasion Coutts' remarkable brain was displayed in court when 'he let himself go with far-reaching results.' Years before, a moneylender in Hyderabad had borrowed around a lakh of rupees from another moneylender, after which he died without repaying his debt. Some fifty years later, when the debtor's grandson had become a rich man, the creditor's grandson found an old bond in the family safe and, in an attempt to turn it into cash, went to the nizam of Hyderabad, placed the facts before him and suggested that a special court be constituted to try his claim. In addition, he requested that the nizam issue a firman,[3] providing that the law of limitation should not apply to the case. Somewhat surprisingly, the nizam agreed to these requests, whereupon the debtor's grandson 'packed up all his movable wealth and fled to Madras.' The creditor's grandson received a decree from the ad hoc court in Hyderabad for the full amount of the debt which, with compound interest at a high rate for the entire period since the original transaction, amounted to 'a fabulous sum.'

At this point the creditor's grandson had the temerity to file a suit in the Madras High Court on the foreign judgment. The case came before Coutts who, in a few 'terse, biting sentences', summarised the course of events, then pointed out that the nizam was 'an absolute sovereign' who could if he chose pass a decree making forfeit the wealth of any of his subjects, but:

> to characterise such a confiscatory decree as a judicial act, merely because it was clothed in a travesty of judicial forms, was absurd. It was no more than the arbitrary act of the supreme executive, perfectly valid within the Nizam's own dominions, but absolutely valueless as the foundation for a judicial proceeding in the courts of another nation.

As Sidney recalled, 'Thus in a judgment of a few paragraphs which said everything that needed to be said and contained not one word which could be improved in any way, Coutts exposed the action of the Nizam to the critical gaze of the public' and, more specifically, to the government of India, who insisted that the ruler put his house in order. Sir d'Arcy Reilly of the Madras High Court was despatched to overhaul the Hyderabad judiciary and Sir Theodore Tasker[4] (also a Madras civilian) was made a member of the nizam's executive council. Other British officers were placed in strategic positions in the state, to ensure that in future the administration would be run 'on more orthodox lines.'

Every Saturday morning it was Sidney's job to take 'an accumulation' of administrative files to Coutts to get his orders, much as had been the case when he was private secretary to Lord Willingdon. However, whereas Willingdon was both punctual and efficient, Coutts was unpunctual and more eager to relate 'funny stories' to Sidney than to issue orders. At ten o'clock Sidney would arrive to find him 'just dressed and regarding his breakfast with a look of unutterable disgust—clear signs of a hang-over which in a man of less equable temper might inspire forebodings.' Nevertheless, he would gradually become more cheerful, and by the time the files had been produced he would be in the 'full flow of reminiscence' and the work (which should have absorbed half an hour or so) would provide 'a nominal occupation for the best part of three hours.' His stories were intrinsically good and never repeated, but it was saddening to see 'this brilliant and most likable man visibly disintegrating.' After Sidney left the High Court office, Coutts' health deteriorated very rapidly and his capacity for work decreased still further. Two years later, in 1929, he was put on a ship in Madras harbour with two nurses in attendance and he died at sea a week or so later, to Sidney's 'very great grief.'

Although Coutts was the 'outstanding personality', there were other notable figures on the Madras bench at the time. Mr Justice Cheruvari Krishnan was 'a tall, upstanding man with as fair a complexion as many

Europeans'. He belonged to the caste of Tiyyans[5] from Malabar which permitted its women to form liaisons with men of a higher status and to bring the children up in the mother's family house. In colonial Madras this practice resulted in a significant infusion of Brahmin and even European blood into the community, which, according to Sidney, occasionally 'produced men of great ability'. Sidney was informed that Krishnan's grandfather was an English duke and he certainly appeared to have a strong strain of European blood which revealed itself in his complexion and features. It was claimed that due to his heritage his mind would welcome the 'realistic and practical' answer to a problem while all his Indian colleagues would 'naturally be attracted to the idealistic and theoretical solution'. To Sidney he was 'rather stiff with the bar', having no favourites. When a nephew of his was starting a junior practice, his cases were handled by Krishnan just as unsympathetically as those of the rest of the bar. In fact, it was said that the judge made a point of throwing out his nephew's cases 'so as to discourage those who were hoping for favouritism.'

Krishnan was the only Indian judge of his generation who died soon after leaving office, while no fewer than three of the European judges failed to live long enough to enjoy their retirement. Sir Charles Spencer was one of the early casualties and the others were Sir William Phillips and Sir Francis Oldfield. The death of Sir William was a great surprise 'for an apparently fitter man one could not imagine.' Thin and wiry, and a good cricketer in his youth, 'as he got older he used to work off his superabundant energy by hunting, shooting, fishing and strenuous singles at tennis and he seemed absolutely tireless.' However, one day, having played eighteen hard holes of golf in the morning and several 'vigorous' sets of tennis in the afternoon, 'he sat down and just died'. Sir Francis was of a very different type. Tall, round-shouldered with a long neck and a great beak of a nose, he was known as 'the paddy bird' because of his crane-like appearance. Although a gentle, kindly soul of a rather studious nature, he had little regular education in law, but made up 'by natural aptitude and private reading for what he lacked in academic and forensic training.' When he retired, he was appointed professor of comparative jurisprudence at Manchester University, but died before he had had time to acquire a reputation as an academic lawyer.

Among the other Indian judges on the bench when Sidney was registrar was V. V. Srinivasa Iyengar,[6] who resigned from the bench after two or three years and resumed practice. When Sidney retired from the service he was still practising, although nearly eighty, retaining his 'physical and mental vigour' to a degree which was almost unprecedented in India (where men aged considerably faster than in Europe) and never losing his sense of humour, which helped him to craft a number of skits on the vagaries of Indian administration. It was a pleasure to see the old man stride into court 'with the figure and gait of a young man and the alert look and readiness for battle of the old warrior that he is.' Another judge was Mr Justice Madhavan Nair, with whom Sidney had a great deal of work when he was secretary to the Board of Revenue and Madhavan Nair was Advocate General. He was a member of the Chettur house of Malabar, whose most celebrated member was Sir Chettur Sankaran Nair,[7] against whom Sir Michael O'Dwyer, Governor of the Punjab, brought a famous libel action claiming that he had been defamed by Sankaran Nair over his handling of the Jallianwala Bagh massacre. Tall, dignified and courteous, Madhavan Nair looked 'every inch a judge'. He possessed the patience and industry which to Sidney were 'even more important judicial qualities than positive brilliance' and his appointment to the Judicial Committee of the Privy Council was most popular. His elder brother, Diwan Bahadur Sir Mannath Krishnan Nair,[8] was public prosecutor and government pleader during the whole of Sidney's five years as district judge of Madura and saved him endless work due to his 'sound judgment and wonderful grasp of facts'.

Perhaps the most talented of the Indian judges in the 1920s was Mr Justice Ramesam, later Sir Vepa Ramesam, who in his old age remained 'full of intellectual vigour and an insatiable thirst for facts'. A Brahmin by caste, he was 'small, lean and very talkative, full of enthusiasm and generally hot in the pursuit of some new theory.' At one time he became particularly interested in a new theory of dietetics and made himself seriously ill by attempting to live on uncooked potatoes. Later, having raised a huge family, he somewhat bizarrely came out as a public protagonist of birth control. With a truly impressive knowledge of the chapter and verse of the enormous mass of Indian case law, he was also a very good mathematician with an extraordinary memory which enabled him to reel out all the stations on the London Underground in their correct order and to list the ships that fought at Trafalgar 'with precise details of their armaments.' In fact, according to Sidney, his chief problem as a judge was his inability to control such a phenomenal memory, with the result that 'the cases cited in his judgments were apt to tumble over each other in never-ending profusion.' However, in his earlier days, when Sidney dealt with him as government pleader, his legal opinions were 'models of clarity and conciseness' which gave a clear indication of the action to be taken. Moreover, he was one of the kindest of men and his 'little eccentricities' most appealing.

There were a number of other legal luminaries on the Madras bench. Mr Justice Beasley (later Sir Owen Beasley) who succeeded Sir Murray Coutts as chief justice was 'a short, stocky and fit-looking man, rather pugnacious, but with many solid qualities hidden behind a somewhat "prickly" exterior.' In his youth he was the captain of the Cambridge University association football team and played cricket for Glamorganshire. He demonstrated his fitness when he retired from the bench in his sixties, shortly before the Second World War, and served with his wife in France as part of the crew of a YMCA canteen, in which he washed dishes until the couple was evacuated shortly before Dunkirk. Thereafter he served as an ARP warden in Kensington throughout the Blitz and became chairman of a pensions tribunal. Sir Charles Odgers was a 'big, bluff, hearty man with a cheery manner and a large voice' who became the leading light of the local dramatic society and served for many years as Administrator-General[9] before he was raised to the bench. G. H. B. Jackson (later Sir Gilbert Jackson) was a brilliant member of the younger generation of ICS judges who also edited 'Madras Occasional Verse' and in his youth acquired a local reputation as a cartoonist, 'producing merciless caricatures of his elders and betters' which were wisely withheld from publication. Finally, H. d'Arcy C. Reilly (later Sir d'Arcy Reilly)[10] who was a contemporary of Jackson and known to be a 'very fair-minded and painstaking' figure whose judgments, although they 'smelt a bit of the midnight oil … were clear, sound and learned.'

One of the minor concerns of Sidney's time as registrar arose from the activities of 'a well-known lunatic' who was a Brahmin of a decent family and fairly well-educated but 'obsessed with the notion that he was the rightful owner of the Guindy race-course.'[11] He started pro

Ventagiri ceedings by prosecuting the stewards of the Race Club for criminal trespass and, when this complaint was thrown out, he drafted a fresh one 'recapitulating the old case with embellishments and adding allegations of unnatural offences' with the result that this 'remarkable document grew like a snowball.' He took it from court to court, and as each authority rejected it, the name of the magistrate concerned was added to the list of persons accused of 'unmentionable crimes.' By the time it reached the High Court, the list of the accused looked 'rather like a page out of the civil list' and Sidney felt quite honoured when his name, with that of the chief justice, was added to the schedule of offenders. So long as the man's activities were confined to the typewriter he was merely a nuisance, yet when he started to make noisy demonstrations in the chief justice's court the police were called in to inform his relatives that if there was more trouble he would have to be sent to a lunatic asylum, after which Sidney never heard of him again, presuming that 'the poor fellow is locked up in some back room, drafting endless petitions about his legal rights.'

In 1925 the Madras bar also contained 'a galaxy of stars', quite a number of whom had business in the Board's office and had also appeared before Sidney in his position of sub-collector. Sidney's oldest friend at the bar was Sir Alladi Krishnaswami Ayyar, 'a small man with an enormous mouth and a pair of greyish eyes which lit up his whole face when he smiled' who, although young, was briefed by the Maharaja of Ventakagiri to appear in an important batch of rent suits in 1916. Out of his large mouth came a 'surprisingly big and rather harsh voice ... backed by a brain of quite unusual range and power' and he succeeded in making Sidney write a judgement in his favour which was 'so complete and convincing that it went all the way up to the High Court intact.' His father was poor, a purohit (family priest) living in a village near Naidupet, and his education was financed with the utmost difficulty. As a result, Alladi must have been 'literally penniless' when he started to practise. But he was already known as a youngster of marked ability and was taken under the wing of an excellent mentor who soon found that his pupil had a 'magnificent legal brain ... which came to maturity at a remarkably early age.' However, notwithstanding all his triumphs in court and the public recognition of his 'great attainments', Alladi remained 'a simple, modest, kindly person, generous to the poor, especially to those who like himself, have to struggle for an education, and loyal to his friends.'

At the same time that Alladi 'burst upon the public gaze like a meteor', another star was ascending 'with at first little suggestion of phenomenal brilliance.' S. Varadachari was a 'rather shy and diffident young man, obviously endowed with a fine legal brain, but apparently lacking in push and assertiveness'. According to Sidney, he appeared 'very much like scores of other Brahmin lawyers, plainly dressed, pleasant but not at all striking in physiognomy, with quiet manners and a complete absence of that masterful demeanour which one associates with a leader of the bar.' But gradually he attracted attention and with 'exceptional powers of gentle persuasiveness' he began to win an unusual number of cases. Shortly after Sidney ceased to be registrar, Varadachari was raised to the bench, and before long 'his judgments came to be quoted with a respect which was quite different from that rather formal deference which is paid to the views of more ordinary judges.' His pre-eminence as a judge received recognition throughout India and he was knighted and elevated to the Federal Court. Everyone in Madras rejoiced at the honour that had been bestowed upon him, but at the same time felt that 'his brilliant abilities were being rather wasted in that rarefied atmosphere, where the volume of work was so small' while there was so much work to be done in Madras and so few judges capable of handling it.[12]

Another luminary, Sir C. P. Ramaswami Ayyer KCIE, had ceased to be advocate-general before Sidney became registrar but, as law member of the Madras government and a personal friend of the chief justice, he maintained a profound influence over judicial matters. Although from a well-known legal family with many influential connections, the secret of his success appeared to lie in 'the versatility of his agile brain and the personal charm which no one seems able to resist'. C. P. was extremely well read, 'with a great knowledge of the world and none of the narrowness of outlook which is the weakness of many first class lawyers.' Possibly influenced by the fact that in 1917 in his thirties he had served as secretary of the Indian National Congress, there were senior British officials known to Sidney who never missed an opportunity of criticising the lawyer. One such official came to serve under 'his pet aversion' but in a matter of weeks was won over by the Indian and became a close personal friend. Following his time in the Madras government, C. P. served as law member of the executive council of the viceroy (at that time Lord Willingdon, under whom C. P. also served in Madras) from 1931 to 1936 before being appointed diwan of Travancore in 1936. During his tenure many social and administrative reforms were made in the princely state, but C. P. also ruthlessly suppressed a communist uprising and resigned in 1947 followed a failed assassination attempt. In September 1966 he left for England to undertake research on a book entitled 'A History of My Times' at the India Office Library where he suddenly slumped on his armchair while speaking to a reporter and died instantly. Also involved in politics and serving as a notable president of the Congress in the 1920s was S. Srinivasa Ayyangar, whose political experience undoubtedly left its mark on the style of his advocacy, in that he was inclined to address the court as though it was a public meeting. Srinivasa Ayyangar was advocate-general of Madras from 1916 to 1920 but resigned his post and returned his Companion of the Order of the Indian Empire in 1920 in protest against the Jallianwala Bagh massacre. At that time he joined the Congress and participated in the non-cooperation movement, before joining a breakaway faction which later formed the Swarajaya Party in January 1923. The party opposed Gandhi's suspension of all civil resistance in 1922 following the Chauri Chaura tragedy (in which 22 or 23 policemen were killed by a mob of protestors), firmly believing that the non-cooperation movement should not have been discontinued over an isolated incident of violence and that the remarkable success of the movement was close to breaking the back of British rule in India. In Madras the Swarajaya Party emerged as the single largest party in the 1926 and 1934 Assembly elections but refused to form a provincial government under the existing dyarchy system.

In Sidney's time there was also still a 'small but vigorous' European bar. The 'great' Eardley Norton,[13] who was a member of the committee which drafted the constitution of the Indian National Congress and a champion of the creation of a United Kingdom wing of the Congress under the leadership of the MP Charles Bradlaugh,[14] had by 1925 left Madras for a 'more lucrative sphere' in Calcutta. In his shoes had stepped Nugent Grant, a 'wonderfully fine advocate and an admittedly poor lawyer' who, when a legal point of any complexity arose, declared that 'his learned junior' was infinitely better qualified to deal with it. Although 'capable of a brilliant exhibition of fireworks, he did not trust to pyrotechnical displays to take the place of solid work' and, despite being in private a kind and generous man, in court could be 'devastatingly offensive if he thought the interests of his client required it.' On one occasion he became decidedly impatient with the proceedings and 'in those audible asides of which he was much too fond, he made several disparaging remarks about the interpreter's renderings.' However, upon receiving a 'well-merited reproof' from the Bench he immediately made an open and complete apology and later sought out the interpreter ('a very competent and conscientious man') and 'humbly asked to be excused.' In Sidney's opinion most of Nugent's occasional irritability was due to the fact that he was suffering from cancer and after a number of operations was so weak that it was necessary to prop him up with cushions to address the court. His extreme generosity was displayed after a train tragedy in Moplah on the Malabar Coast in 1921 in which 61 out of a total of 90 Mappila Muslim rebels suffocated in a railway wagon while being transported to prison. The government of India decided to make a scapegoat of a certain Sergeant Andrews who was in charge of the van, and Nugent travelled to Coimbatore in the west of the Madras Presidency where he successfully defended the man without a fee. He also conducted the civil suit against a young zamindar who had turned King's evidence in the criminal case following the murder of Clement de la Haye, principal of Newington College in Madras, and succeeded in getting reasonable compensation for de la Haye's widow.[15] The lawyer had literally hundreds of friends and Sidney was particularly impressed by 'the large number of Indian gentlemen who came to pay their last respects at his funeral.'

Although the work of the registrar was largely administrative, the post required certain judicial functions. Twice a week Sidney sat in the library to attend to a large number of formal applications dealing with such issues as adding parties to litigation proceedings, appointing guardians ad litem[16] and sending for additional documents. Although not intellectually rigorous, these duties did bring him into contact with junior members of the bar, some of whom rose to eminence. Another branch of work which provided similar opportunities was connected with the control of the cause lists. The system on the appellate side was to put cases into the 'ready list' as soon as all the printing and preparatory work had been done. From this list the 'rough list' was prepared, to warn advocates of the work which was likely to come into the cause list in a few days' time so that they could read their briefs. In practice, however, the 'rough list' acted mainly as a reminder to lawyers to collect the balance of their fees and, 'as the Indian litigant is one of the most reluctant payers in the world', Sidney was besieged by requests to take cases out of the list for a week to enable the advocate to get 'instructions'. He was forced to point out that, although if a lawyer went into a Madras court without his fee he would more often than not have to work for nothing, the more leniency that was given to adjournments the more difficult it would become for the lawyers to collect their money. Fortunately, a working understanding was achieved with the 'very reasonable and friendly body of men' on the Madras bar.

11

CHINGLEPUT 1926–28

At the end of 1926 Sidney found himself in the district of Chingleput,[1] taking his seat for the first time as a district judge or, in his other capacity, sessions judge. Murder cases, for example, were tried by a sessions judge, whereas a district judge dealt with the most important civil suits. He had original jurisdiction in serious cases and heard appeals from second- or third-class magistrates and subordinate civil judges (often Indians) in others. The city of Madras was not included in the Chingleput district limits, although a large portion of the population of the district lived in what were more or less suburban areas, resulting in 'a certain vagueness' as to the whereabouts of the headquarters. The collector's office was lodged in an old 'garden house' in Saidapet (a Madras suburb), the district superintendent of police had 'come to anchor' at St Thomas' Mount three miles further out, and the district judge and most of the other district officials were stationed at Chingleput, about thirty-five miles from Madras on the great trunk road to the south.

The move started 'rather inauspiciously'. There was no other European official in the area, and Sidney and Olive knew none of the missionaries, so decided to move straight into their house. Depositing their belongings on two large lorries in the morning, they set out by car after lunch, expecting to arrive just in time to supervise the unloading. But upon arriving at the house, which was pleasantly situated on a small hill outside the town, they found the house completely empty and 'not a sign of our goods and chattels or servants'. About an hour before dark the missing lorries turned up, their occupants having left the road for a meal and siesta in the shade. Somehow or other it was possible to open all the boxes to find the lamps before darkness descended and they were able to assemble their beds and produce some sort of a meal which, 'after four years of comparative civilisation ... seemed an unnecessarily rough reintroduction to the primitive joys of upcountry life.'

Chingleput was a 'small, undistinguished town', subsisting largely on the indirect profits from the courts and offices located in the area. Its inhabitants comprised 'clerks, lawyers, touts, typists, eating-house-men, petition-writers and all the riff-raff which accumulates inevitably on the fringe of the law. There was also a fairly large representation of that class always to be found in the neighbourhood of rich wet lands—people who call themselves agriculturists, but do precisely nothing except collect their grain rents twice a year and quarrel among themselves.' Within the confines of the town was an old fort which had once been an important frontier post for Madras, attractively situated on the bank of a large lake, the level of which had been artificially raised for irrigation purposes. Beyond the lake and on the other side of the town were ranges of low, forest-clad hills which remained green even in the middle of the hot weather, while the low-lying land in the cold weather was 'a sea of brilliantly green paddy ... broken only by the double line of graceful coconut palms which border the main road.' At harvest time the road was used as a threshing floor and any traffic was forced to negotiate piles of straw, heaps of grain and a continuous procession of men, women and boys carrying bundles of straw on their heads. Sidney describes the colourful picture in the evening light, 'the golden straw, the paler tint of the grain heaps, the bright reds and pinks of the women's clothes and overhead the lovely fronds of the coconut palms'.

The fort was surrounded by a moat fed from the neighbouring lake. Within the confines of the moat but outside the entrance to the fort there was a small mahal or palace which was once the residence of the local raja before it was used to accommodate the courts. Inside the fort was a large reformatory school for boys. When Sidney and Olive first visited the school, they were shown around the classrooms, dormitories, kitchen, weaving sheds and carpenters' shop, and the brass band was then paraded for them, playing as an exhibition piece 'Show me the way to go home', which under the circumstances was remarkably apt as, one Christmas as an experimental measure, all those boys who had homes to go to were allowed to return for a week's holiday. They travelled without escort and every one of them came back punctually, which was a fine testimony to the success of the institution. Sidney spent a fair amount of time with the boys, playing cricket and organising two scout troops, and found them 'as decent a crowd of boys as any other', yet almost all of the pupils had at least two convictions, mostly for theft. He left Chingleput convinced that juvenile crime in India was largely the result of a bad environment and few of the boys had 'inherent criminal tendencies', but had taken to crime out of poverty or peer pressure; the percentage of boys who reverted to crime after three or four years in the school was very low.

Sidney was particularly interested in one small Anglo-Indian boy who at the age of twelve had made a living by travelling on the railways without a ticket and stealing from the other passengers. When he arrived at Chingleput, he looked 'forlorn, sullen and half-starved' and the superintendent (himself an Anglo-Indian) failed to know how to treat him, as he was reluctant to see him eat and live like the 'cooly-class boys' who made up most of the school. However, it became apparent that what the boy needed was 'discipline, good food, education and a congenial occupation and his social status could safely be left to look after itself', therefore he was let loose among the rest of the inmates and, although he was as dark in colour as many of them, the superintendent marked him out as 'a distant relative of the ruling race' by giving him a topee to protect him from the sun. Remarkably, the other boys did not resent this, as the newcomer appeared to be of a different caste from themselves and they thought it quite natural that he should wear the headgear of his own community. When it came to teaching him a trade, at that time very few Eurasians became carpenters, weavers, blacksmiths, gardeners or farmers, which appeared to eliminate most of the trades taught in the school. It was then found that the boy was musical and he was put into the band where he learnt to play the cornet. In a matter of weeks he improved dramatically and appeared to be 'well on the way to being turned into a decent, useful member of society.'

About two miles away on the other side of Chingleput was a large leper settlement run by missionaries of the United Free Church of Scotland. In Sidney's time it was managed by a man named Wilson, who had a very different background to the majority of missionaries, starting life as an assistant in one of the big trading firms on the Malabar Coast. He did so well that by his early thirties he was able to retire from business in order to take up the life for which he felt a calling. He went up to Cambridge and, despite his late start, 'succeeded in getting a first class in the moral and metaphysical sciences tripos, a very notable achievement for one who had spent ten years or so buying copra and selling piece-goods.' He was then ordained and returned to South India in charge of the leper settlement during the absence of the regular manager. Wilson was 'a man of brains and ability' besides having much experience of affairs in South India, and when the mission, which observed a strict demarcation between senior and junior missionaries, treated him 'more or less as a juvenile', he not unnaturally resented it. Dr R. S. Donaldson, the young Scot in charge of the medical work of the settlement, backed up Wilson. The Wadsworths knew nothing of the rights and wrongs of the situation, but were highly aware of the 'cleavage' amongst the missionaries who were their only European neighbours and the undercurrent of ill feeling. In the end both Wilson and Donaldson left India and 'the mission lost the services of two very good men.'

The inmates of the settlement were for the most part in the advanced stages of leprosy, which not only disfigured the body, but, according to Sidney, also had 'a most unfortunate effect on the mind.' In his experience, lepers were 'almost always cantankerous, ill-tempered, impatient folk, who display no gratitude towards their benefactors and strongly resent the constraints and suffering inseparable from the treatment', which was very prolonged and often involved deep and painful injections. The daily work of nursing, feeding and caring for the patients must have been 'a weariness to the flesh', and he had the utmost admiration for Margaret Salmond, the nursing superintendent, who hardly left the settlement except for her annual much-needed holiday in the hills. Without fear of infection, she refused to wear gloves while doing her dressings until compelled to do so by being threatened with dismissal if she persisted in taking unnecessary risks.

Sidney was of the opinion that the amount of concealed leprosy in India must have been very great, particularly in the early stages of the disease when it was said to be at its most infectious, and he received a number of anonymous petitions alleging that one clerk or another was a leper. Although he usually put such petitions into the waste paper basket, he always insisted on a medical report and in some cases the allegation was justified. The disease seemed to affect all classes and was very common among Brahmins, 'notwithstanding their scrupulous personal cleanliness.' The village people appeared to be less frightened of leprosy as might have been expected, possibly because it was so slow in developing that its contagious character was not appreciated. However, the risk of contracting it was obviously well known, as lepers could always travel on the railways without tickets because no railway employees would touch them to turn them off the train.

While Sidney was at Chingleput there was a strike at the leper settlement. The patients had been receiving a very generous ration of rice, out of which they were saving a substantial portion and trading it through the fence for toddy. As alcohol was supposed to be extremely bad for their condition, Wilson reduced the rice ration and made up the difference in vegetables. Immediately, the majority of the inmates walked out of the settlement and some hundreds of them descended upon the city and 'parked for the night in any vacant space they could find—verandahs of houses and shops, temple precincts and office porticoes.' The strategy of the local inspector of police in dealing with the invasion was both original and effective. At night his men rounded up all the lepers and marched them down to the railway junction. As each of the numerous night trains rolled into the station, he packed twenty or so of the lepers into it, without tickets, leaving it to them to decide where they would alight. Within a week or two, practically all of them were back in the settlement. As Sidney pointed out, the necessary legislation to segregate all lepers in a contagious condition did exist in India, but was not enforced 'for the simple reason that the available institutions could not deal with a tenth of the cases.' Moreover, there was the danger that compulsory segregation would drive the disease underground even more effectively than was already the case.

During his time in the district, Sidney was faced with a murder case against a leper which caused him great consternation. A man who had 'a handsome and rather luscious wife', and a daughter aged six or seven, was fatally stabbed one night in front of his house. The wife swore that the accused, a leper, had been lodging in their house and had been making immoral overtures to her. She also swore that she actually saw the leper stab her husband and this evidence was corroborated by the little girl. There was the usual 'dying declaration' implicating the leper as the assailant, alleged to have been recorded from the deceased by the village magistrate; while the government doctor, having examined the leper's deformed fingers, expressed the opinion that it would have been quite possible for him to have inflicted the wound by clasping the knife between his two palms. Sidney was troubled by a number of matters: dying declarations were often recorded in a village after the alleged deponent was dead, especially if the accused was a person against whom there was some 'popular feeling'; it was unlikely that the child, who was too young to be effectively cross-examined, and her 'highly sexed, passionate' mother would have had a leper as a lodger; moreover, it was most probable that the woman would have repelled the leper's advances (if he made any) and quite possible that she was shielding another man; and, finally, since the accused was quite unable to use the fingers of either hand, it was doubtful whether he could have gripped the knife with sufficient firmness to have inflicted a deep abdominal wound.

In South India, murder cases were not tried by jury except in the High Court. Sidney sat with four assessors who gave their opinions separately, but the responsibility for the decision was his alone. With no positive evidence in support of his suspicions, he contacted his friend Dr Donaldson, the foremost authority on leprosy in South India at the time, who agreed to appear without a fee 'in the interests of humanity and justice.' In the presence of the entire court he made a careful examination of the leper's hands and studied the post mortem documents with 'a truly Scottish deliberateness' before declaring that the man could have held the knife, 'but not with sufficient force to have caused so deep a penetration.' Sidney now had no doubt that the leper had been chosen as a victim because the village wished to get rid of him. The leper went free, but the real murderer was never discovered.

Sidney was sent to Chingleput to learn the civil work (largely new to him) rather than to deal with criminal law, and the number of murders in the area was in any case small. However, while there he had to try one of most sensational cases which came before him throughout his career. The story revolved around the 'strange personality' of Adinarayana Rao, a Brahmin of a respectable but impoverished family who at the outset earned a fairly precarious living as the clerk of a country lawyer. He was 'a tall, strikingly handsome man who spoke English very fairly and was equipped with a pair of piercing eyes which evidently played havoc with the other sex.' He had a wife, 'a poor, down-trodden, half-starved creature', and a small child. His relatives were involved with the Theosophical Society and he was therefore familiar with the story of Annie Besant's attempt in 1909 to launch her fourteen-year-old protégé, Krishnamurti, as a theosophical Messiah.[2] Perhaps influenced by this, Adinarayana Rao abandoned his ill-paid profession and came to Madras with his family, evidently in anticipation of a more illustrious career. He was the guest of his uncle, Venkata Krishnayya, the assistant secretary of the Young Men's Indian Association, which was an organisation started by Annie Besant on the lines of the YMCA but with a theosophical and nationalist leaning. Living with Venkata Krishnayya at the time was his niece called Chandramati, 'a clever and good-looking girl of some education', who was separated from her husband. Once in Madras, Adinarayana Rao began to assume a 'semi-divine status', supporting his claims by producing forged '"messages"' from Mrs Besant, from her 'bishop', Charles Webster Leadbeater,[3] and, finally, from the Archangel Gabriel himself. With the help of these documents and 'the power of his soulful eyes and glib tongue' he was able to get himself accepted as a 'budding Messiah' by several gullible female theosophists from whom he extracted money and jewels, and from Venkata Krishnayya who gave him money. However, the uncle began to realise that his nephew was a fraud and threatened to expose him. Adinarayana was forced to leave Madras and, with his wife and child, stayed with a cousin, Subba Rao, who was a railway clerk in the suburb of Villivakam to the north of Madras. An 'undersized, insignificant-looking fellow and miserably poor', Subba Rao appeared to be completely under the influence of the dominant personality of the '"Messiah".'

Early in November 1926, Venkata Krishnayya consulted a leading theosophist in an effort to challenge his nephew. In the first week of December, Adinarayana, who had already pawned all his wife's 'ordinary' jewels, took from her 'the sacred marriage tali (which no Hindu wife will sell, even if she is starving)' and sold it to a goldsmith for a little over five shillings. On the same day, an ounce of strychnine was purchased from a chemist by an unknown man with a forged doctor's prescription, and three days later Subba Rao turned up in Nellore at the house of Adinarayana Rao's mother-in-law, Subbamma, and persuaded her that her daughter was ill. Subbamma left for Villivakam and unfortunately took with her a younger daughter, both of them wearing all their jewels, 'as is usual when Brahmin women go on a visit.' On the same day, Subba Rao wrote inviting the old uncle Venkata Krishnayya to stay with him in order that Adinarayana Rao, with the help of his mother-in-law, could settle the uncle's claims.

Subbamma and her daughter arrived at Subba Rao's house in the evening and were never seen alive again. The next day a neighbour saw people digging in Subba Rao's back yard and some young banana trees were planted there. On the same day, Adinarayana Rao ordered a new tali (necklace) for his wife, and he and his cousin sold the jewels which Subbamma and her younger daughter had been wearing, 'raising a substantial sum at various Madras shops.' That evening the 'ill-fated' Venkata Krishnayya arrived at Villivakam, accompanied by his niece, Chandramati, who disappeared to Hyderabad before the police arrived, but was subsequently traced. According to her evidence, she and her uncle were given 'a curry made with bitter gourds' for supper. She took one mouthful and spat it out, declaring that it was too bitter. The old man ate all his curry and shortly afterwards 'was taken ill, with fearful cramps and muscular spasms, and in less than an hour he died in extreme agony.' The next morning Venkata Krishnayya's body was publicly cremated. No attempt was made to conceal the death, which at the time caused no suspicion.

Meanwhile, Subbamma's relatives in Nellore were becoming suspicious when she failed to return home. A report was made to the police, after which Subba Rao was placed under 'surveillance', and two days later he told the police the entire story. The banana plants were dug up, the corpses of the women and child were found beneath them, and some of their belongings were discovered in the well. All the jewels were recovered from the numerous shops in Madras where they had been sold, and the shop assistants identified both Adinarayana and his cousin, incontrovertibly proving the case against them.

The court was packed throughout the trial and the spectators had much to discuss. As Sidney described:

> Firstly there was the striking appearance of the self-styled Messiah. He really was a remarkable man to look at, with his tall erect figure, his fine features, his weird eyes and the long black beard which Hindus always associate with the holy man. Then there was Chandramati, young, distinctly pretty, clever and mysterious—everyone was speculating about her part in the strange story, but she gave nothing away. Then there was the downtrodden wife, cowering in the dock with her child in her arms—she was implicated as an accessory but was acquitted. Finally there was the day at the end of the long trial when the two principal accused appeared in the dock guarded, not as before by the ordinary police, but by a strong force of armed reserve constables; and the story gradually leaked out that there had been a fearful struggle in the jail the previous evening, when Adinarayana Rao had tried to murder his cousin.

The issue was never in doubt and in the end both men were hanged 'as they richly deserved'. However, Sidney was never able to ascertain the true mental state of the 'Messiah'. For a Brahmin to take the life of another Brahmin was a sin much greater in Brahmin eyes than any other murder, and the 'very cruelty and (to Hindu notions) the sacrilege of the crimes make one wonder how far the main perpetrator was a person with instincts and mental processes like those of ordinary human beings.'

One civil suit which particularly interested Sidney concerned the rights of irrigation from a river which served villages belonging to three parties: the government, the temples of Tirupati city and its surrounding area[4] (eighty-six miles northwest of Madras), and the Raja of Kalahasti.[5] The river Swarnamukhi had changed its course, upsetting all the old mamuls or customs, and what was required was not a legal decision regarding existing rights, but 'the formulation of a new scheme, settling in a reasonable way the future distribution of water from what was in effect a new river.' Sidney was aware that any attempt to decide the matter on ambiguous evidence in court would result in dissatisfaction and the futile waste of money in appeal. He therefore asked the lawyers on all sides if they would agree to accept him as an arbitrator on the condition that he made a careful local inspection, a suggestion which was welcomed. It was an arduous trip involving seventy miles by car and eight miles across country by horse, then 'a long tramp around the affected area and much talking to the local peasantry.' Finally, he prescribed 'a dam of a certain height with vents of certain dimensions, each vent serving the channel of particular villages.' Despite the fact that this was 'all more or less guess-work', there was no grumbling and years later, as far as he knew, the arbitrary decision still governed the water rights of the locality.

Most of Sidney's time in Chingleput was spent on appellate work, consisting of criminal appeals from the decisions of first-class magistrates[6] (whose powers extended to sentences of two years' imprisonment and a fine of Rs 1,000), from civil appeals from the judgment of district munsiffs[7] (who corresponded roughly to county court judges) and from judgments in the smaller suits tried by subordinate judges. He also did as much original civil work as possible, including certain classes of work which he was unable to delegate, such as those dealing with religious endowments, guardianship and matrimonial issues. Most of his problems came from Conjeevaram, a large town of great religious significance about 15 miles north of Chingleput.

In his experience 'some of the most quarrelsome and fractious people in India were to be found among the priests and office-holders in the big Hindu temples' and the root of the discord lay in the constitution of the shrines. Many of the temples had very large endowments which came partly from ancient grants from former rulers and partly from gifts and legacies from pious worshippers. The temples usually had several trustees who were often, but not always, hereditary. They worked through a manager to control the funds and festivals, subject to the vested rights of the priests and officials whose offices were all hereditary. Most of the trustees regarded their office 'not merely as a position of honour, but as one carrying perquisites and financial advantages' and many of them were systematically dishonest, especially those whose office was 'the sole remnant of a once rich heritage.' In Sidney's opinion the priests were 'a lot of lazy fellows, whose emoluments are just sufficient to prevent them from ever having to work and whose duties, even when they perform them conscientiously, are not sufficiently onerous to keep them out of mischief.' Constantly on the look-out for more fringe benefits, their religion was 'largely a matter of forms and ceremonies' with little regard for personal ethics. Assisting them in milking the system were the 'hereditary cooks, mahouts, lamp-lighters and musicians', not to mention the hereditary dancing girls who spent much of their spare time in prostitution. According to Sidney, it was only since the publication of Katherine Mayo's book *Mother India*, which attacked Indian society, religion and culture,[8] that the position of such women within the temples was 'admitted on all sides to be a disgrace to Hinduism' and legislation was introduced to end their extramural practices. In his opinion it was remarkable that, notwithstanding the corruption of the personnel, the great temples 'continued to inspire the reverence and respect of millions of Hindus and to be centres of true religion.'

Doubting whether 'there was a single temple in the whole of India with a more deplorable record of factious disputes than the great temple of Sri Devarajaswami at Conjeevaram', Sidney traced the history of the disputes of the temple in official records going back to the early eighteenth century, long before the power of the East India Company extended beyond the limits of the city of Madras. The basic cause of the quarrels appeared to hinge upon the fact that, although the temple was sacred to the god Vishnu, there were two sects of Vaishnavites who 'differ only in minute points of ritual but accentuate their differences by wearing different namams [caste-marks]. One sect is called Vadagalai and wears a namam on the forehead shaped rather like a large V; the other sect is called Tengalai and wears a namam rather like a T, but with two upright lines one at each end of the cross-stroke.' Unfortunately, the trustees of the great Conjeevaram temple were a family of Brahmins belonging to the Vadagalai sect, while the priests and nearly all the temple servants belonged to the Tengalai sect, with the result that for about 250 years there had been a constant battle between the two parties as each tried to establish its own ritual and insignia. Every ten years or so 'the battle flares up in a new form; it is dragged into the courts and rarely dies down again until the matter has reached the High Court, if not the Privy Council.'

The ludicrousness of the situation was illustrated by the fight over the temple elephant, which occurred many years before Sidney presided over the area, when the mahout, a Tengalai, painted 'an offensively large' Tengalai namam on the elephant's forehead. The trustees ordered him to remove it and substitute a Vadagalai namam. He refused and was backed up by his entire sect. The trustees then filed a suit in the local munsiff's court where it was decided that the elephant was a Vadagalai. There was an appeal to the district judge, who refused to pass judgment on whether the elephant belonged to one sect or another as he had no jurisdiction to decide questions of 'ecclesiastical ritual.' This pleased neither party and the matter was taken to the High Court, which some years later came to the conclusion that the elephant, like its mahout, was a Tengalai. In response the Vadagalais raised the large sum necessary to take the case up to the Privy Council which, 'after hearing very learned arguments, finally decided that on the true principles of law, the elephant was, like the trustees, a Vadagalai.' The officer of the court 'duly supervised the removal of the offending emblem from the elephant's brow and the substitution of that which their lordships of the Judicial Committee thought proper.' However, the very next day, although the elephant was seen marching through the great courtyard of the temple still bearing the Vadagalai namam, 'no one could see it, for over it was draped a white cloth on which was painted an enormous Tengalai emblem.' The battle in the courts then reconvened.

To escape such cases, which consumed 'an unconscionable amount' of time and required all the patience he could command, Sidney escaped from time to time to the nearby coast. Fifteen miles away was Mahabalipuram (mentioned in Chapter 6 as the chosen spot for Lady Willingdon's picnic) with its Seven Pagodas, one of which had disappeared into the sea. These tiny temples, most of them monoliths, were situated among casuarina trees along the shore. Dating from about the seventh century AD, they were, in Sidney's opinion, 'far more beautiful than any later Hindu architecture in South India', and near them were 'wonderfully naturalistic sculptures in relief, carved on the living rock, depicting scenes of animal life with complete fidelity—monkeys hunting for lice in each other's hair, a cow gently licking its sucking calf and so on—all beautifully executed without a trace of the grotesqueness or conventionality of more modern Hindu art.' About five miles further south was the small Dutch fort of Sadras, 'deserted but in perfect preservation, enclosing a little graveyard with elaborately carved coats of arms on the tombstones, the lettering of which is almost as clear cut as if it was ten years old instead of two hundred.' Sidney imagined that the fort must have been very similar in size and design to the original Fort St George which disappeared when the town grew around it and was protected by battlements. Whether or not this was the case, Sadras was 'a perfect specimen of the fortified trading settlement of the 17th and 18th centuries', dealing mainly in the export of high-quality muslin. There must have been 'little comfort and no liberty' for the early traders in its cramped quarters, making it highly likely that they quarrelled with 'regularity and fervour.'

Also while in Chingleput Sidney found a welcome diversion from fractious legal disputes in his increasing involvement in the Scout Movement.

12

SCOUTING

During his brief connection with the Duke of Connaught during the duke's visit to Madras in 1921, Sidney had learnt that there were two types of scout enthusiast in India: one was 'the ardent disciple of Lord Baden Powell, believing in the scout movement simply because it made boys healthier, happier, more honourable and more useful; the other was a politically minded individual who saw in the scout movement essentially a machinery for training boys to become good nationalists.' Although the rival organisations joined forces at the time of the Duke's tour, the two widely differing approaches persisted. Sidney himself had nothing more to do with the movement until shortly after his arrival at Chingleput when he received a visit from his friend A. J. Leach, who was manager of a Madras firm of merchants and devoted practically all of his spare time to the Boy Scouts. Leach was endeavouring to enlist Sidney into the movement in the hope that he would undertake the organising of the scouts of the local district, who were now too numerous for the Madras branch to manage. Despite Sidney's protestations that he knew nothing about scouting, Leach provided him with three small books with the assurance that, if they were read carefully, Sidney would know as much as those with whom he was to work. He also pointed out that the movement needed a person whose position would command respect and Sidney 'unable to think of any more excuses ... agreed to have a shot at it—somewhat reluctantly'.

In a week or two, he found himself 'a fully warranted district commissioner' and, having acquired a superficial knowledge of the contents of the little books, he started his duties, which he was soon to find extremely interesting. In Chingleput itself there were troops of scouts at the local high schools, in the reformatory and even in the leper settlement. The last troop must have been 'almost unique', consisting as it did of about a dozen boys and a scoutmaster, all of whom were lepers. Their activities were naturally limited by their physical disabilities and they were unable to join in any general rallies or other gatherings, but 'it must have done much to brighten up their otherwise drab existence.' There were also troops in all the other larger towns of the district and Sidney was able to visit most of these when on his rounds inspecting courts.

There was no difficulty in recruiting Indian boys to join the scouts and it seemed possible to enrol them in hundreds, especially if there was help to provide them with uniforms. The problems arose when they made little progress with their training and were stuck at the elementary stage, 'not dropping out of the movement but failing to advance any further'. It was quite common to find a troop of thirty or forty boys out of whom only two or three had passed the second-class test while not one in a thousand ever became a first-class scout. Some of the troops would become quite proficient at one or two particular branches of work or play and 'could put up most entertaining turns around the camp fire', but when it came to passing tests and earning badges they appeared unable to summon up the necessary energy and enthusiasm. Sidney suspected that the Indian schoolboy's life was overshadowed by examinations which were 'absolutely necessary for his future livelihood', with little point in working for additional tests after school hours. Moreover, the Indian parent tended to suffer from 'a very serious examination complex, all the more powerful because it is vicarious. He is never happier unless his unfortunate son is sitting over his lessons and will keep the boy nominally at work for ridiculously long hours, with the inevitable result that he becomes dead stale, loses interest in his studies and often goes sick.'

There were similar difficulties with the scoutmasters, a few of whom were 'splendid', but most 'barely adequate.' In two of the Chingleput high schools the headmasters themselves were keen scouters and the result was a generally high level of efficiency. However, in many of the other schools, the teacher ('generally middle-aged and often physically unfit') who was put in charge of the scouts regarded his troop as an extra class in a subject which did not count for the school examinations. Sidney and his helpers did their best by running camps for the training of scoutmasters 'at which every effort was made not merely to teach them the technical side of scouting, but to instil into them something of its spirit.' Some of the younger lawyers were encouraged to join the movement but the response was not encouraging. There appeared to be a 'great dearth of well-educated Indians who were prepared to give up their spare time for public service without any hope of personal benefit'.

Another difficulty was to get the boys out into the country. None of the towns of the Chingleput district were very large and there was much interesting country within easy reach. Moreover, Indian boys were good at rigging up temporary shelters, lighting fires and cooking their own food. For most of the year the climate was almost ideal for outdoor activity, being warm but not too hot, and dry. In spite of these advantages, most of the scoutmasters 'persisted in parading their troops in the school yard and never stirring out of it'. In an effort to improve matters Sidney rotated from troop to troop, 'urging the boys to aim at a higher standard of efficiency and persuading the scoutmasters to organise small week-end camps in the adjoining countryside.' These efforts met with some success and Sidney did not feel that his time was wasted. What is more, it was work which was totally different from that for which he was paid and he was brought into contact with people he would not otherwise have met, declaring that, 'Revenue work had made me fairly familiar with the tillers of the soil. Court work had given me an extensive acquaintance with lawyers, litigants and criminals. But hitherto I had had little to do with either boys or their teachers.' Despite preferring the boys, he made some good friends among the teachers and 'greatly admired the work of the best of them', but felt that the most able men were not recruited into the teaching profession, not least because of the low pay. It was quite common in Chingleput to find village schoolmasters trying to live on the equivalent of a pound a month, while most of the secondary school teachers were getting little more than a pound a week, sapping any 'originality and initiative'.

Several very successful rallies were held at Chingleput on the playing fields beneath the ramparts of the fort. The proceedings would start with a completely empty field, then 'on the sound of a whistle, several hundred scouts would rise from their hiding places all round the field and all rush together towards the flag, yelling their patrol calls at the top of their voices.' They would then form up and march past in troops before splitting up into patrols, each of which would 'do a show of its own choice in skills such as gymnastics, blindfold boxing, tent-pitching, gipsy dancing, bridge-building, first aid work and half a dozen other different stunts.' The boys were delighted to show off their prowess and the scene resembled 'a large scale circus, with several dozen rings in action at the same time.' At dusk the campfire would be lit and the boys would squat on the ground in a large circle for more or less impromptu singing, varied by special turns provided by the different troops. Some of the entertainment was extremely good; in Sidney's view there was much comic talent among the people of South India and some of the boys were 'surprisingly funny.' There were 'imitations, conjuring tricks, skits, torch drill, costume dances and so on till the time came for supper when all would join in God Save the King and the Indian National Anthem, both sung rather out of tune, not because Indian boys cannot be taught to sing in tune, but because there was usually no one who knew precisely what the correct tune was.'

A good reason for such a celebration arrived when Sidney received a letter from the chaplain to the Commander-in-Chief, East Indies Squadron, to say that Vice-Admiral Bertram Thesiger,[1] who was spending a few days in Madras with part of his fleet, would like to visit the Chingleput scouts. The admiral, himself a keen scouter, went first to see the scouts in the leper settlement and the reformatory, both very unusual troops as neither set of boys could be allowed to roam at large. Many of the lepers had deformities, making it difficult for them to operate like other scouts, but 'the spirit of the movement was in them and they made a brave show.' The reformatory boys were 'most expert at the things which could be taught in the school grounds and were very smart to look at. They were perhaps a shade better disciplined than a scout troop should be, but they were always cheerful'. Later in the day both groups participated in a district rally which despite only two days' notice proved to be quite impressive.

When Sidney was transferred to his next posting in Madura, a district in the south of the Madras Presidency adjacent to the princely state of Pudukkottai,[2] he wanted to continue his scouting activities and, as a well-known local lawyer had already been appointed as district commissioner, Sidney became his assistant. There were roughly 2,000 scouts in the district, which was far more than one commissioner could effectively supervise. However, as Sidney had to inspect all the civil courts once a year, he was able to visit many of the more remote troops at the same time, where he found the standard of scouting 'deplorably low.' Many of the scouters were men who had been recruited by Annie Besant's organisation and Sidney felt that some of them were more keen on politics than scouting. Nevertheless, they did undertake a great deal of useful work, particularly in helping the authorities at the great festivals. The movement was also 'a potent force in softening the rigidity of caste distinctions', since the scouts were of all castes and 'it was no mean feat to get hundreds of them to sit down and eat together without any complaint either from the boys or their parents.' Caste appeared to be the dominant factor of social life in South India and Sidney had frequently seen small boys and girls doing their lessons on the verandah of the village school because they were 'pariahs' and not permitted to come inside. It was also quite common to see 'untouchable' witnesses at a sub-magistrate's court standing on the verandah and shouting their evidence through the window. Only during the first decades of the twentieth century were 'these so-called Hindus of the lowest castes' allowed inside the great Hindu temples.[3] In Sidney's opinion the Scout Movement did much to pave the way for Mahatma Gandhi's campaign against untouchability.

In Madura, Sidney undertook the experiment of forming a scout troop unconnected with any school or institution, and run by a scoutmaster who was not a schoolmaster. Like most of his predecessors in the office of district judge, Sidney was lay trustee of the English church which was located in the railway colony, 'surrounded by the quarters of the guards, engine drivers, ticket-collectors and other upper subordinates of the railway, most of whom were Eurasians.' In the execution of his duties as a part-time, unpaid curate (since the chaplain only visited once a month) he got to know quite a number of the railway employees and discovered that a scout troop for the boys in the colony would be welcomed. About two thirds of the domiciled community were affiliated to the Roman Catholic Church and Sidney gained the cooperation of the priest to start to recruit his troop, which at first consisted of a dozen boys. He filled the role of scoutmaster himself until he found a young telegraph operator who had had some scout training in Madras and could take over from him.

As the troop grew it began to 'shape very well' and the boys camped in Sidney's large compound where they cooked their own food. Recognising the fact that nearly all Eurasians were musical, he started a 'whistling band' using fairly rudimentary equipment, and in a short time its members had made themselves into 'a tuneful and lively orchestra, playing their miscellaneous collection of instruments with a verve which Toscanini himself might have envied.' Moreover, at a district event the boys not only supplied the music, but also 'put up a first class boxing display which was quite the best performance of the rally' and Sidney began to congratulate himself on having built up a very good independent troop. However, his rejoicing proved to be premature, as he came to the conclusion that the Eurasian exhibited 'a strange mixture of good and bad; he is generally a friendly sort of fellow, a sportsman, a regular church-goer and a musician; on the other hand he is too often lazy, touchy and shiftless.' When Sidney left Madura on six months' leave he left the boys under their new scoutmaster, but found upon his return that the troop had ceased to exist and had not met once after his departure. The boys would obey Sidney 'cheerfully and willingly', but they would not take anything in the nature of an order from 'one of their own kind.' Sidney did not have the strength of mind to start again and thus ended his only attempt to run a troop of scouts.

When he went to live permanently in Madras, Sidney was asked to join the Provincial Scout Council, and for some time he attended its meetings regularly and tried to do what he could to help the movement. However, he found the meetings 'a weariness to the flesh and a great waste of time' with endless talk and little to show for it. Many of the members were thinking 'in terms of nationalist politics rather than of scouting', and so much time was spent on questions such as 'whether the scouts should promise to serve the king, whether they should use the Union Jack or the congress flag, whether spinning (Mr Gandhi's panacea for India) should be taught as a scout craft and so on.' In the end Sidney decided that the Council was doing little to further the cause of scouting and resigned, despite an active connection with the movement which had lasted for nearly ten years. He had no regrets over the loss of leisure time, believing scouting to be 'a great moral and educational force'. However, it was a force which depended for its success upon 'the existence of a sufficient number of public-spirited individuals of the right type to act as leaders' and he could see 'little likelihood of South India producing such men in sufficient numbers to make scouting really effective on a large scale.'

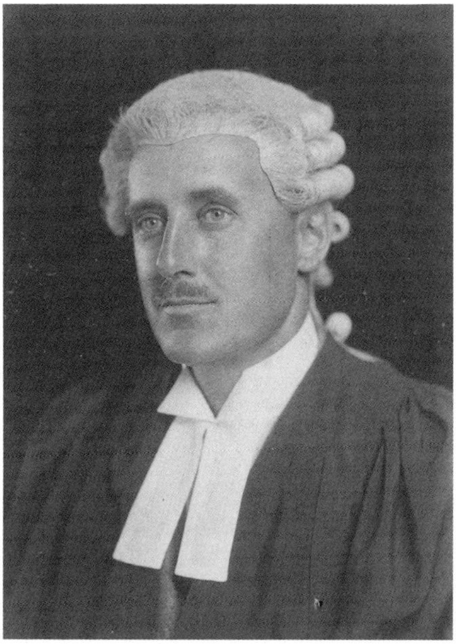

Sidney Wadsworth, Barrister, c. 1925

Sidney Wadsworth, High Court Judge in full-bottomed wig c. 1936

Sidney Wadsworth in formal Court Levee attire, c. 1938

Sidney Wadsworth in Court Session Robes

14 THE TIMES OF INDIA ILLUSTRATED WEEKLY.

INDIAN SOCIAL EVENTS IN PICTURES.

Photograph by Willie Burke, Madras.

The Wadsworth-Clegg Wedding in Madras, at which H. E. Lord Pentland was a guest. He is seen on the left.

Sidney Wadsworth and Olive Clegg: Wedding, Madras, 1916 (l to r: Lord Pentland, Lady Clegg, Sidney, Olive, Sir Arthur Clegg)

The Senate House and Marina Road, Madras. 1918

The Chepauk Palace, Madras. 1918

The Senate House, Madras (top), 1918, The Chepauk Palace, Madras, 1918 (bottom)

Sidney Wadsworth, Madras, c. 1925

Sidney Wadsworth, Isle of Man, 1925

Robert (11), Olive, Elsie (9), Sidney, Margaret (7), Isle of Man, 1928

Sidney (45) and Olive (38), Isle of Man, 1933

3 Generations of Wadsworths in Birmingham in 1952: (l to r): Simon (5), Sidney (62), Tim (8), Suzette (31), Olive (57)

Sir Robert and Lady Clegg in the Isle of Man, 1929, with Robert (12), Elsie (10), Margaret (8)

Reverend Henry Wadsworth, Sidney's father, aged 74 (1929)

13

MADURA 1929–33

In 1927, anticipating by two years the statutory revision of the Montagu-Chelmsford reforms, the British government appointed a commission under the Liberal politician Sir John Simon to recommend a further reform of India's constitution. In an act of gross tactlessness, the commission chose not to appoint any Indian members. As a response to this slight, a committee under Motilal Nehru, father of Jawaharlal, produced an alternative report which demanded immediate self-government within the British Commonwealth. During 1929, the second Labour minority government came to office in Britain, and Labour's more conciliatory policy towards India's constitutional aspirations enabled the Viceroy, Lord Irwin, to make an unequivocal gesture of friendship to India. This included a clear statement, the Irwin Declaration, stating that the natural end of India's constitutional progress would be the attainment of dominion status. A second concession to Indian nationalism took the form of an announcement in October 1929 of a proposed Round Table Conference, at which the princely states and all sections of opinion in British India would be represented to discuss the means of achieving further constitutional reform in the subcontinent. However, the Congress was far from convinced that dominion status was well within its reach; moreover, in the view of Jawaharlal Nehru and other radical nationalists, dominion status no longer satisfied their definition of *swaraj*. It was therefore decided to boycott the 1930 First Round Table Conference, and in March of that year Gandhi launched a new civil disobedience campaign.

The campaign attracted a number of groups who had not previously participated. Most significantly, perhaps, were the inroads which Gandhi now began to make into South India where, according to district collector Sir Christopher Masterman, he had 'extraordinary influence over the masses for social and religious reasons rather than political reasons and it was easy to persuade the ordinary ryot in Madras ... that they were getting nowhere with dyarchy'.[1] Non-Brahmins were securing more places in the government and universities, and Tamil poets and intellectuals had helped to create an increasingly confident South Indian culture. The Congress leadership worked energetically to build bridges to the South Indian populace and by the mid-1930s the party had become the dominant political organisation in the area. The second civil disobedience campaign culminated in the Dandi Salt March in the state of Gujarat in defiance of the Raj's salt monopoly. While Gandhi marched along India's west coast in March 1930, his close associate, Chakravarti Rajagopalachari[2] (later to be closely involved with Sidney), organised the Vedaranyam salt march in parallel a month later on the east coast. His group started from Tiruchirappalli (200 miles south of Madras city) to walk to the coastal village of Vedaranyam and, after making illegal salt there, he was arrested by the police. Due west of Vedaranyam was the city of Madura, where Sidney had arrived two years earlier to take up his next posting as district judge.

Madura (now Madurai) in the late 1920s was a congested town of about a quarter of a million inhabitants,[3] situated on the main trunk road 300 miles south of Madras and seen as 'a great pilgrim centre and a regular stopping place for tourists "doing India" in a month or two.' The town was built around the great temple of the fish-eyed goddess Meenakshi.[4] One of the biggest temples in the world, the Madras civil servant Geoffrey Lamarque described the huge surrounding gopurams (monumental towers) as 'covered with a bewildering entanglement of elaborate carvings of gods, goddesses, and animals of all shapes and sizes.' A feature of the temple was the so-called Hall of a Thousand Pillars (in fact somewhat fewer) and the building was 'invariably packed with people, many of them beggars, intermingling with a few temple elephants who padded about bedecked with tinkling bells.' However, Lamarque 'found the whole place eerie, and indeed sinister, and was always glad to emerge again in the light of day.'[5] To Yvonne Fitzroy, on tour with the viceroy, the building revealed the Hindu architect to be 'a master of detail, but builds too as a giant would build; tier upon tier the gopurams tower; block upon block climb the pillars; the corridors wind and cross; dark doorways lead to dim and haunted recesses; again widen into lofty halls, and every step of the way the rock is hewn, not so much into figure, pattern or design, as into a tremendous exuberance of life.'[6]

The streets of the city were laid out in concentric squares surrounding the temple at gradually increasing distances, eventually reaching a comparatively wide set of streets which followed the line of the old battlements, demolished in the middle of the nineteenth century apart from one large bastion, which in Sidney's time was occupied by the district hospital. The bulk of the population lived within the perimeter of the old walled city and was 'incredibly concentrated.' In the mornings and evenings when Sidney had to make his way to and from the courts, 'the streets seemed to be packed with a dense medley of men, women, and children, cars, buses and jutkas, handcarts, buffaloes and donkeys, with here and there a couple of ducks or even a gaggle of geese to add variety to the concourse and to test one's skill as a driver.'

Like Lamarque, the famous Meenakshi temple failed to inspire Sidney, who found it a 'grim, dirty, gloomy structure, impressive by its size and the barbaric splendour of its sculptures, but completely devoid of either sanctity or beauty.' The great gateways of the temple were packed with shops and stalls selling 'flowers, fruits, idols, toys, lamps, glass bangles, sweets—anything likely to appeal to the crowd of worshippers and sightseers' which inevitably reminded him of Christ's words in the temple at Jerusalem that the holy site had become 'a den of thieves'. Sidney suspected that many pious Hindus regretted the desecration of the Meenakshi temple, however, the building relied on the shop rents for the bulk of its income and 'in the east, as in the west, economics are apt to prevail over good taste.' The temple administration provided Sidney with a great deal of tedious work. Although not cursed by sectarian disputes, as was the temple at Conjeevaram, the Meenakshi temple was often the 'storm centre of local politics, which usually revolved round personalities rather than policies.' When matters came to a head, the district judge would be asked to call the appropriate temple trustee to account and his court would be packed for days on end, while 'long-winded advocates would make the roof ring with their sonorous periods, all professedly aimed at the protection of true religion and the sanctity of the temple, but in fact inspired for the most part by personal rancour and factious spite.'

It amazed Sidney how the most mundane of temple disputes could be guaranteed to fill his court, while a 'comparatively sensational' murder case would empty it. But 'murder was not news in Madura.' He averaged sixty-three murder cases a year during his five years in the city and, allowing for the fact that many were not detected or prosecuted for want of evidence, there must have been a murder in the district roughly every other day, making it hardly surprising that 'the local idlers got bored with the spectacle of a man on trial for his life.' Sidney became 'desperately tired of the monotonous diet of blood and hatred' and most of the cases were essentially uninteresting in that the same crimes came up again and again in a slightly different setting. Moreover, it was extremely hard work, as the judge was forced to take down all the evidence (usually delivered in an extremely difficult foreign language) in his own hand. Of course there was always an interpreter, but waiting for the interpreter before starting to write slowed down the pace of the court, with the result that cases could drag on for days and the work would get into arrears. Sidney had enough Tamil to follow the evidence fairly well, but Tamil was at best 'a very indistinct language, with an excessive number of liquid sounds and a multiplication of almost meaningless words which are tacked together in endless profusion', and to understand a toothless old peasant woman talking Tamil, one needed 'not only an unusual familiarity with the local idiom, but a super-sensitive ear.'

All the principal courts in Madurai were situated in Tirumal Naick's palace, 'an enormous structure built in the time of Charles I and originally intended to house the Rajah, his zenana, his court and secretariat, as well as his elephants and a large part of his army.'[7] When first erected in a blend of Dravidian and Islamic styles, it extended almost up to the temple, as could be seen from the elephant stables (of which the columns still existed) about a furlong away from the palace, but even in its diminished size it was very impressive. The main portion was built around a huge courtyard flanked by vast pillars, some six feet in diameter, supporting a massive terraced roof. Between the pillars were wide and lofty verandahs 'always crowded by chattering throngs', leading to the various dark and noisy rooms occupied by most of the courts. Since Madura was the headquarters of two large districts, there were normally nine or ten courts working in the palace (nearly as many as in the High Court at Madras) and, although the palace was a very fine old structure, it was 'grotesquely unsuitable' for the courts it had to house.

Sidney's court was the only one in the building which was truly habitable, situated in a small wing to the rear of the main courtyard and 'quiet, cool and dignified.' It opened on to a pleasant small garden and was chiefly notable for two great monolith pillars of polished granite which were nearly thirty feet high and about three feet in diameter. Interestingly, these pillars were made of a stone found only in the Trichinopoly district, more than 100 miles from Madura, and 'the task of transporting them from the quarry to the palace at a time when there were no metalled roads and no bridges over the numerous sandy rivers, must have been formidable.' It seems likely that they were 'dragged on rollers by elephants and crowds of slaves' and the transport of each must have taken many weeks.

Looking down upon Sidney were two interesting portraits: one of a former district judge called Thomas Weir, known to generations of lawyers as the author of *Weir's Criminal Rulings*, 'one of the earliest and most authoritative collections of Indian case law'; the other of Sir Philip Hutchins, who had a particularly varied and distinguished career. Like Sidney he had been in the Secretariat and the Board's office before becoming a judge. After some years as a district judge, he became secretary to the Madras government before being elevated to the High Court. Having served for several years as a High Court judge, Sir Philip became a member of the Governor's Executive Council, was promoted to the Viceroy's Executive Council and finished his career as a member of the Secretary of State's Council in London. Sidney doubted whether any other member of the ICS had achieved a similar number of jumps between the executive and the judiciary branches, no doubt to the horror of 'constitutional purists'.[8]

Sidney never really appreciated the charm of his court hall until the viceroy, Lord Irwin, came on tour to Madura and was shown around the palace with his wife. For this occasion the hall was converted into a drawing room, with the dock and dais hidden behind large banks of foliage and flowers. All the court furniture had been removed and replaced by the contents of the Wadsworth drawing room with a floor covering of good Persian rugs, and the viceregal party had an opportunity to rest in peaceful surroundings during a long day of sightseeing and public functions. Sidney expressed his amazement that 'this picturesque and comfortable lounge was the very room in which twenty-four hours previously I had sentenced four murderers to death.'

On the other side of the rear part of the palace there was a much larger wing containing two very interesting apartments. One was a sizeable octagonal room which was used as a record room for the courts and, shut off from any possible breeze with the only light and air coming through small windows under the roof, was once the home of Tirumal Naick's zenana. Sidney's record-keepers used to complain bitterly about the heat and, when heavy hangings blocked the doorway and country oil lamps were used as the only source of light during the 'sultry evenings' of the raja's reign, conditions must have been appalling. An enormous hall with a sunken floor, which was commonly known as the bathroom, occupied the rest of the wing. It was lit by a clerestory, under which ran a gallery, and tourists were told that the women of the zenana would disport themselves in the bath while Tirumal Naick 'ogled them from the gallery above.' In Sidney's opinion this was pure fiction and the hall had in fact been used for dramatic and other entertainments, with the audience sitting in the well and the performers occupying the raised platform at the end, which was subsequently used by one of the courts.

It was also said that in the hot weather (lasting for the best part of nine months) Tirumal Naick used to sleep in a swing cot, 'suspended by long chains from the lofty vaulted roof.' One night 'a clever and daring thief made a hole through the solid masonry of the roof, climbed down the chain of the cot, removed all the jewellery from the person of the sleeping monarch and escaped by the route by which he had entered.' Tirumal Naick, filled with wrath at the impudence of the theft and the outrage to his dignity, issued a proclamation to the effect that any person giving information which would lead to the detection of the offender would receive the grant of a whole village as his reward. Hearing this proclamation, 'the impudent thief presented himself at the palace, did obeisance to the Rajah, announced that he himself was the thief and claimed the village.' Tirumal Naick could not go back on his word and ordered his diwan to make out the promised grant, whereupon he sent for his executioner and directed him to chop off the offender's head. This operation was 'duly performed, to the delight of the assembled courtiers and the enhancement of the Rajah's prestige.'

Sidney owned a fine William Daniell print which showed the great hall as it was 160 years earlier when the well or auditorium was half full of earth and cattle were tethered in it. The 'barbaric mouldings' which adorned the walls in Sidney's time were absent from the print, but it was possible to see the holes in which ornaments of some kind must have been fixed. The decoration of the hall was the result of a restoration carried out under the orders of Lord Curzon, 'that great restorer of India's historic buildings',[9] and in Sidney's opinion the ornamentation was probably modelled on the sculptures in the Meenakshi temple. Little was known about the building of the palace, but it seemed likely that Tirumal Naick employed Italian architects, as the great courtyard with its massive columns was unlike any other South Indian building and its general architectural style was to some extent European. Apparently it was well established that European architects and craftsmen were working in India under Mughal rule.

To the southeast of the old city of Madura on the road to Ramnad[10] there was a very large and 'extremely beautiful' teppakulam or sacred tank.[11] It was of the traditional design, square with steps going down to the water on each side and a small shrine on an island in the middle of the water, but to Sidney 'the proportions and the background of coconut palms' made it particularly attractive. At the time of the 'Floating Festival' the idols of the Goddess Meenakshi and her consort Lord Sundareshwarar were taken on an illuminated raft across the water to the central shrine, and all the steps and parapet walls were lit by thousands of tiny oil lamps as a dense crowd filled the surrounding roads. However, this spectacle paled in comparison with the Chittrai festival which was celebrated in Madura in the middle of the hot weather. A gold image of the god Alagar (Lord Vishnu, the elder brother of Meenakshi) seated on a horse was brought in a procession from the temple bearing his name at Alagar Koyil, a village about thirteen miles outside Madura. The route was lined by mantapams[12] or pavilions, each held in trust by some local notable who stood in its shade to receive temple honours as the procession halted for a short time on its long journey. According to legend, the object of the god's journey was his attendance at the marriage of the goddess Meenakshi to Shiva in the dry bed of the river Vaigai and, as Sidney described it, each year the marriage was celebrated with 'great magnificence, when, by a convenient convention, one of the officiating priests sneezes—a highly inauspicious action which enables the wedding to be postponed for yet another year.'[13]

Outside his court work in the palace, one of the duties of the district judge was to serve on the board of visitors of the central jail, which involved visiting the building whenever there was time and attending the regular meetings of the board. Inside the double gates and forbidding walls, a large Indian jail was 'a surprisingly pleasant-looking institution' and far more open and rural than the long, resounding corridors and individual cells of its English counterpart. In Madura the jail buildings were laid out in lines radiating outwards from a central office which commanded a view of the whole precincts. As a rule the prisoners lived in large rooms, each of which accommodated a dozen or more inmates and each prisoner had a cement platform on which he spread his sleeping mat. Such an arrangement was not unusual for a working-class Indian, who liked a hard surface on which to sleep, and it was undoubtedly much cooler than a soft bed. Individual cells were used only for special cases such as prisoners undergoing solitary confinement (a form of punishment which was 'rapidly becoming obsolete' in Sidney's time) and others who had to be kept separate for particular reasons.

Prisoners under sentence of death were kept in a series of cells known as the 'condemned cells', the last of which was nearest to the execution enclosure. There was 'rather a gruesome practice of using these cells as a sort of queue, the unhappy men moving up one place whenever the end cell is vacated.' Sidney himself never went inside the execution enclosure, believing that the less he saw of the final scene the better he would be able 'to treat the case objectively and decide it according to the evidence.' In Madura jail, executions were always held on a Monday morning and, as the jail served three 'decidedly murderous' districts, there was work to do on most Mondays. There was no question of a highly salaried executioner travelling from prison to prison, as happened in England. In an Indian jail, convict warders did almost all the internal duties, and one such duty was the execution of the death sentence.

The prisoners were employed on a variety of tasks. In some of the jails they made 'excellent' carpets, the men working in gangs with a foreman calling out the stitch. In Madura the main industry was weaving on handlooms the rough cotton cloth to be used for prisoners' uniforms and bundling up records in government offices. Other men made the coarse tape used in offices and the string bags which held rupees in banks and treasuries. There was also a cabinet makers' shop for school and office furniture, which required a great deal of supervision because of the sharp tools involved, and many prisoners were employed in the jail gardens which produced all the vegetables consumed by the prisoners. The one job which the prisoners universally hated due to its tediousness was 'working at a sort of hand-mill which has to be kept rotating horizontally by a gang of men, each of whom has to give a handle a sharp push as it passes him.' However, even this task was not excessively taxing and, taking into account 'the number of men working as cooks and cleaners in the wonderful fly-proof kitchens and all the other soft jobs waiting for men who behave themselves', Sidney doubted if the average man doing a sentence of 'rigorous' imprisonment worked as hard as an unskilled labourer outside. The punishment was 'not really the hardness of the life, but the loss of liberty, separation from wife and family and the deprivation of tobacco.' The food was excellent and the accommodation 'at least as comfortable' as the homes of most of the prisoners.

Apart from daily meetings in court and office, Sidney's contacts with Indians were confined to athletic activity (such as cricket of 'a rather mixed quality'), and when the Wadsworths arrived in Madura they discovered that their social life tended to be divided up into a number of 'almost water-tight compartments' within the considerable European community. The couple therefore made it their main goal 'to mix things up' and make friends with all the various groups. The divisions were partly geographical. Sidney and Olive had a large house on the racecourse, which was no longer used for racing but provided space for a good cricket ground and a rough golf course. On and near the racecourse were the houses of most of the officials, the bank agent and all the 'superior staff' of the Madura Mills, except for the manager, who lived in 'solitary splendour in a magnificent house five miles away to the south of the town.' The collector of Madura had a 'strange old house, known as the Tunkum, which was originally a sort of summer house for the rajahs of Madura.' Its most remarkable feature was 'a handsome drawing room, which had once been the Rajah's cockpit, octagonal in shape and built on an outcrop of solid rock' which raised it to a level with the first floor of the rest of the house.

The residents of the racecourse formed a natural group, all living within easy distance of each other with the club in the middle. Another group was made up of the technical staff of the mills, who lived in a separate colony called Kochadai, two miles to the southwest of the town and with a club of its own. While some of the Kochadai residents were 'a bit rough', most were 'extremely nice folks and it seemed wrong to us that they should live in almost complete social isolation.' There was also a very large missionary population, mostly belonging to the American Madura Mission which was historically connected to the Arcot Mission and similarly staffed mainly by Americans of Dutch extraction. They too were divided geographically into three groups: those living in the college to the north of the town, those at the hospital in the city and the directing staff who lived near the Mills manager to the south of the town. In addition to the Americans, there was a Swedish mission which mixed with no one, and a large number of Catholic priests and nuns who were mostly French and Belgian and belonged to one of the oldest missions in the subcontinent, the records of which provided the best sources for the history of South India during the period preceding the arrival of the British. Sidney's ICS contemporary Humphrey Trevelyan noted that Catholic missionaries 'sensibly went much further than the Protestants in assimilating the ceremonies of the church to the local scene', recalling that, 'Their churches were often hardly distinguishable from the Hindu temples, and the processions in honour of a favourite saint, such as St Antony or the Virgin, might have been Hindi processions in honour of Vishnu or Mariyamma', the south Indian goddess of rain.[14]

Whatever the differences, fraternisation among these different groups was limited and, since driving through the crowded streets of Madura was 'a slow and wearisome business', the community tended to stick to its topographical sections. Anxious to break down the barrier between the various circles, at a large Christmas party the Wadsworths assembled the officials, the bankers, both sections of the Mills' employees and 'all the younger and brighter members of the missionary community.' Sidney reported that it was a huge success. The young men of the Mills found that there were some 'very attractive daughters' in the bungalows of the American Madura Mission, and 'the ice having been broken … there were no fewer than four engagements between the guests' at the party, among whom was 'a modest and amusing' Scotsman called Jimmy Doak who would become 'one of the biggest commercial magnates in India'.

Perhaps the most interesting person in Madura was a man who lived alone in a large house near the teppakulam. When Sidney first met Robert Ffoulkes, or 'Bertie', he was 'in his middle fifties … short, round-shouldered and rather tubby, with a thick, grizzled moustache and a heavy brow' and his rather sallow complexion 'indicated a slight mixture of Indian blood.' His father had been chaplain of Madura in the 1860s and had married one of the daughters of Robert Fischer, a descendant of one of 'those interesting adventurers who came out to India in search of a fortune some two hundred years ago.' The original Fischer acquired a considerable fortune, married a begum and became the zamindar of two estates, one in Madura and the other in Salem.[15] Robert Fischer was a wealthy man of great local importance who built the old English church in the centre of the town (later handed over to the Tamil congregation 'greatly to Bertie's indignation'), and when he died Bertie inherited the Madura estate and his brother inherited the estate in Salem. There were also two other brothers: one a colonel in the Indian Medical Service, who was murdered by tribesmen on the northwest frontier, and the other an achiever of high rank in the army. All the brothers were educated at good English schools and Bertie entered the survey department, retiring when he came into his inheritance. Settling down in Madura, he soon became very influential in the area and was for many years the president of the district board,[16] close to Hindus and Muslims in a way which no transient Englishman could hope to emulate.[17] When his wife died, he buried her in the garden of his own house, 'beneath a beautiful marble tomb which was the work of a well-known Italian artist', and after her death Bertie became something of a recluse. His house was like 'a rather neglected museum', including a fine collection of ancient Rajput paintings which 'must have been originally illustrations of some old Persian story book.' It was suspected that, when he died in Madras some years later, many of his valuables were stolen and certainly some of his 'curious French china' was being sold by the Madras hawkers a year or two after his death. Sidney felt that the last years of Bertie's life must have been 'very gloomy'. He became heavily in debt, 'being sufficiently a man of the country to value his prestige higher than his solvency' and, at loggerheads with the rest of his family, his health broke down. Sidney preferred to remember him as he was when they first encountered each other, 'a man of great taste and refinement, full of enthusiasm for the welfare of the people of his district, well-read and much travelled, with a fund of good stories about the many interesting people he had met.'[18]

Sidney and Olive spent five 'very full and in the main very happy' years in Madura. The climate was hot and the work unceasing, but the couple had many friends and an interesting life. However, tragedy clouded their last year. The collector of Ramnad, John Gray, came to live almost next door to Sidney and became a great friend, as both wives were back in England with the children. Gray then fell ill and within a week was dead. Sidney confessed that 'His death filled us all with sadness and I was glad when the time came for me to depart.'

14

SOME CRIMINALS

When Sidney looked back on the 'enormous mass of serious crime' which passed through his hands in Madura, he was struck chiefly by the way in which matters easily 'disappeared into the realm of things forgotten'. A case would be studied 'with intense concentration for a day or two, a decision would be reached and judgment pronounced' before swiftly moving on to the next legal challenge. However, there were a few cases which were not easily forgotten.

Not long after his arrival in Madura, Sidney had a most challenging criminal appeal. A rich merchant, Muthu Chetty, who was prominent in local politics and therefore had many enemies, owed a comparatively small sum to a tradesman, paid the bill and obtained a receipt. He was therefore surprised when, a year or so later, the tradesman filed a suit claiming the same amount. Muthu Chetty through his lawyer put in 'the obvious defence of discharge' and filed with his written statement the relevant receipt. Nevertheless, the suit came on for trial; the tradesman denied the authenticity of the receipt and swore that he had never been paid, and Muthu Chetty swore that the receipt was genuine. At the next hearing the plaintiff examined two post office experts in order to prove that the stamps on Muthu Chetty's receipt were of an issue which was not on sale to the public until some months after the sale of the receipt. On the strength of this evidence, the suit was decreed and an application to prosecute Muthu Chetty for fabricating false evidence was granted. When the case came before the magistrate, on the circumstantial evidence Muthu Chetty was sentenced to a term of imprisonment. He appealed to Sidney's court and C. Brooke Elliott, an English barrister from Madras, was brought down to contest the case. He 'rightly laid great emphasis on the wealth of his client and the futility of risking a forgery to escape payment of a sum which he would never have missed' and suggested that the appellant had many enemies, one of whom might have tampered with the receipt. However, he was unable to explain how this could have happened when the receipt was in the custody of the court.

Sidney was 'distinctly worried and reserved judgment' but, having time on a Sunday, he closely examined the receipt with his wife and noticed a slight crinkling of the paper under the stamps as if it had been dampened, and ink marks under the stamps which did not correspond with the writing of the signature across them. It appeared that Muthu Chetty's enemies knew of the existence of the genuine receipt when the suit was filed, and with the help of a confederate in the office of the munsiff's court the stamps were removed from the receipt and stamps of a later date affixed, with part of the signature forged upon them. It was 'a clever trick which completely defeated the handwriting expert who had examined the document in the bad light of the magistrate's court.' Muthu Chetty was acquitted 'but did not live long to enjoy his triumph. A few years later he was stabbed to death in the dark by an unknown assailant, so his enemies got him in the end.' Sidney failed to establish the identity of the clerk who had betrayed his trust, although he had 'a pretty good idea who it was and had him removed to a place where he had less opportunity for mischief.'

In Sidney's view, false cases were 'deplorably common' in most parts of India. It was apparently a common saying in the 'murderous districts' of the south that you should 'never waste a corpse'. One case which provided a good example of this maxim occurred in the lower Palni Hills,[1] where a large area was devoted to fruit farming and coffee plantations on a fairly large scale. One of the Indian planters, a big man with many enemies, died suddenly. The corpse was buried and two days later a report was sent to the police 'alleging that he had been murdered through the machinations of a well-known rival.'

Eventually the case came before Sidney. The medical evidence was inconclusive as, by the time the corpse had been exhumed, it was too decomposed to arrive at a diagnosis of the cause of death. The prosecution examined 'a very wild and woolly snake-catcher who swore with many gesticulations and a great sense of dramatic effect' that at the request of the accused he had extracted venom from the poison glands of a cobra. Another witness had carried the dried venom up to the hills to an agent who was seen by yet another witness to pass it on to the dead man's cook, and it was proved that the victim died that night after eating his supper. Unfortunately for the prosecution, the defence examined a leading doctor who 'swore that the consumption of dried cobra venom in food would cause nothing worse than slight indigestion' as the poison only acted when injected into the blood stream. In fact there was little doubt that the victim had died of carbon monoxide poisoning, since the night of his death was cold and he had gone to sleep with his head very near a charcoal brazier in a little room with no ventilation. It appeared that the cobra venom story was 'nothing more than a bright idea for making good use of an otherwise unfortunate accident.'

Sidney never completely understood why 'murder in South India always seemed to be prevalent in the foot-hills and neighbouring valleys and to be comparatively rare in the open flat country.' One explanation was that 'the tearing monsoon winds' which raged through the valleys during the hot weather played 'havoc with the nerves and tempers of the inhabitants' and led them to commit violent acts. However, the greater number of murders in hot weather might have been due to the fact that it was 'a time of idleness.' There was also the fact that the initial ploughing which began with the first showers of the monsoon brought to a head any disputes about ownership of land which had proved to be a very frequent cause of fatalities. However, after many years of experience Sidney came to the conclusion that 'a great deal of murder is due to nothing but convention' and that in certain communities and areas, custom required that 'comparatively trifling wrongs should be wiped out in blood'.

The strangest example of conventional murder in his experience was triggered by 'a terrible custom prevailing in the virile and violent community of Maravars.'[2] If two men had a fierce argument, each firmly convinced that he was in the right, one would 'take one of his own children by the feet, bash its brains out on the nearest rock and lay the corpse at the feet of his adversary, whose perversity in argument is thus thought to have brought the blood of the child upon his own head.' This appalling custom was mentioned in the Madura District Manual, and Sidney himself was involved in one such case. Perhaps more understandably, there appeared to be a requirement for 'the injured husband of an unfaithful wife to chop her head off and place the head and the chopper in the nearest police station.' Also explained by convention was the blood feud or vendetta, displayed at its worst in a village called Combai at the foot of the Travancore Hills in the Madura district, which used to provide a murder roughly every six months, 'the two factions taking it in turns to supply the victim.' The Combai inhabitants usually employed hired assassins for their murders and Sidney had one of them before him no fewer than three times. On the first occasion he had quite clearly shot two men, but the case was complicated by the introduction of false evidence to implicate his alleged employers. Due to a lack of agreement by the two judges on the bench there was a retrial, by which time the evidence was 'stale' and the man ultimately got off. A year or so later he came up again, when Sidney 'came to the conclusion that though he was a scoundrel, he was not the particular scoundrel who had done that murder' and he was duly acquitted. Soon afterwards he was in Sidney's court for the third time, not as an accused, but as a witness for the prosecution. It appeared that the police, having failed to book him for murder, 'were keeping their eye on him by employing him to track down other murderers.' The character rather appealed to Sidney, who viewed him as 'a brave man and loyal to his employers and there was nothing of the sneak about him.'

The most interesting case which Sidney had in Madura was known as 'The Umbrella Case', involving an elaborate scheme of impersonation. A ploughman driving his oxen along a country lane in the early morning was suddenly roused when his bulls shied violently at something lying by the roadside. Upon investigation it proved to be the corpse of a man dressed in a long white cassock, which in India was the mark of a Roman Catholic priest or friar. The dead man had obviously been half strangled and then beaten on the head with a blood-stained stone which lay beside him, 'but the strangest feature of the case was the fact that the tip of an umbrella was sticking into the dead man's cheek. Apparently the assailant had jabbed at his victim's head with the ferrule of the umbrella which had stuck in his cheek and broken off.'

The ploughman informed the village magistrate and in due course a highly intelligent police officer arrived. Having established that no one was able to identify the corpse, he sent it to Dindigul, forty miles north of Madura, for a post mortem examination and, taking the umbrella tip with him, went round the Catholic mission stations in the neighbourhood to see if he could collect news of suspicious strangers. At a village some three miles from the scene of the murder, he discovered that a young Christian known as Arul Prakasam, who had once been employed as a cook by a priest in the area, had arrived the previous evening asking for a night's lodging. He was apparently 'carrying an umbrella with a white imitation ivory handle and no tip.' As Arul Prakasam was talking to some of the mission staff, a snake was seen and the newcomer killed it with his umbrella, breaking the white handle into two pieces in the process. The police officer was taken to the place, where the two pieces of the handle were lying where they had fallen.

The police now had the tip of the umbrella and its handle, but needed to find the rest. To Sidney's satisfaction, 'By one of those extraordinary mistakes which the cleverest of murderers so often commit, the culprit did not discard the umbrella in the middle of a prickly pear bush where it might have lain for ever, but took it to Dindigul, leaving it behind in a friend's house, when he disappeared as soon as he learnt that the police were investigating the crime.' The police obtained possession of the object and it was established that the tip taken from the cheek of the victim and the white handle broken on the back of the snake both fitted the part of the umbrella which had been abandoned by the wanted man. It therefore seemed 'fairly clear' that the man known as Arul Prakasam was the murderer, but less clear was the identification of the victim and the motive for the crime. The police knew well that 'to try and prove a murder by circumstantial evidence without establishing a plausible motive was a very tricky business'. However, the corpse was then identified by two Roman Catholic priests as that of a young monk who had studied in a seminary in the town of Trichinopoly to the north of Madura and, bizarrely, had given as his name the same, rather uncommon, name of Arul Prakasam.

This problem required weeks of patient investigation. It was finally established that about fifteen years previously there were two boys who were sent to the same school in the Ramnad district with the idea that they should both be trained for the priesthood. One, Arul Prakasam, behaved so admirably that he was passed on to the priests' sanctuary at Trichinopoly and eventually became a monk. The other, a reprobate called Susai, was expelled and, unable to become a priest himself, became 'the next best thing, that is the cook of a priest' who had a church in a village near Dindigul. Years afterwards, when Susai was in his twenties, he was driving the priest's bullock cart to a local festival and gave a lift to a boy who happened to be a cousin of Arul Prakasam. Discovering that Arul Prakasam had been separated from his relatives for many years while training for the priesthood, Susai on the spur of the moment pretended that he himself was the long lost young monk and was duly invited to the cousin's home. Word was sent to Arul Prakasam's mother, Arulayee, who, having not seen her son since his college days, 'fell on the neck of Susai and wept tears of joy over him', never suspecting that he was not her own son.

Susai, 'who hated work, saw a chance of free food and kept up the deception.' Arulayee fed and clothed him at her home in Kallurni, and when he pressed her to arrange his marriage, she sent for her other son, who was working in Penang, to return and finance the wedding, which was 'celebrated with due eclat', the bride and groom continuing to live with Arulayee. When some months later the young wife announced that she was going to have a baby, it was decided that Susai must find a job and Arulayee gave him a letter to an influential merchant in the next village, soliciting his help. However, upon presenting himself to the merchant as Arul Prakasam of Kallurni, the man declared that he had been at college with a student of the same name and that Susai was lying. He subsequently produced 'a rather morbid group photograph, taken at the funeral of a fellow student, with the garlanded corpse propped up in an armchair in the middle' which proved without doubt that Susai was a fraud and the merchant announced that he was intending to expose him as such.

Susai appeared to have been 'in mortal terror of exposure and ... decided that his only safety lay in doing away with the man he was impersonating.' At the monastery where the real Arul Prakasam was living, Susai told the porter that he was Arul Prakasam's brother who had come to inform the monk that their mother had died 'and he wept bitterly, hiding his face in his upper cloth.' The next morning, Susai greeted Arul Prakasam with more tears and the latter seemed to accept the fact that Susai was none other than the brother whom he had not seen since his boyhood. They departed together for the railway station, where Susai 'must have told his intended victim yet another lie to induce him to go to Dindigul and journey thence to the scene of his death.' The two men were seen together on the Dindigul platform and in the end the whole story unravelled in a way which left no possible doubt as to the result. Sidney stated that, 'The priests afterwards told me that Susai met his fate with courage and sincere repentance.'

15

THIEVES, USURERS AND SNAKE-CATCHERS

Surrounded for five years by the inhabitants of the 'huge area' of which Madura was the centre, and 'listening day after day to accounts of their quarrels and their crimes, their loves and their hates, their customs and their beliefs', Sidney felt that in his memoirs he was obliged to record 'this mass of human material'. He chose to comment on three of the 'more interesting' communities as samples of the people among whom he was living and working, 'who with their manifold divisions and diversities make up the patchwork of a South Indian district.'

First place was given to the Kallars, a 'very large and influential community of hereditary thieves, who, strange to say, occupy many positions of trust and influence.' The god Alagar, mentioned in the description of the Chittrai festival in Chapter 12, was held in special veneration by the Kallars, who invoked his aid when setting out on a robbery and gave him part of the proceeds. In Sidney's time the members of the community could be numbered in the hundreds of thousands, living mainly in the country between Madura and the town of Trichinopoly, eighty miles to the north. They played a leading role in rural life, occupying such responsible positions as village magistrate and temple trustee, and the most distinguished Kallar family was that of the Raja of Pudukkottai, who ruled over a state in the Madras Presidency as large as one of the smaller English counties.[1] Nevertheless, the Tamil word 'kallan' means thief, and it was said that 'even in the most respectable Kallar households, convention requires the head of the house to go through the form of committing a sort of notional theft every year, to show that he has not abandoned the calling of his caste.' Even the Raja of Pudukkottai ('the most urbane and civilised of men') admitted to the British officer Geoffrey Lamarque that he had fulfilled this requirement by 'pinching a trinket off his sister's dressing table.'[2] While there were many Kallars who lived honest and respectable lives, a substantial part of the community still depended for its livelihood on 'organised theft and extortion.' It was the custom of the caste to live at the expense of their neighbours, and its members 'systematised their extortions to a degree which would not be possible in a community which was not basically trustworthy.' Yvonne Fitzroy suggested in 1926 that, according to the authorities:

> circumstances and not natural depravity had driven them to crime. For they are agriculturalists in a country that has no rivers and no artificial irrigation. Their cry, and a very conscious cry, is for water. Further they have no railway … and so even such produce as they can raise cannot find a market. It has been, and often still is, a case of Starve or Steal, and being a people of spirit they naturally prefer to steal.

The government was working to educate them and to help agricultural practice, but 'the fringes of the problem only have been attacked … the Kallars are still a primitive people, primitive and predatory.'[3]

Throughout the Madura country, the Kallars had the 'customary right of kaval' which allowed them to exact fees in return for watching and guaranteeing the safety of crops and household effects. If the fee was paid regularly, the Kallars would, in case of theft, either recover the stolen property or make good its value. If the fee was not paid, property would be stolen and there would be no remedy but 'a certainly troublesome and probably fruitless complaint to the police.' The system existed even inside large towns, where Kallars claimed the kaval rights in particular streets. It was said that Clive had his horse stolen by a Kallar during the Trichinopoly campaign; in Sidney's view he was presumably 'too confident of his position to take out the customary insurance.'[4] While Sidney was at Madura, David Gillespie, the manager of the Madura Mills, employed a gang of Kallars as watchmen and gardeners at his house. One night the house was forcibly entered and a sum of Rs 500 was stolen. Gillespie called up the head Kallar who declared that the job must have been done by Kallars in another district and that if he was given three days leave he would recover the money. On the fourth day he returned and without a word placed the missing money on his master's table. Sidney never knew that he himself was involved in 'this ubiquitous form of blackmail' until he discovered after some time that his old and not particularly efficient gardener in Madura was a Kallar, but did not have the courage to dismiss him to see what would happen.

The kaval system covered crops and household effects, whereas the cattle stealing industry was run on different lines. The Kallar had a great love for cattle, and the creatures played a significant part in his domestic life, his agriculture and his sport. The Kallar people handled them so expertly that thefts were made in complete silence and it was rare for an owner or his men to hear their removal from the stall in which they slept. Particularly popular was the theft of oxen from a moving cart. Long-distance traffic in South India moved largely by night so that the oxen did not suffer from the heat, and for safety the carts travelled in convoy. There would often be a string of a dozen or more carts 'rumbling along at a steady two miles an hour in close formation', and it was unusual for any of the drivers except the man in the front of the convoy to be awake in the early hours of the morning. At this time the Kallars would 'softly overtake the last cart of the string, and, handling the bulls so as not to cause them the least alarm … stop the cart, unyoke the bulls, prop up the shaft of the cart with a piece of wood and disappear into the darkness with the valuable animals.'

It was after the theft that the 'ingenious system' of tuppukuli or ransom came into play, a system 'so well established that there is a special section of the Indian Penal Code to deal with it.' The owner would make no report to the police; he knew that if he did, he would be unlikely to see his cattle again. Instead, he examined the ground carefully to identify by the tracks the direction in which his cattle had been taken and, accompanied by his younger brother, set out on that course, asking all the Kallars they encountered whether cattle of a particular description had been sighted. After twenty miles or so a Kallar would declare that he knew the place of the missing cattle and was able to retrieve them if 'paid for his trouble.' Thus began 'a process of bargaining, the customary tuppukuli being approximately half the value of the cattle, which, of course, the owner tries to keep as low as possible, for he is now in the position of a buyer.' The bargaining would continue 'pleasantly and without rancour' for an hour or two, when a figure was reached which was acceptable to both parties. The owner would return home to borrow the money and, at an appointed time and place, hand it over to a 'go-between' without any guarantee other than the good faith of a Kallar, which was always upheld. The bulls would then be found 'quietly grazing' at some selected spot with no one apparently in charge of them.

The beauty of this arrangement was that 'the owner never knows who is the thief, the go-between is never in possession of the stolen property and there is nothing which can legally be called extortion.' The owner was so delighted to get his bulls back that he never complained about the cost and the police rarely heard of the thefts as the actual thieves were seldom seen driving strange cattle far from their homes. It appeared that the continuing success of the tuppukuli system was 'a great testimony to the essential honesty of the Kallar community' who stole because it was the custom of their caste, but were also absolutely reliable in their subsequent dealings and in handing over the stolen property, displaying 'a standard of commercial honesty which would do credit to many insurance companies.'

Sidney much admired the Kallars as 'a virile, courageous and essentially self-respecting community who, in spite of their depredations, have retained the respect of their neighbours to an astonishing degree.'[5] They were cheerful, sociable and sporting, and their women were handsome and 'generally chaste', possibly due to the ease with which a divorce could be obtained by a simple financial settlement. Their traditional costume left the breasts bare, but they covered the upper part of their bodies when going to town. In Sidney's view it was strange that 'these handsome, upstanding women disfigure themselves by stretching their earlobes into great loops, sometimes nearly two inches in diameter, the hole being gradually expanded by inserting first a small pin or peg and later a roll of palm leaf of steadily increasing size.' To him the earlobes looked 'hideous' when the women were in their working clothes, but 'when they are all dressed up in their finery and their ears are loaded with massive gold jewels, the effect is one of barbaric splendour.'

It was said that to see the Kallars at their best, one should see a jellicut, 'an ancient form of bullfighting ... called the Indian rodeo'. As a spectacle, the jellicut provided 'all the colour and much of the excitement of a Spanish bullfight with none of the cruelty. The competitors run considerable risks for very small prizes, the chief reward being the smiles of the fair damsels who according to time-honoured custom, choose their husbands from those of the young men who display courage and skill in the contest.' The course was nearly half a mile long and about four yards wide, formed by two long lines of country carts placed end to end, each one full of women and children in their best clothes and festooned with jewels. Between the two lines of carts the men squatted on the ground five or six deep on either side, leaving a six-foot passage in the middle ('maintained by the strenuous exertions of a small army of stewards ... armed with thin canes and whips of banana fibre') down which the excited bulls 'gallop and plunge.' The women on the carts 'hold on to each other for fear of an upset, take turns at nursing the babies, hand round sticky sweets in grubby hands, drink copious amounts of water out of the family chembu and chatter away like a flight of green parrots.' Among them were young girls who were evidently less interested in the spectacle than surveying the 'slim, clean-built youngsters who, with chests and backs bared for the fray, parade up and down the course as the competing bulls are led backwards and forwards for the appraisement of the spectators.' Throughout the proceedings:

> the drums beat deafeningly, Kallar dancers entertain the crowd with rhythmical 'toe and heeling', stewards shout, bulls snort, babies cry, girls laugh, officious constables rush about and get in everybody's way, late-comers try and squeeze into places where there is not sitting room for a fair-sized flea, the dust rises, the heat increases and at last the word is passed that the first bull is coming.

As the animals appeared, brave young men attempted to catch their tails or grab their humps, trying to secure a hold to slow the beasts down in order to grasp the gold-laced cloth which was wrapped tightly around their horns. As they failed in this pursuit, a trail of competitors was left rolling in the dust as the bulls flashed down the course. For those who partly succeeded before being sent flying into the crowd, there were consolation prizes for a sporting effort even if they failed to stop the bull, after which it frequently had to be chased for four or five miles by its owners as it escaped from the course. The jellicut lasted for about two hours and there was no betting of any consequence and 'nothing which could be described as cruelty'. Although risks were run by the competitors and the front ranks of the spectators, the sport was less dangerous than it looked, as the footwork of the bulls was remarkably precise in avoiding the scores of people who 'seemed to be in imminent danger from the galloping hooves.' One or two of the bulls turned on the combatants with their horns or kept them at a distance with 'a smart kick', but on the whole 'they obeyed the unwritten laws of the game and trusted to their speed and bucking powers to ward off their pursuers.' In Sidney's opinion, 'One came away from the meeting with the feeling that one had witnessed a clean and manly sport which calls forth the best qualities of an ancient and virile race.' Moreover, it turned out to be an event at which the decorum of the Kallars could be demonstrated. Yvonne Fitzroy recounted the story of one particular jellicut which the local European police officer was anxious to attend. At first the Kallars hesitated, 'as it had been decided to grace the occasion by a particularly desirable murder, but in the end courtesy triumphed, the Police Officer was invited and the murder was cancelled altogether in honour of his visit.'[6]

The second community in the Madura area of particular interest to Sidney was that of the neighbours of the Kallars, the Nattukottai Chettis.[7] In his view it was hard to find a greater contrast. The Kallar was 'essentially a sportsman and a fighter' and the Nattukottai Chetti was 'a man of the pen and the account book.' The Kallar tended to stay close to his roots and his forays were 'limited to a couple of days' march from his own village.' The Nattukottai Chetti was 'accustomed from his boyhood to spend long years in foreign parts' and, although found all over southeast Asia and even as far afield as Africa, they never settled abroad. Sooner or later 'they pack up all their belongings and with their papers and accounts return to their native villages, where their wives and families ... have been patiently waiting for their return.' To Sidney they were 'a strange race', known sometimes as 'the Jews of the East', and were quite different from the other Chettis or merchants of South India. Like the Jews, their lives were governed by 'the most intricate rules of customary law', being 'very religious, incredibly parsimonious in small matters, magnificent in their public charities, merciless towards their debtors, but as a rule honest in their dealings.'

It was said the first word that a Nattukottai Chetti child learnt was the word 'vaddi' or interest. The whole objective of the community appeared to involve money and the interest it would earn, and at every stage of their domestic life 'sums of money are set aside to carry interest for someone or other—wedding presents, dowries, birthday gifts to children, maintenance allotments, women's savings—these and many other small sums go into the family firm and carry compound interest at the market rate.' The accounting of Nattukottai Chettis, although 'complicated and cumbrous', was almost perfect and was written with a pointed stylus on palm leaves, tied together with string. Nothing was omitted—'every postage stamp, every bottle of medicine or packet of sweets bought for the children, every anna given to a cooly, all figure in the accounts side by side with transactions running into many thousands of rupees.'

The children of the community went to school until they could read and write, and at that stage their scholastic career was over, even if their parents were wealthy. By Sidney's time, a few of the largest families had given their sons an English education, but this was an innovation and higher education for girls was practically unknown. According to the practice of the caste, the boys learned to keep accounts before they were twelve, and at about fourteen they were sent abroad to work as junior clerks in the firm of some relative, usually in Burma or Malaya. They would stay there for three years before returning home to be married, which was the occasion for 'a most elaborate procedure, every item of which is governed by custom.' Normally the boy married his paternal aunt's daughter; however, endless negotiations preceded the final ceremony and the 'precise amount which each party shall contribute by way of presents, the jewellery to be ordered for the bride, the firm in which the cash presents shall be invested, the money to be spent on the wedding feast—all these are matters which are only fixed after much hard bargaining and there is no more zealous bargainer than a Nattukottai Chetti.' The actual marriage ceremony was equally intricate in that every action of every party was laid down by rigid rules and 'the caste has a peculiar vocabulary of its own to describe all the presents and visits and other items of the accompanying ritual.'

After the marriage the young couple lived in the house of the bridegroom's parents, as was the Hindu custom, but whereas in normal Hindu households the son and daughter-in-law shared family meals and lived as junior members of a large family 'mess', the Nattukottai Chettis allotted separate quarters in the family house to the young couple, where they provided their own food and the young wife did her own cooking. The father would allot a 'barely adequate quantity of grain and provisions' and a small sum of money to his son. If the son wished for more money he could have it, but it was debited against him in the accounts and carried compound interest. When the son of the house had acquired sufficient experience, he usually went abroad again as the agent in charge of the branch of a firm. This entailed an absence of three years, during which he was responsible for lending out the firm's money on good security and collecting the firm's dues. Every transaction was entered not merely in the accounts of the branch, but also in a 'weekly abstract' which went to 'the village' (as the headquarters of the firm was called) and was subject to the most detailed scrutiny by its head who, 'by means of regular letters, written in the most vague and involved language, keeps up a running commentary on the deeds and misdeeds of all his foreign agents.'

After the three years' period a new agent came out, scrutinised every detail of the business and, having decided which of his predecessor's transactions were sound, took them over. The rest were left in 'the old account' and remained the responsibility of the outgoing man who set sail for India 'laden with a large bundle of accounts and a parcel of gifts (which he hopes to debit to the firm) for his master's household.' There then followed an elaborate audit of the agent's accounts and, if the result was satisfactory, he received the balance of his salary and a bonus depending on the amount of the profit. If there was a loss, the agent had no bonus and might even find that the loss was debited against his salary. However, normally he received a substantial sum which he deposited at compound interest until he had accumulated sufficient capital to launch out on his own. At the end of each foreign tour, the Chetti usually stayed at home for a year or two, 'enjoying the pleasures and troubles of family life', before going abroad for another three years until he was 'a big enough man to sit at home and employ others as his agents.'

The entire life of the 'incredibly industrious' Nattukottai Chettis was made up of the 'work of money-making', family affairs and the glorification of their temple. It was true that the richer men often added variety to their lives by keeping an expensive dancing girl as a mistress, and some owned racehorses and built 'extravagant palaces', yet these pursuits were largely a matter of prestige. The influence of a Nattukottai Chetti was 'strictly proportionate to his wealth' and there was much rivalry among the most successful men. If one man acquired 'a fat and bejewelled mistress', his rival must necessarily acquire one 'still fatter'. The same applied to houses: if one man built a palace with two towers, his rival would build a 'still bigger monstrosity with four towers.' Such rivalry was also evident in their benefactions, which were 'no doubt designed for the glory of God, but there can be equally little doubt that they are designed also for the glory of the Chetti.' The community had spent many lakhs of rupees on the restoration and extension of the big Shiva temples of the south, but in Sidney's opinion these benefactions lacked taste as, 'instead of encouraging the art of the best sculptors and craftsmen, the Chettis have spent their money lavishly on plaster, gilding and whitewash, often with the most deplorable aesthetic results.'

In appearance the Nattukottai Chetti tended to be 'square, rather squat, with a big shaven head and very shabby clothes'. However, his distinguishing feature was his 'poker' face. Sidney recalled that he had watched Nattukottai Chettis for hours in the witness box under the stress of prolonged cross-examination, without being able to detect 'the slightest sign of emotion of any kind.' Normally a witness displayed visible signs to an experienced onlooker when a question was near the mark ('a shuffling of the fingers or toes, beads of perspiration on the brow, or a sidelong glance into the body of the court in the hope of succour'). But none of these signs were to be seen when the Nattukottai Chetti was being pressed hard and his face remained 'absolutely wooden and expressionless', giving no help to the cross-examiner. To Sidney such complete control over emotions and facial expression must have been the result of a lifetime of training and 'part of the equipment of the successful money-lender', contributing to the role of this comparatively small community in effectively controlling a very large part of financial activity throughout southeast Asia.

Sidney's third example of the castes of the Madura district was 'just as insignificant as the other two are important.' The Pamulas were a wandering tribe of snake-catchers, said to be a subsection of the widespread gypsy tribe of Koravars, who traversed a great portion of India and practised trades such as 'fortune-telling, salt-hawking, basket-making and the vending of quack medicines, their speciality being the cure of piles.' They were not particularly numerous, but there was usually a gang of them somewhere in the neighbourhood of any large town. For clothing, 'the Pamula is satisfied with a piece of dirty white cloth, perhaps eighteen inches long and six inches wide, held in position by a string round the waist; he may also have a dirty white cloth wound round his head and he usually carries a ragged country blanket neatly folded up on his shoulder.' He carried with him the tools of his trade: 'a gourd pipe, a flat-topped round basket for carrying snakes and a small cloth bag, in which he puts his magic stone for curing snake-bites, his potent root which will reduce an angry snake to subjection, his tweezers for pulling out thorns and other odds and ends.' His accommodation was as simple as his clothing, consisting of 'a strip of matting about four feet by eight, pegged down to the ground at both ends and held up in the middle by a horizontal rod resting on two forked sticks, making a primitive tent just big enough to provide a sleeping shelter for himself and his wife and a child or two.'

The first sign of a visit from the Pamulas was the sound of the pipe with which they announced their arrival. If a potential client lived in a street they would produce cobras from their baskets and proceed to play with them for amusement. If one had a garden they would on request catch snakes in it, put them in their baskets and use them for future exhibition. It was suspected that the snakes caught in a garden had been planted earlier by the Pamulas, which may have been true. Sidney's own garden in Madura was full of snakes and he always insisted that the Pamulas caught at least four before they were paid, to be certain that there was no trickery. On one occasion he set them to catch a particular cobra with a stumpy tail which frequented a large banyan tree and they were most successful. The procedure was fascinating to watch. The Pamula:

> advances on tip-toe with a slow and stealthy step, playing on his pipe a strange medley of sounds, in which one notices a sort of chirrup, like

> the call of a small bird. All the time his keen eye is watching the ground and all of a sudden he leaps forward with the speed of a bird of prey and literally pounces on the snake in the undergrowth, seizing it by the tail; then whirling it round, he flings it on to some open ground, where his assistant rapidly drops his blanket on top of it. Once covered by the blanket, the reptile lies still and the Pamula runs his hand under the blanket, finds the tail and works his hand up the body until he has a safe grip around the back of the neck.

The snakes in Sidney's family compound were nearly all cobras or Russell's vipers. The vipers went into the basket, but the cobras were always played by the Pamula who, 'armed only with his pipe and his small cloth bag, would squat in front of the angry snake, playing on his pipe and occasionally teasing the cobra by pushing his pipe at it, causing the snake to strike furiously at the offending object.' Sidney believed that the real purpose of this exercise was to cause the cobra to eject most of its venom by a series of attacks on the pipe. When the reptile had been worked up into a state of fury, the Pamula took up his cloth bag and pushed it gently under the very nose of the snake. Presumably the potent root inside the bag had a powerful smell, as 'the snake instantly collapses to the ground like a pricked balloon, to rise up again full of fight as soon as the obnoxious bag is taken away.' In an even more theatrical display, the Pamula would take a small piece of the root out of the bag and, holding it between his thumb and first finger, would thrust his bare hand within an inch or two of the flickering forked tongue of the cobra which immediately forced the snake to subside in a 'vanquished' state to the ground.

On one occasion the Pamula chief's youthful assistant, who was carelessly taunting a particularly lively cobra despite warnings from the Wadsworths, was bitten on the thumb. Olive understandably thought that the boy would die and begged the Pamulas to take him to the hospital. The Pamula chief merely smiled, scratched the bite with a finger nail until it bled, then produced from the cloth bag a small black pebble which he pressed on to the bite until it stuck there. The boy meanwhile 'had turned a sick grey and showed every sign of an imminent collapse.' However, instead of dying on their hands, his colour gradually returned, he ceased to perspire and his groans became less frequent. After about half an hour, he was greatly improved and the

Pamulas asked for a little milk, which was held under the boys thumb until the stone dropped off and fell into the milk. The milk at once turned green, 'presumably as the result of the poison extracted from the wound by the stone.'

Whatever the efficacy of the snakestone, Sidney did not believe that the boy was ever in serious danger, as apparently the venom in a cobra's poisons gland was only sufficient for one or two fatal bites, and after it had been ejected, the natural process of replenishing the glands took a day or so. If a cobra had been teased for a considerable period and repeatedly struck a pipe which had been thrust at it, the snake would probably have ejected most of its store of venom and become relatively harmless. However, Pamulas did occasionally die from snakebites, proving that the snakestone did not invariably work. Cynically, Sidney came to the conclusion that the boy who was bitten at his house was staging a show in the hope of extracting more money than would normally be forthcoming for a mere display of snake catching. Whatever the circumstances, no Pamula would ever kill a snake, declaring that it would be unlucky for them to do so. Sceptics were of the opinion that they needed to put snakes back into the wild to catch them again at a future date, but it was quite apparent that they were so able at catching them that they could 'replenish their stocks in a perfectly legitimate manner.'

16

KODAIKANAL

The Madura district was divided into two parts by a mountain barrier running from west to east, pierced in one place by a narrow valley through which the railway ran. On the east side of this valley were the Sirumalais (little mountains), while to the west rose the 'mighty mass' of the Palni Hills, taking their name from the sacred town of Palni which lay beneath their northern slopes. These hills, like most of the mountains of South India, remained relatively unexplored until the middle of the nineteenth century when they were opened up by European and American activity. The American Madura Mission first built houses on the 'lofty central plateau' in about 1845 and 'started to develop the wonderful country which they found there as a place of refuge from the heat.' In Sidney's time, much of the best land in the main town of Kodaikanal still remained in the hands of the mission and other missions which followed its lead, while at a slightly lower level there was an extensive area which was developed and brought under cultivation by the Jesuits and other orders of the Roman Catholic Church.

Until 1915, when the thirty mile long ghat road[1] was opened, Kodaikanal was very difficult to access and 'summer visitors had to travel some forty miles by bullock cart from the railway and then climb a steep bridle path for nine miles more, either riding on ponies or being carried on chairs lashed to stout poles'. The inaccessibility of

Kodaikanal had the effect of keeping it relatively inexpensive, which was a great consideration for the mission and, apart from the missionaries, there were then few visitors other than the officials and other Europeans living in the adjacent district. However, when the new road opened, it became possible to travel by car or bus in four hours or so from the railway to the top and 'the charms of this most beautiful of hill stations began to attract a much wider public.'

When Sidney first drove from Chingleput to Kodaikanal, it was a decidedly adventurous trip. The main road to the south was still 'languishing in the complete neglect which followed the development of the railways' and, apart from the great bridge over the Cauvery river,[2] there was apparently not another crossing on the 105 miles from Chingleput to Trichinopoly. He became 'badly stuck in the swift waters of the Coleroon river',[3] having successfully negotiated many lesser obstacles, yet with plenty of willing helpers his party emerged safely. There were no serious difficulties south of Trichinopoly until they began to climb the ghat road, the first seven miles of which were something of a test both for car and driver. Sidney described how:

> The road twists and turns along a ledge cut in the face of a mighty cliff. The gradient is steep, there is rarely a view for more than forty yards ahead and in this part of the road there were then comparatively few places where two vehicles could pass. On one side of the road was the face of the cliff, on the other a low and very unsubstantial wall separating you from a drop of hundreds of feet. Moreover the road was so steep and curly and the surface was so rough that the mere process of getting up without boiling away all the water in the radiator, required considerable skill.

By the time that Sidney left Madras, the road was considerably wider, with a good surface, and car engines had improved so dramatically that the journey had 'lost most of its terrors.'

It was a fascinating drive for anyone coming from the scorched plains in the middle of the hot weather. Having risen about 2,000 feet:

> the air begins to get noticeably cooler and you plunge into deep forest, with tall trees and a tangle of creepers and undergrowth, the luxuriant tropical jungle which one expects to find in India and so rarely sees. If there has been rain, torrents cascade down the precipitous cliffs and the whole forest resounds with the din of countless cicadas,

> while monkeys chatter in the tree-tops. A few miles further on comes a stretch of less precipitous, undulating country, which extends for miles towards the north, all covered with fertile plantations of coffee, bananas and oranges, with gay little houses surrounded by scarlet hibiscus and sky-blue morning glory. A few miles more and the road again begins to rise steeply as you pass through lofty forest trees, shading plantations of cardamums [sic], which are low plants rather like large aspidistras, yielding a spice which is much esteemed in the east not merely for its peppery qualities, but because it is believed to have value as an aphrodisiac.

After rising to about 4,000 feet, the road plunged down into the steep valley which lay at the bottom of 'a majestic mountain', the Perumal Peak. It was a long climb around the contours of the mountain and, leaving the forest behind, the wide panorama of mountain and valley opened up until one reached the level mile of Neutral Saddle and could look down upon the deep cleft which separated Perumal from Kodaikanal, with a view of Palni and the purple plains 5,000 feet below. There was a final climb above the banks of 'a turbid torrent, lined with tree ferns and festoons of morning glory', which at such a high altitude retained much of its colour throughout the day. In the crannies of the rocks by the roadside were wild begonias and 'an endless variety of delicate ferns and mosses.' After the first houses and the large Jesuit seminary of Shembaganar there was still nearly 1,000 feet more to climb and four more miles to traverse before the road skirted around the edge of the bazaar and reached the picturesque lake which was the centre of the European town of Kodaikanal.

Although Kodai, as it was called, was originally a missionary sanatorium, for many years it possessed a small resident population made up mainly of retired officials, and large numbers of other people unrelated to missionary activity came up each year for a holiday. The two communities, while very friendly, tended to keep apart in their social activities with separate clubs. Although it was said that 'Kodai-carnal and Kodai-spiritual do not mix', each year the two clubs fought 'a great battle on the tennis courts in the friendliest of spirits ... followed by an international match, British Empire v. America, in which there are usually two or three missionaries playing for the Empire.' Kodai was always a friendly place where newcomers were introduced all round.

Later in the twentieth century, Indians increasingly came to appreciate the advantage of a holiday in the hills and many joined the English Club to take part in the social and athletic life of the station.

When there were no cars and no golf, people would spend most of their days on the lake, which had 'a well-run boat club with rowing-boats and punts imported from the Thames.' It was 'a very attractive stretch of water, narrow in the middle, with arms extending into the various branches of the main valley, so that it gives the effect of a broad river, rather than an artificial lake.' The lake was used mainly for transport, since houses were built up the slopes of the valley in which the lake lay and the easiest way of getting from one place to another was often by water. There was a simple arrangement whereby one would get into any boat which happened to be tied up nearby and row across, leaving the boat for anyone else who might want it. If there were no boat handy, one would stand on the water's edge and shout 'Michael' until one of the lascars from the boat club, all of whom appeared to answer to the name of Michael, would row across to help.

On the east side of Kodai, many houses and the three principal churches were built on the top of a high ridge from which there was an almost sheer drop down into the valley 1,000 feet below, giving 'the most wonderful panorama'. To the northeast rose the 'noble outline' of Perumal and in the south a large part of the lower Palnis could be seen as well as the line of the ghat road. Further south were glimpses of the old 'cooly ghat' or bridle path winding down a steep wooded valley to the little town of Periakulam and, looking over the last spurs of the hills, 'miles and miles of hot red and purple plains, dotted here and there with the bright silver of an irrigation tank with its adjacent patch of vividly green paddy.' On clear days it was possible to see as far as Madura, seventy miles away. Beneath the houses on the ridge ran Coaker's Walk, from which a phenomenon known as Coaker's Ghost could be seen. The ghost made its appearance when there was mist rising up the valley and a setting sun behind the onlooker, whose shadow was thrown on to the wall of mist producing 'a most convincing spectre.'

The Kodai climate was ideal, as the town was sheltered from the full force of the southwest monsoon, so the months of June and July, which in Ootacamund were 'cold, wet and miserable', were in Kodai 'fairly dry and extremely bracing'. However, in the period of the northeast monsoon, which normally began in the middle of October and petered out just before Christmas, Kodai was to be avoided as the rain came down in 'solid lumps' and it was quite usual for small landslides to put the ghat road temporarily out of action. Otherwise the climate was 'as near perfection as a climate can be.' During January, February and March there were slight frosts at night and glorious sunshine by day with normally no rain at all. April and May were the summer months, with cool nights and hot days, relieved by an occasional thunderstorm. August, September and the first half of October were like 'a second and milder summer.' Unusually in May 1930 the town experienced a violent cyclone which 'in the space of an hour wrought tremendous havoc'. It tore most of the roof off the golf clubhouse and roads were blocked in all directions by huge eucalyptus trees which came down like 'the proverbial nine-pins.' One of the pinewoods on the downs was an extraordinary sight after the storm as it was partly protected by a ridge of high ground and the trees had all been snapped off some ten or twelve feet above ground level, as if 'some gigantic scythe had shorn right through the wood.' But in general Kodai cyclones were far less common than on the east coast, where one tended to occur somewhere or other nearly every year.

Sidney recalled that one of the worst storms in the Palni hills during the past few years occurred early in February, a month when there was usually settled fine weather. He was in Madura and was expecting the chaplain, the Reverend F. B. Jamieson, to stay as usual for his monthly visitation. However, on this occasion the chaplain was coming a day earlier as he had a wedding to celebrate. By 5 pm he had still not arrived and an agitated Eurasian bridegroom and best man turned up at the house. Fortunately they were able to get hold of the Tamil priest to perform the ceremony and the next evening Jamieson appeared, having walked all the way down the 'cooly ghat' and travelled the last distance by bus. He had set out by car from the hills the previous day and had no idea that there was a problem until he came upon a huge landslide. Concerned about the wedding, he had left his car and had attempted to walk, but 'after struggling over dirt, boulders and fallen trees' he was forced to make his way back to Kodai. In fact 'the landslide had blotted out more than five miles of road and the torrents of water washing huge boulders down the hill streams had completely destroyed four substantial bridges.' Fortunately there were no inhabitants at the scene of the storm and the road was empty at the time, so there were no casualties.

In Sidney's day, most Indian hill stations consisted of 'a cluster of houses and hotels perched rather precariously on the top of a high mountain with little or no room to spare'. The Palnis, like the Nilgiris, possessed many miles of 'steeply undulating, grass-covered downs', all above 6,000 feet and so extensive that it was impossible to see more than the comparatively small portion which could be reached by road. When the Wadsworths first went to Kodai, there were no roads going more than five miles out of the town, but before they left it was possible to do a forty mile round trip by a road which wound and twisted along the southern edge of the plateau, 'giving the most enthralling glimpses of the Cumbum valley and the Travancore High Range.' Many hairpin bends made it a challenging road, but 'from the scenic point of view it has few rivals.' For Sidney it was unfortunate that, unlike the terrain of Ooty, 'the Kodai downs were too steep and the grass too tussocky for hunting' and fishing also was a disappointment. The lake contained some large carp, but they would not take a fly or a spinner and attempts to introduce trout into the small rivers on the downs had not been successful due to cannibalism, although there was no particular reason why trout could not thrive as well as they did in the nearby High Range.

Three miles out of Kodai on the southeast corner of the plateau was 'a most attractive golf course, beautifully situated on the edge of the downs and bordered with plantations of pine trees, fringed with mimosa' with nine holes, although cleverly duplicated to produce eighteen, all 'very different and extremely sporting'. The club was in effect the creation of one Scot, E. O. King, who had been secretary, architect and 'moving spirit' from its inception. E. O. held for many years the 'enviable position' of representative of a group of London financiers from whom the Raja of Ramnad raised money on debentures. One of the conditions of the loan was that the representative of the debenture holders should be on the spot to attend to the regular payment of the interest and, if necessary, to take possession of the estate in case of default. Since the Raja paid his interest with regularity,[4] E. O. had what was virtually a sinecure and was able to live at Kodai and 'devote his abundant energy and ability to the development of the golf club that he loved.' It was one of the few courses in the world where a tiger had been seen on the fairway; 'sambhur' or sambar deer were still seen occasionally on the wooded heights and the large number of wild boars created a considerable problem for those responsible for the upkeep of the fairway. Sidney regretted the fact that golf was a game which attracted few Indian players, possibly due to the lack of good courses on the plains. Since those who had taken to the game played it well, he saw no reason why a nation which had produced so many fine cricketers could not also produce excellent golfers, and hoped that, with the decline of the European population, the golf clubs they had built up would not 'languish for want of players.'

All forms of sport and social life in Kodaikanal owed much to the members of the Pudukkottai ruling house, who always spent the hot weather there. When Sidney knew Kodai, the sole survivor of the older generation was Captain B. R. Dorai Raja, brother of the late Raja, and affectionately known to many Kodai people as 'The Do'. The late Raja, Martanda Bhairava Tondaiman, and his brothers were largely brought up by their English tutor, Frank Crossley, and his wife who, according to Sidney, 'did their job well and taught their charges to play all the games and do all the things which young Englishmen learn to do.' Unfortunately, this dedication to western sporting pursuits was not appreciated by the government of Madras which in a letter of August 1897 declared that the Raja was 'more like a coloured European gentleman, with entirely European tastes, than a Native Prince', and as a ruler he had made no real effort to gain insight into the administration, the wants of his people or the expenditure of state funds.[5] At the end of his life, 'The Do' lived permanently in Kodai and, as 'one of the kindest and friendliest souls in India', knew everybody and was universally liked. He played or had played every game and always ready to help with umpiring or organisation. He was 'a wizard at the bridge table—scorned all conventions, called at times in a most unorthodox way, but never forgot a card or failed to draw a reasonable inference, with the result that he was continually winning tricks which most people would lose.' Although it was suggested that he was particularly lucky, in Sidney's view he had 'a natural card sense developed by a lifetime of practice, until his mental processes had become almost automatic and unconscious.'

There was no doubt that over the course of years, life in a hill station tended to breed eccentrics as a result of 'an adherence to bygone fashions and manners by people who have grown old in a small and isolated sphere.' Few villages in Britain were as small or isolated for six months of the year as Kodaikanal and there were some 'interesting relics of an earlier generation' among its residents. 'Old "Daddy" Proud, who spent his youth in sailing ships and his middle age as a pilot on the Rangoon river, lived on in Kodai until he was ninety-five and, by virtue of his nautical training, exercised the power of an admiral over the fleet of the boat club almost to the end.' Mrs Muter, known in her youth as 'The Kodai Lily' and widowed soon after her marriage, lived alone in a small house overlooking the lake for the next fifty years, 'her style of dress and her outlook on life changing so little that by the end she had become almost a museum piece.' Also Munro Maiden and his sister, who as children had survived the 1864 great tidal wave that swept over Masulipatam, drowning many thousands, and who could remember 'cowering with their parents in the upper storey of their house while the waters crept steadily up the stairs.' In addition, Kodaikanal contained two political prisoners on whom the sub-collector had to keep his eye since they were forbidden to leave the town. One was a pretender to the Afghan throne, 'a glamorous if ruffianly looking figure', and the other was the exiled maharaja of Nabha, 'an eccentric whose house was, for some reason or another, kept blazing with electric lights all night'.[6]

The 'most juvenile septuagenarian in India', Ernest Logan, was linked to the foundation of a remarkable irrigation scheme, the Periyar system, which, despite being 'a most ingenious and successful irrigation project', received little publicity. The Periyar river rises in the Travancore High Range about fifty miles south of Kodai and, until the end of the nineteenth century, flowed down the western side of the mountains where its waters spilt into the Indian Ocean and were wasted. At that stage the Madras government obtained a lease of the upper valley from the Travancore State and a mighty dam was built across it, creating 'a huge lake with long branches extending up various subsidiary valleys.' At the head of the lake a tunnel was bored through the solid mountain with a sluice at its mouth, so that the impounded water was spilt down the east side of the mountain barrier rather than the west, roaring out of the tunnel into the bed of the Vaigai river. It flowed along the riverbed for some fifty miles before meeting another dam which diverted it into a high level canal from which 'feeder channels take off to irrigate an enormous area of what was once a famine-stricken district, but is now for six months of the year a great expanse of rich and lovely crops.'

According to Sidney, two mistakes were made in planning this great work. One was the complete omission of any provision in the agreement for the use of the water for hydro-electric purposes, which led to 'a most unfortunate and expensive dispute between Madras and Travancore'. The case was eventually referred to arbitrators who decided that, according to the lease, Madras had not acquired the right to use the water drawn from the lake for generating electricity. Since Travancore could not use the water without the cooperation of Madras, the result was that no power could be generated until the two governments came to a fresh agreement. The second mistake was the decision that the water from the Periyar should be distributed through existing small tanks and channels. This caused endless trouble since many of the tanks were the property of small zamindars who successfully claimed the right to charge cultivators for water for which they had already paid a substantial water rate to the government. As a result, 'the wretched tiller of the soil often has to pay twice over.' However, in a hot, dry country to pay twice was infinitely preferable to going without the water. During the course of Sidney's work, he often had to trace in considerable detail the favourable economic history of families whose lands had been affected by the Periyar system. In the 1890s impoverished families were selling their land at about Rs. 150 an acre, but with the arrival of water they mortgaged all their assets to level their remaining fields and make them fit for irrigation. Within ten years of the opening of the project, all their mortgages had been cleared and they were buying and selling their land at ten times its previous value. Unless they were foolish enough to become involved in litigation, the families were soon in a position of 'considerable affluence.'

Although very inaccessible, the Periyar Lake was well worth a visit. The journey was 100 miles by road from Madura, 'ending in a very tricky little ghat with a number of awkward hair-pin corners.' While on holiday the Wadsworths had a narrow escape when turning up a narrow drive with deep trenches on either side, a sign of the considerable damage wreaked in the hills by wild elephants. Arriving at the travellers' bungalow, they discovered that they had come to the Travancore State bungalow instead of that belonging to the Madras Public Works Department. As Sidney was turning to go back, 'the steering wheel of the car span right round in my hands; the ball and socket joint controlling the front wheels had worn so badly that it had come right adrift. If this had happened at one of the hairpin corners, the chances are that we should have crashed through the low parapet wall and been precipitated into the deep valley beneath.' Abandoning the car, he walked to the Madras bungalow and sent a mechanic back to deal with the vehicle. Half an hour later, it reappeared supposedly 'fixed'; however, on starting up, exactly the same thing happened. All that had been done was 'to push the worn ball back into the worn socket and presumably the only thing that had saved them from a dive into the elephant trench was the absence of any sharp bend.'

The Wadsworths went down to the lake and embarked on the Public Works Department launch. Crossing the lake they spent 'a delightful time' at the bungalow built near the dam, with a wonderful view not only over the lake, but also down the lower Periyar valley almost to the west coast of India. All the banks of the lake were covered with primaeval forest and kept as a game reserve by the Travancore state. Sidney described:

> Roaming about the water in the launch, you can watch herds of wild elephant, bison and sambhur from quite close quarters. The muddy banks are covered with tracks of a great variety of game which comes down to the water to drink. The only inhabitants are an incredibly primitive race which has taken to wearing clothes only within living memory. These people live in huts built up in the branches of trees, for safety from elephants and other wild beasts; and they subsist mainly on roots and forest fruits and fish caught in the lake, which they navigate on crude rafts.

At the end of the holiday, the Wadsworths were fortunate enough to be able to borrow a car from the assistant engineer to take them back to Madura. They left their own car with their 'very inexpert' driver, who was given strict instructions to wait until spare parts arrived from Madras, while the servants and luggage were to come down by bus. The day after their return, Sidney was:

> astonished to see our car drive up, loaded to capacity with servants and luggage. My worthy driver, with the courage that comes of ignorance and a complete lack of imagination, had got the defective joint tied up with a bit of copper wire and, though he had never driven a ghat road before, he had brought the car down that dangerous road with perfect confidence. Mercifully the wire held. The driver was quite hurt when I abused him for taking unnecessary risks. He was extremely pleased with himself for having saved me the cost of bus fares!

17

CHITTOOR AND BANGALORE 1934–35

After nearly five years in Madura, Sidney was approaching the end of his term as district judge and was posted to the city of Chittoor on the main road linking Bangalore to the west and Madras city to the east, 'a pleasant place of no particular importance' other than the fact that the district judge of Chittoor was also an additional judge of the court of the resident of the princely state of Mysore and Additional Judicial Commissioner of Coorg.[1] In these two capacities he visited Bangalore, capital of Mysore state, once a month and functioned as 'a miniature High Court' for the Bangalore cantonment and the 'curious little province' of Coorg, of which the Mysore resident was the chief commissioner. As a result, for a little over three weeks in each month he had a 'very leisurely existence' in Chittoor, while for the rest of the month he was involved in difficult and responsible work in Bangalore. Most of the work he did alone, although the resident (Colonel Charles Plowden)[2] joined him for murder appeals in order to make the required bench of two judges. Sidney's visits to Bangalore were made very pleasant by the hospitality of the resident and his staff, and the assistant resident, Lieutenant-Colonel Cosmo Edwardes, who was later Resident for the South Indian States.

Sidney already knew Chittoor well as it was the headquarters of the district in which Madanapalle was situated, formerly the North Arcot district which had been split in two before he arrived in India. Vellore was made the capital of the more important new region, while Chittoor retained 'most of the pleasant uplands and a very moderate share of the work.' Earlier, Chittoor had possessed a small garrison and was a fairly important station. However, when the Wadsworths lived there, it was little more than a big village with a few offices and courts 'to give it a fictitious importance.' The area had a much better climate than its 'bigger and more prosperous' neighbour Vellore, but at only 1,000 feet above sea level its hot weather was 'rather severe and the place was apt to get very deserted when my three neighbours, all touring officers, used to escape to the Palmaner and Madanapalle plateau, leaving the judge to endure the heat in solitude.'

One very attractive feature of Chittoor was the reserve forest which adjoined the small European quarter. It was an 'entirely artificial creation', full of interesting trees and laid out like a wild park with pleasant paths in all directions. With much time on his hands, Sidney walked for many miles exploring the woods, often accompanied by Joan Brisles, the eight-year-old daughter of the collector and 'a most delightful companion.' She introduced him to the 'hitherto unknown sport of tracking centipedes, which leave a trail in the sand rather like a miniature railway line and seem to travel great distances.' The pair also acquired a good knowledge of the many birds which frequented the reserve, including the 'most beautiful of all the birds of South India, the paradise fly-catcher, with its lovely tail of two long, trailing feathers of the softest dove-grey colour.'

Such work as there was in Chittoor came mainly from two sources. One was the holy town of Tirupati with its big and wealthy Govindarajaswamy temple, attached to the shrine on the top of the sacred Tirumalai hill:

> the sanctity of which was exploited on a commercial scale; so much so that there was a thriving trade in human hair, derived from the countless devout women who in pursuance of vows used to have their heads shaved before ascending the holy mountain. Many of these women were widows making the pilgrimage for the benefit of their husbands' souls; but most of them were young women who had taken a vow in the hope of offspring and used to spend the night sleeping on the hard floor of the shrine on the hill-top, confidently expecting an auspicious dream.

By tradition the management of the Tirupati temples was vested in the mahant (abbot) of the mutt (monastery), which was somewhat loosely connected with the temples, and it was the custom for each mahant to nominate his successor when he was getting old. The inmates of the mutt were immigrants from North India and were supposed to live lives of chastity dedicated to the service of God but it was said that 'their practice sometimes fell far short of their precepts.' The mahant of Sidney's time was 'a clever, worldly wise, English-speaking gentleman, who, if it were not for his sanctimonious attire, might well have been mistaken for a prosperous lawyer. He kept an establishment at Bangalore and seemed to spend much of his time travelling backwards and forwards by car.'

The other main source of work was the derelict Karvetnagar zamindari, 'an ancient estate which had fallen on evil days and come into the hands of a very rich and eccentric money-lender called Lodd Govindas.' Like many Indian usurers, he was 'a Shylock to his debtors, but sought to make the best of both worlds by ostentatious charities and religious benefactions.' Under his control the estate was stripped of most of its forests, and its irrigation works were allowed to disintegrate before it was sold in separate villages to a number of impecunious speculators who were always late with their revenue. As the whole estate was a single unit for the purpose of revenue, and there was often considerable doubt as to the ownership of many of the villages, 'the most dreadful legal tangles used to come before the courts ... also constant boundary disputes, resulting from the existence of large areas of forest which had never been properly surveyed, so that no one knew where one village began and the other ended.' Unsurprisingly, Sidney found this work less than appealing and 'was thankful that the worst of it was done by my worthy subordinate judge.' The truth of the matter was that the district court of Chittoor seemed 'rather small beer' after the crowded days of Madura, with its 'vigorous bar' and multitude of subordinate courts. In Madura the process staff alone was 'nearly as big as a battalion and the task of keeping up a moderate standard of honesty in its ranks used up much of my energy.' In Chittoor, on the other hand, there were only six civil courts in the whole district, and crime was very light. Being somewhat underemployed, Sidney realised that he was also 'feeling rather stale and getting restive.'

One of the main players in recent Chittoor history was W. S. Whiteside, who was gazetted to the district as chief revenue officer and magistrate in 1877 and, in Sidney's opinion, must have been a man who exercised an extraordinary 'hold over the minds and imaginations' of others to have been remembered so well by the people of the district in which he served for many years. Whiteside was one of those fortunate men who were able to spend most of their time in a single district with which they became intimately identified. However, mere length of service did not explain his fame and he was evidently a man who believed in 'judicious display', never going into camp with less than eighteen cartloads of possessions and an enormous pot garden which he used to carry with him on tour to surround his tents.[3]

Sir Christopher Hughes Masterman, in the Madras ICS from 1914 to 1947, recalled this earlier, and decidedly more elevated, progress through the Indian countryside when, on tour as the young subordinate of the collector Charles Todhunter, they travelled with five horses, two bearers, a cook, a waterman, a sweeper and five syces. The party would start on horseback early in the morning, inspecting crops, settling irrigation disputes and encroachments on government land by illegal cultivation, and visiting any schools, jails or hospitals en route. Returning at midday for a large meal which was a combination of breakfast and lunch, Masterman was subjected to a cross-examination on crops, methods of cultivation and sources of irrigation. Todhunter then retired to his tent, with strict instructions not to be disturbed until dinner in order to deal with his tappal (mail delivery) which had arrived in wooden boxes from headquarters during the morning.[4] Sidney, on the other hand, was forced to adopt the modern practice of rushing around from one rest-house to another in a Ford car, taking nothing which was unable to fit in the boot, envying the 'Indian Civil Servant of former days who lived like a rajah and exercised almost autocratic powers, may have been feared, but he was certainly respected and admired; while his essentially personal rule was something that the common man understood and liked.'

One hundred miles from Chittoor was the city of Bangalore, where many thousands of British troops had been stationed. The route was via a good road, most of which was on a plateau, with a great change in the countryside as one left the Madras Presidency and entered the state of Mysore. The hills became barren and rocky, there was less irrigation and the villages all possessed ornamental gateways, on which the name of the place was engraved in stone. The language changed from Telegu to Canarese, and the population contained a fairly large proportion of Hindustani-speaking Muslims, remnants of the Mughal armies and the forcible converts of Tipu Sultan. The city of Bangalore was peculiar in that it had the cantonment in the centre, almost surrounded by a mile or two of bazaar, and to all intents and purposes consisted of two towns: Bangalore cantonment, which was under British administration, and Bangalore city, which was under the control of the Mysore durbar, with no visible line of demarcation between the two areas. This situation could have resulted in endless questions of international law, but fortunately the police on both sides of the border worked in close cooperation, and criminals who attempted to obstruct justice by dodging across the boundary soon found that there was little to be gained.

When Sidney was working in Bangalore, the question of the retrocession of Bangalore cantonment to the Maharaja of Mysore was under discussion and, to safeguard the handover for all concerned, Humphrey Trevelyan (then secretary to the resident in Mysore) worked on a document of 700 printed pages before it 'sank without trace' in the hands of the government of India. Eventually the cantonment was peacefully given back to the Mysore government after the Second World War with no safeguards or conditions.[5] It contained a reasonably large number of permanent residents of European or Anglo-Indian race, 'none of whom had the slightest doubt of their British nationality.' However, it appeared that when the state of Mysore had surrendered the administration of the cantonment area to the British, there was no surrender of theoretical sovereignty, so that those thousands of people who thought themselves British subjects and had always been treated as such, were really Mysoreans. Trevelyan noted that in the Bangalore cantonment, 'the Indians could bathe their brown bodies in the swimming-pool and dance with the English girls, since the cantonment was in the Mysore State, but even Indian officers with the king's commission were not allowed to vote at the club meetings and the combined efforts of the resident and the general commanding the district were not strong enough to get the rules changed.'[6]

Sidney knew the Maharaja of Mysore, Krishnaraja Wodeyar IV, only slightly, describing him as 'a man of high personal character, … [who] had shown great wisdom in the choice of his diwans and had given them every support in their schemes for the betterment of the state.' As a result, Mysore was probably the most progressive and best-governed state in India. It did of course have many advantages. The state was large, its finances rested on the royalties from the Kolar gold field, which was entirely worked by British companies, and it had benefited for many years from direct British rule following a civil insurrection in 1831 and the services of British officers after the subsequent rendition to Mysorean rule in 1881.[7] However, it was certain that Mysore progressed to a remarkable degree under the benign rule of the late maharaja and his two great diwans, Sir M. Visheshwarayya and Sir Mirza Ismael, 'both men of marked ability and originality'.

Much of the work which Sidney undertook in Bangalore originated from Coorg, 'a tiny province tucked away in the hills between Mysore and the district of South Kanara.' He much regretted never having visited Coorg, having little work to do there, as apparently it possessed many features of interest and considerable beauty. It was said:

> One of the proud boasts of the people of Coorg is that they are not a conquered race. Protected by their geographical isolation from being involved in the wars of the eighteenth century, they came under British rule at their own request and have always held their heads a bit higher as a consequence. They are an attractive race, physically strong, virile in spirit, pleasant mannered and independent … [with] all the fighting qualities of the Punjabi, combined with a great degree of intellectual power.

Trevelyan recalled that in Coorg it rained 'steadily for three months of the year, which depressed the planters who were always in low spirits, being hopelessly in debt on account of the low coffee prices'. He observed that the Coorgis were

> staunch believers in conspicuous expense. They took their native climate with equanimity and invariably dressed in smart mackintoshes. Their estates were all mortgaged to support their ideas of how a gentleman should live. They bred generals of the Indian army after independence and appeared to have nothing in common with the people living round them … They are a most intelligent and agreeable people, endowed with a happy mixture of courage and improvidence.[8]

The civil appeals coming from Coorg gave Sidney much hard work, as the area had a unique system of land tenure with which he was entirely unfamiliar and there was also a 'curious sort of joint family which retained a kind of fictitious union long after it had become divided for all every-day purposes and the precise extent of this remnant of joint rights seemed rather nebulous; at any rate it did result in all the members of the larger group having a right of preemption over all the original family lands'. One of the difficulties of dealing with the peculiarities of Coorg lay in the fact that the decisions of the Judicial Commissioner's court were not reported and, rather than a bound and indexed set of decisions on Coorg tenures and customs, there was only a bundle of typed judgments to fall back upon when a dubious point arose. However, there was a 'small but competent specialist bar' to assist in avoiding mistakes.

It was the difficulty of the Coorg work which gave rise to the system under which the Chittoor judge was attached to the Mysore resident, since few residents possessed much training either in law or revenue matters and on the whole they knew none of the South Indian languages. Sidney was 'horrified by the delays in the judicial branch of the Resident's office', which were due not so much to the congestion of the actual court work, but the process during which, after the case had been heard and decided, the office often took some considerable time to produce the decree, 'without which the successful party could do nothing.' Early in his association with the office, a batch of decrees was put up for signature and he noticed to his great anger that they all related to cases decided some two years previously. The clerk pleaded overwork, and when Sidney told him that he was 'either very corrupt or completely incompetent', he looked hurt; however, by simplifying the form of decree and duplicating many of the forms, all the arrears were cleared off in a month or two. It was suspected that 'the arrears were nothing more than a dodge for extracting bribes—the successful party had to wait for the fruits of his victory until he had greased the palm of the clerk who drafted the decree.' The same scheme had occurred in the High Court office where Sidney had also enforced punctuality, believing that there was 'no more powerful lever for extracting bribes than a state of continual arrears.'

Sidney had been in Chittoor for only eight months when he learnt that his name was being submitted to the King for appointment to the Madras High Court in a permanent vacancy which was to arise in June

1935. He was asked to give the customary undertakings that he would resign on reaching the age of sixty and would not practise as a barrister in Madras after his retirement. He felt that he had been 'extraordinarily lucky both in getting on to the High Court at the age of 46 and in not having to undergo the customary purgatory of acting and reverting for a year or two before finding a permanent footing.' He was also well aware that, had he stayed in the executive branch of the service, in all probability he would have had to wait another seven years before reaching such heights. Having the permanent appointment more or less in his pocket, he was also able to take a little leave and 'have another glimpse of my little-known offspring.'

18

THE HONOURABLE MR JUSTICE 1935–47

Sidney's appointment to the High Court of Madras was to begin in the middle of the vacation. Being 'diffident' about suggesting that he should take the oath in London, he duly presented himself before the vacation officer at Madras, was sworn in and proceeded to Kodaikanal to play golf for over a month. He regretted that it was only after he was installed at the High Court that 'the excellent practice was introduced of swearing in a new judge in open court before a Full Bench clad in scarlet robes and full-bottomed wigs', as it seemed to him that there was 'something unseemly in treating the office of one of His Majesty's judges as if it were on a par with a routine affidavit.' However, when he first arrived he doubted if there was a judge on the Madras bench, with the possible exception of the chief justice, who possessed a full-bottomed wig, and he never saw a wig worn all the time when he was registrar. A later move was made for all judges doing criminal work to wear scarlet robes and bench wigs, but this innovation met with much opposition as the robes concerned were 'extremely hot draperies for a man who is working really hard in a hot, moist climate.' There was also the practical difficulty in adopting scarlet robes for criminal appellate work, in that the bench frequently switched from criminal to civil cases and a great deal of time would be wasted in a change of apparel.

Sidney often wondered to what extent 'the ordinary man in South India is impressed by what has been irreverently described as judicial haberdashery.' The Englishman was certainly used to associating the administration of justice with 'sartorial anachronisms' but it was doubtful whether Indians were equally influenced. The average Indian was 'impressed by power and most conscious of personality, but is almost completely indifferent to dress and appearance, except perhaps on big state occasions.' For Sidney:

> How else can one explain the extraordinary reverence always paid to the late Mr Gandhi, surely the worst dressed national leader in the world? Moreover the maharajahs of India, though they wear the most magnificent habiliments at great ceremonies, are very simply clad at other times, generally wearing the long white coat and trousers of an ordinary Indian gentleman … [and] many of the British officers who have exercised the greatest influence amongst Indians, have been men who were distinctly careless about their external appearance.

Much could be said for the wearing of a judicial uniform; but 'surely this would be equally impressive if it were simple, cool and dignified, instead of the hot, semi-ecclesiastical and mediaeval costumes of the English courts, the historical significance of which is completely lost on the Indian litigant.'

Sidney gave the following description of the establishment in which he was to play a significant part:

> The Madras High Court is historically a composite institution, being the successor not only of the old Supreme Court, which was founded by royal charter, but also of the East India Company's appellate court, which was known as the Court of Sudder Adaulat.[1] The latter court exercised jurisdiction over all the Company's courts outside the city of Madras. The Supreme Court was really a branch of the King's Bench, exercising jurisdiction only within the city of Madras and having at its disposal all the prerogative writs which could be issued by the judges in London. As a result of this historical evolution, the High Court of Madras has two 'sides', the Original Side representing the Supreme Court and the Appellate Side, more or less representing the Sudder Adaulat; and these two sides used to be completely distinct as to jurisdiction, procedure, bar and staff. But of recent years this distinction has been considerably softened down. The Original Side is no longer the preserve of barristers and attorneys, its procedure has been assimilated to that of the other courts and its staff has become practically interchangeable with that of the Appellate Side; but it still retains the termi-

> nology of the English courts, which is apt to be rather confusing for those who have been brought up on the Code of Civil Procedure.

Sidney spent most of his first two years as a judge on the Original Side, which was of great benefit as he had very little experience of the trial of original suits other than rent suits and those matters which went before the district judge. There were usually two judges on the Original Side. One dealt with commercial work, company law, actions in tort and the considerable chamber work arising from these subjects. The other dealt with cases under Hindu and Muslim law, bankruptcy and chancery work. The commercial judge was Frederick Gentle (later Chief Justice of Madras and Judge Advocate General of the Armed Forces) and Sidney was in the other court where the work was much like that in the districts. The two men lived together for some time and were very good friends; Gentle could help Sidney with new procedures and English practice, and Sidney could offer advice on 'strange customs, weird names and Dravidian tongues.'

Much of the work proved to be extremely interesting, some of it dull and one area 'positively repulsive', consisting of insolvency work, most of which was 'petty, futile and degrading.' Many of the parties and witnesses in the insolvency court at Madras were criminals and 'one or two of the lawyers who specialised in that branch of work needed a lot of watching.' To Sidney:

> Most of the insolvents were men who sought the protection of the court only after carrying out an elaborate scheme of fraudulent alienations. Many of the creditors were claimants under bogus debts, acting in collusion with the insolvents so as to reduce the rateable share of the genuine creditors. The genuine creditors were more often than not Shylocks who had taken notes for more than the sum advanced and claimed interest at rates ranging from 24% upwards. The debtors with few exceptions secreted their assets and falsified their accounts. Most of the creditors were Marwaris, who kept their accounts in a sort of loose leaf album, written in Indian ink on hand-made paper, neither of which fade, so that a new page could be substituted without the change being apparent.

Moreover, Marwaris wrote in a language which was understood only by the court interpreter, and professed ignorance of English and Tamil, so as to prevent effective cross-examination and to gain time to perfect their answers. Like his ICS contemporary F. W. A. Morris, who had an intense dislike of 'sitting for hours in a court room with the dubious breeze from a punkah to lessen one's irritation with the mass of contradictory lies from the prosecution and defence witnesses',[2] Sidney came 'to loathe Mondays, which were insolvency days, and the atmosphere of fraud, falsehood and pettifogging chicanery'.

Some years before Sidney arrived in India, a major European mercantile bank Arbuthnot & Co. crashed, bringing great misery to large numbers of depositors and severely affecting the credit of European firms in general.[3] Every few years the Official Assignee would declare a minute fractional dividend, 'so small that the rateable share of the small depositor was not worth the cost of swearing an affidavit and engaging a lawyer.' These minute unclaimed dividends in the Arbuthnot insolvency mounted up over the years to a huge sum, the interest on which was sufficient to pay most of the cost of the Official Assignee's establishment. It seemed to Sidney that 'there was an obvious need for some simple provision that dividends of small amounts might be sent by money order to the person apparently entitled at the discretion of the Official Assignee, without requiring elaborate proof of heirship or formal application.' If there was still no one to whom these small sums could be paid, the court could be empowered, not to treat the money as being in effect the property of the state but to add it to the fund available to satisfy the creditors who were prosecuting their claims.

The 'babel of tongues' was an astounding feature of the Original Side of the Madras High Court. The official language of the court was, of course, English, but 'comparatively few of the witnesses are sufficiently at home in that language to depose in it; and of those who speak English fairly fluently, quite a lot prefer their own vernacular because of the extra time which the process of interpretation gives them, to think out their answers in cross-examination.' The largest and most important body of invaders of Madras had been Dravidians, settling into four major language areas, each with a distinctive Dravidian tongue and distinctive script. North of Madras were Telegu speakers, south of Madras Tamil speakers, in the centre of the peninsula towards the west coast were Canarese speakers and on the southwest coast Malayalam speakers. Since Madras city was on the borderline of the Tamil and Telegu territories, these two languages were in constant use.

Most of the interpreters could translate both and Sidney himself was fairly familiar with them. There were also witnesses who spoke Canarese and Malayalam, which were similar enough to Tamil and Telegu to enable Sidney to have 'a vague idea of what the witness was saying if the story was familiar'. Many of the Muslim merchants of Madras city spoke Hindustani, of which Sidney knew 'at most forty words', and the Marwari moneylenders spoke a dialect of Gujarati which was unfamiliar to virtually everybody.

The worst 'linguistic muddle' Sidney had to tackle was a strange case between two Armenians. Many years earlier there had been a flourishing colony of Armenian merchants in Madras. In the middle of the nineteenth century a wealthy Armenian died, leaving a bizarre will which provided that his estate should be left to accumulate for sixty years and should then be distributed in a certain manner. It was possible that the will could have been challenged as contravening the rule of perpetuities, but in fact no one did challenge it. The estate consisted of a number of houses (by Sidney's time impossible to identify) and a large sum deposited in an Italian bank which had ceased to exist many years before. After the sixty years' period had expired, the First World War was still in full flood and the number of heirs had risen to well over a hundred who were scattered all over the world. When peace finally returned to the countries of the Near East, two lawyers who were connected with the family set to work to trace the various heirs. One of the lawyers came from Istanbul and the other from Beirut, and each purported to represent about fifty or more of the heirs. In 1935 they arrived in Madras, hunting for the lost estate, and both seem to have failed to find it. However, the Istanbul man applied for letters of administration of the will and the Beirut man opposed the grant.

Sidney was to hear the application, and the first question concerned the language in which the court was going to work. The court did not keep an Armenian interpreter, but Sidney suggested that the parties should agree to one of the half-dozen Armenian residents in the city being sworn as an interpreter for this case. Unfortunately every one of these people was an adherent of one or other litigant and therefore unacceptable. Neither of the litigants could speak English or French with any fluency, but both professed to be able to talk Arabic and Turkish. There was a Muslim clerk in the High Court office who could speak Arabic, but his Arabic was quite unintelligible to the two Armenians and no progress was made. When it was suggested that Turkish might be tried, a Muslim schoolboy whose mother was Turkish was sent for, but it transpired that he was quite incapable of translating Turkish questions relating to the administration of a will. As a result, Sidney was forced 'to take on the job himself and the case proceeded in a manner which threatened to degenerate into broad comedy. The advocates put their questions in English. I translated them into French of a sort. The witness replied in a mixture of pigeon [sic] English and halting Levantine French, which I did my best to render into comprehensible English.' The many 'loungers' who thronged the corridors crowded into the court to see the fun, and it seemed to Sidney that there was not the remotest likelihood of any of the property or funds being recovered. In the end he threw out the petition for want of the proper proof of the petitioner's authority to represent the heirs.

Every now and then there was a case which referred back to the early history of Fort St George. One suit related to the title to some small houses situated in a blind alley off the China Bazaar Road where there had been a massacre of a British regiment which had retired in the face of superior French troops and, turning into what they presumed was a thoroughfare, found no escape. Sidney's involvement was with the current occupants of the houses who were (and always had been within living memory) servants of the nearby Chennakeswara Temple. The question was whether or not the temple owned the houses and the land they occupied. It was proved that the temple itself had originally been situated on the northern glacis of Fort St George and apparently 'the authorities had foolishly allowed all this land to be built over, thereby masking the guns of the fort.' Following the capture of Fort St George by the French in 1746 and its rendition under the Treaty of Aix-la-Chapelle, it was decided to clear the glacis as far as the Esplanade in order to provide a field of fire for the guns. It was also proved that the Chennakeswara Temple originally had houses for its servants when it was near the fort and that the East India Company had provided the temple with its present site. There was no positive evidence of the grant of the disputed land for the use of the temple servants, but taking into consideration the history and the fact that they had been living in the present houses without question for many years,

Sidney held that it must be presumed that there was a grant of land for the temple servants similar to the grant for the temple itself. The case was particularly interesting in that incidentally it showed how the government came to have at its disposal the land on which the High Court and the Law College were built.

While on the Original side, Sidney had to try a case which was one of the largest account suits tried in South India. Raja Sir Annamalai Chettiar, the defendant, was the most prominent of the Nattukottai Chetti bankers, 'a man of great wealth and ability and one whom the government had delighted to honour. Not only was he a brilliant financier, but he also had charming manners and great social gifts'.[4] However, his financial importance and the great power that he exercised made him 'the target for a good deal of criticism and at the same time inspired considerable fear.' He had a brother who died young, leaving an infant son as heir to his extensive business interests, and it was apparent that Sir Annamalai had been managing his minor nephew's firm. When the minor came of age, he regained his business and filed a suit against his uncle and others alleging that he had been defrauded of a vast sum. The allegation was 'that the estate had been handed over to him, not on the basis of the true accounts, but a set of false accounts manufactured under the orders of Sir Annamalai for the purpose of defrauding the income tax department.' The plaintiff therefore formally requested the court to order an account to be assessed on the basis of the true books and 'to require Sir Annamalai to pay him the difference which, if all the allegations were substantiated, would have amounted to close on half a million sterling.'

The case was filed in the court of the subordinate judge of Devakottai, who had jurisdiction over most of the Chettinad (the region due east of Madura to which the Nattukottai Chettiars migrated in the thirteenth century following a massive flood). It then came before a succession of other judges who passed a series of preliminary orders, 'all of which were made the subject of elaborate proceedings in revision before the High Court.' At the end of six years, the actual trial had not begun and the case began to resemble a contest to determine which party was the wealthier. At this stage Sir Vepa Ramesam officiated as chief justice for a short time and transferred the case to the file of the High Court. Sidney was set to try it and recalled that, 'The record was truly terrifying. There were thirty-two large printed volumes of documentary evidence, mostly extracts from accounts and correspondence.' The defendant had briefed a formidable array of counsel, among them Mandakolathur Patanjali Sastri, who was an expert on Chetti accounts and became a close personal friend of Sidney.[5] The plaintiff's team was 'less imposing', but led by S. Doraiswami Iyer who, in Sidney's opinion, had been quite the best advocate on the Original Side for some years and 'endowed with something of a genius for making obscure things clear.'[6]

Determined that there should be no more delay, Sidney refused to hear more requests for adjournments and, as the trial progressed, he began to appreciate the formidable challenge of writing the judgment. Fortunately the case was 'admirably presented' and he was taken through the various clauses of the plaint in a most methodical way. Each clause was in effect a separate case in which it was necessary 'to take up a transaction, follow it through the accounts of the various branches of the firm, illustrate the accounts from the voluminous correspondence, all written in the most obscure phraseology, and collect the inferences from odd phrases and entries to establish the existence of the other set of accounts which, according to the plaintiff, had been suppressed.' Days were spent chasing a sum of thirteen lakhs of rupees (nearly £100,000) which represented the assets of a branch in Cochinchina[7] which had been closed down. This large sum was remitted from branch to branch, changing its currency several times, until at last it went to Rangoon, where it disappeared. There was much 'enlightening' correspondence about the preparation of special income tax accounts and letters were sent to the foreign branches asking for examples of their particular notepaper and ink, 'alleged to be required for the fabrication of false correspondence in support of the new accounts.' As the case developed, Sidney's notebook (of which he was very proud) gradually assumed 'the form of an elaborate index of all the hundreds of documents referred to, with a brief abstract of each and a cross-reference to other evidence on the subject … with the help of which I succeeded in giving an impression of omniscience which was very far from the truth.'

The end came about a month after the trial began, when Sir Annamalai was cross-examined at length and appeared to admit that separate income tax accounts had been prepared, while denying that these had been used to cheat the plaintiff. It was undoubtedly understood that this was 'very dangerous ground' and the next day the case was compromised. Sidney had no official knowledge of the terms of the settlement, but understood that 'the plaintiff was entirely satisfied with the result.' He himself was greatly relieved to be able to 'pronounce a final judgment in two sentences, instead of having to struggle for weeks in a probably futile attempt to describe clearly and convincingly the inference to be drawn from this huge mass of obscure evidence.'

In the middle of 1937, when Sir Lionel Leach[8] came from Rangoon to succeed Sir Owen Beasley as Chief Justice, Sidney was moved over to the Appellate Side and, except for a few short spells as judge of the criminal sessions, never again sat on the Original Side. He could only remember trying one case of any particular interest at the High Court Sessions, the only time a European was before him on a charge of murder. The accused (unnamed, as he was still alive at the time Sidney wrote his memoirs) was a private in the regiment stationed in Fort St George. He seemed to be a youngster of 'very little education or intelligence' and it was obvious to Sidney that at the time of the incident he was suffering from 'what the French call le cafard—a much more expressive phrase than the English equivalent "browned off".' It was in the middle of the hot weather and 'the poor lad was evidently down and out, hating the climate and the army and the barracks and thoroughly homesick.' His only consolation was a pet mongoose which was killed one day by a dog belonging to a man in the same block. The tragedy seems to have completely upset the mental stability of the private, who appeared 'to have been overcome by a wave of unreasoning hate for the man whose dog had caused all his misery. So he got his rifle out of the rack, loaded it … and shot the owner of the dog dead.'

The facts were clear. Although it was suspected that the soldier's mind was 'unbalanced by his troubles', there was nothing that could be called insanity in law and no defence of insanity was attempted. Instead, his counsel put forward what appeared to be 'a hopeless plea of "grave and sudden provocation".' Sidney summed up, suggesting that there was not provocation from the deceased at all. The only provocation came from the dog and even this, though grave, was not 'sudden'. However, he later admitted that he had underrated 'the power of the average juryman to shut his ears to the law and listen only to his sympathies' and to his surprise and relief, the jury found the accused guilty only of 'culpable homicide not amounting to murder.' Some time afterwards Sidney asked one of the jurymen how he had arrived at this surprising result. He replied that 'there were three of us who had been in the army and we knew exactly how the poor devil was feeling and we didn't think it right to treat him like an ordinary murderer.'

Sidney gave the accused ten years, and about eight years later, quite by chance, he heard from an officer in the same regiment that the man was expecting his release from prison very soon and was 'full of hope for the future.' Sidney saw no reason to doubt that he would be 'perfectly well behaved when at liberty.' In his opinion:

> Contrary to the general impression, homicides (except for a few professionals and maniacs) are usually excellent citizens and not in the least likely to repeat the offence. In fact in the penal settlements of the Andaman Isles, murderers were usually employed as domestic servants and even instead of nursemaids for the families of the staff and they were found to be entirely reliable.

Although biased by having performed most of his criminal work without a jury, Sidney declared with much feeling that he 'hated' working with one. He was never able to understand the mental attitude of other judges who would 'shrink from the responsibility of deciding on the guilt of a fellow man on trial for his life' in favour of leaving the decision to a jury. As far as he was concerned, when working with a jury there was a double responsibility: first it was necessary to decide personally as to the guilt of the accused; then there was the added responsibility of guiding a jury to their decision, 'with the extremely difficult task of determining just how much guidance it is fair and reasonable to give them.' Moreover, a trial by jury robbed the accused of an appeal on the facts, and he believed that in India there were far more miscarriages of justice in jury trials than in trials by a judge or magistrate sitting alone. For Sidney, juries in India were 'quite incalculable.' In Madras the quality of the jury seemed largely to depend on the intelligence of the two or three Europeans who were normally found on it. In the districts, where they were entirely composed of Indians and mostly employed in theft cases, they would often convict 'on the most meagre evidence, because they knew quite well that if an alleged thief was up before the sessions, he must have a pretty lurid record.' Besides, in cases where the accused was wealthy there was often widespread bribery of Indian juries. In fact, in one case (not before Sidney) he was told long before the case was over 'not only what the result would be, but what would be the precise majority in the jury.'

Although in Sidney's view there was not much of general interest in appellate work, he did in fact find a good deal that interested him. His first two years were spent mainly in single judge work, consisting of second appeals and revision petitions in civil suits, broken by a few short periods on the criminal appellate bench and an occasional call to make up a full bench. Sidney had had his fill of murder in Madura and was glad that in the High Court he was employed mainly on civil work, which he found more attractive. He declared that, contrary to popular belief, mortgages were more interesting and varied than murders in that the latter possessed a 'soul-destroying monotony ... and it is only the rare murder case that presents anything like an intellectual problem'. In his opinion 'mortgages nearly always make the brain work hard, especially when they run two or three deep and third parties have acquired an interest in portions of the properties mortgaged.'

He did not enjoy the position of junior judge in a full bench. There was nearly always a mass of conflicting authorities which could only be reconciled or distinguished by 'a hair-splitting process which often demanded more subtlety of mind than I possessed.' In addition, 'the pace of a full bench was apt to be the pace of the slowest judge and as my own brain makes up in speed for something of what it lacks in subtlety, I was apt to get bored if one of my colleagues spent what seemed to me to be an inordinate time chasing hares up side-alleys.' Generally, the bigger the bench, the slower the pace at which it moved. The advocates naturally wanted to be certain of all the judges and tended to concentrate on those who asked more questions and required the most explanations. For this reason Sidney particularly enjoyed second appeals, which were restricted to points of law and 'if one was quick in getting hold of the facts, one would frequently find that the point of law did not really arise, so that the case could be finished in half an hour. If there was a genuine legal point, it was often interesting and as there was only one mind to make up, the process was not unduly prolonged.' Moreover, many of the appeals dealt with questions of land tenures, irrigation and encroachments, about which he knew a great deal.

Sidney's 'state of single blessedness' was terminated by a major political event. The Government of India Act of 1935 was born out of the three Round Table Conferences of the early 1930s and the findings of the Joint Select Parliamentary Committee of 1933, and made provision for a federal centre while substantially extending provincial autonomy with ministers now responsible to their local legislatures in charge of all branches of government. The Act was intended to accommodate the wide spectrum of opinion in British India: to secure the cooperation of the Indian princes, to afford sufficient recognition of the communal principle to satisfy the Muslims and other religious minorities, to make enough concessions to the principle of self-government to appease the nationalists and to include sufficient safeguards to placate British imperialists. However, although designed to please everybody, the Act failed miserably. Despite Gandhi's participation in the second Round Table Conference and an earlier pact between the Mahatma and the Viceroy, Lord Irwin, radical nationalists were not satisfied. While the Indian princes paid lip service to the idea of a future federation, it appeared unlikely that they would be willing to surrender their power and privileges or to acknowledge the supremacy of a democratically elected central government. Although most Muslims supported the Congress rather than the Muslim League, there was growing anxiety at the prospect of a Hindu Raj. Finally, British liberals and radicals were frustrated at the lack of Indian nationalist support for the 1935 Act and British diehards thought that far too much had already been surrendered.

Following a resumption of acts of civil disobedience in the early 1930s, in 1937 the Indian National Congress decided to abandon its policy of non-cooperation and contest the provincial elections, with the stunning result of absolute majorities in six of the eleven provinces in British India and the largest single share of the vote in three more. In the elections the Muslim League performed badly and most Muslim voters chose to support representatives of their faith within the Congress party. However, the leader of the League, Muhammed Ali Jinnah, previously a Congress stalwart, bitterly resented his exclusion from power in the lead up to the elections and began to rally Muslims to the cause of communal politics.

The Congress ministry that took office in Madras following the 1937 elections was led by the 'astute and charming' Chakravarti Rajagopalachari (always known as C. R.), who later became the last Governor-General of India. The advent of fully responsible ministers obviously marked a fundamental change in the techniques of government control, although in reality the ICS continued to exercise a remarkable degree of influence at all levels of political activity. The service remained the 'steel frame' upon which government hung, despite the heavy load imposed upon it and the strain to which it was exposed, and, unlike areas such as Bengal and Bihar, the reforms worked admirably in Madras. *The Times* praised Rajagopalachari as a 'leader whose rational approach to most of his problems assures a continuity ... of sound and ordered government'[9] and Sir Christopher Masterman saw him not as an idealist, but 'a sensible and down-to-earth politician' who, in tackling alcohol abuse, although a keen prohibitionist, was also his own finance minister and realised that the loss of considerable excise revenue would be disastrous. He therefore introduced prohibition very gradually, first in the district of Salem, and by 1939 only four districts were dry. In Masterman's opinion C. R. was no 'power politician' but genuinely tried to do what was best for his country, which did not always coincide with the wishes of the Congress.[10]

C. R. also differed from most Indian politicians in that he was conscious of the appalling amount of agricultural indebtedness, which had been doubled or tripled by a recent slump in agricultural prices. As Sidney pointed out:

> The Indian peasant really lives on a grain basis. When he borrows a sum of money, he thinks of his debt as the equivalent of so many measures of paddy or so many acres of arable land. When the price of paddy fell by half and the price of land went down in sympathy, the result was that the debtor had to sell twice as much grain to pay his interest and twice as much land to repay the principal. Of course he could not afford to do this, with the result that a very few years the whole agricultural population was on the verge of bankruptcy.

C. R. pledged to lift this load of agricultural indebtedness and in a most drastic way drafted with his own hand a very short bill which he 'rushed through the legislature at lightning speed' so that in a few weeks it became law as The Madras Agriculturists Relief Act IV of 1938.

Act IV was to be Sidney's 'daily bread' for five years. It provided for the summary reduction of all debts from agriculturists on the basis that, 'for all debts incurred before 1st October 1932, the unpaid interest as on that date should be cancelled ... and after that date the original debt should carry interest not exceeding 6¼%; while all debts newly incurred after that date and before the discussion on the bill began, were to have the past interest reduced to 5%.' There were also provisions for the cancellation of old arrears of rent on agricultural lands and a restriction of all future interest to 6¼%. Although this act was 'a courageous and beneficent measure intended to remedy an economic position of great gravity', it suffered from the haste with which it had been enacted. Being very loosely drafted, 'it prescribed no proper procedure for carrying its provisions into effect and no attempt had been made to anticipate all the legal consequences of the tearing up of vast numbers of contracts; and especially there was no indication of how old payments were to be appropriated in calculating the new debt.' Moreover, the all-important definition of an 'agriculturist' had been 'framed as to include a whole host of people who had never touched a plough' (in Sidney's view probably for political reasons) and it was very difficult to determine who was and who was not entitled to the benefits of the act.

The truth was that, although C.R. had started life as a practising lawyer, he had had little practice in the 'very difficult art of legal draftsmanship and was in too much of a hurry to permit the proper examination of the new statute'. As soon as the new act was passed, cases began to pour into courts all over the presidency and there were the widest differences as to the interpretation and application of the act on many different points. There were also many suits in which the competence of the provincial legislature in enacting some of its most important provisions was challenged. Soon these cases began to 'trickle' up to the High Court, and Sir Lionel Leach, the Chief Justice, wisely realised that a few conflicting decisions in the High Court would soon render the law on the subject 'chaotic' and that 'the task of interpreting the new act consistently and prescribing a procedure was going to require continuity and specialised knowledge.' Therefore he decided that all the cases under Act IV should go before a special bench of which Sydney would be in charge, with Mandakolathur Patanjali Sastri as his colleague, beginning an association of 'complete harmony and cooperation' which was to continue with a few short breaks for nearly five years.

Patanjali was not only a great expert on Chetti accounts, but also for years standing counsel to the income tax department. He was also a 'most profound and clear-headed legal thinker, with a great sense of the importance of pure doctrine and a most acute legal conscience.' Personally he was very shy and reserved, with few interests outside his work and family, but Sidney soon realised that he was working with a man of 'unusual quality and complete mental integrity' and he did his best to win his confidence and friendship. As a result, the time during which the two men worked together to make sense of such a particularly important piece of legislation were 'years of good fellowship and happy and fruitful work.' Neither man was noticeably quicker or slower than the other and in the vast majority of cases they arrived at the same conclusion almost simultaneously. When they were inclined to go in different directions, 'one or other of us almost always realised that he was not so sure that he was right, so that the more confidently held view prevailed'. There was never any question of going back on a view once adopted, and they arrived at a mutually satisfactory way of dealing with the hundreds of judgments, which was a matter of some importance since a very large percentage of their earlier decisions were reported.

Pantanjali was not particularly fond of delivering ex tempore judgments in cases which were likely to be reported. Sidney, on the other hand, found that his ex tempore judgments read better than those which had been 'kept brewing' for several days. Patanjali's judgments filled Sidney with admiration; on legal subjects he could express his thoughts in English which was 'clear, concise and correct', and there was very rarely a phrase which suggested that the writer was not an Englishman. Nearly all of their work was breaking new ground, as they were confronted with a statute which 'destroyed contracts and gave little indication of what was to happen to the broken fragments.' It was necessary therefore to go back to first principles for their law, at the same time keeping a wary eye in case, in dealing with a particular situation, they laid down some rule which might have 'startling results if extended to other circumstances.' Sidney certainly found that the process of working out the consequences of the act in a variety of cases was a 'liberal education in the principles of the law' and he was extremely thankful to have been blessed with such an accomplished lawyer as his colleague.

It took the two men the best part of two years to cover most of the questions which were of frequent occurrence and which during that time filled hundreds of pages in the local law journals. In the process they acquired a unique knowledge of the subject and were frequently able to help counsel with cases which had not yet been reported or had been overlooked. The way of tracing such cases was curious in that Sidney could generally remember what had been decided, but 'not the remotest idea who the parties were.' Pantanjali, on the other hand, could always remember one or both of the lawyers appearing in the wanted case, and by contacting them could reopen the matter. After the first two years they continued to deal with cases involving questions under Act IV, but as a rule the points arising were not new and their work gradually began to resemble that of an ordinary appellate bench. Moreover, one of the disadvantages of their specialisation was that most of the other judges had little opportunity of learning the new law which they had laid down and were inclined to send over to them any case in which Act IV was so much as mentioned.

Looking back on his twelve years on the Madras bench, Sidney realised how lucky he had been with his colleagues. Under the watchful eye of Sir Lionel Leach the standard of work was steadily rising and the arrears falling, with 'a noticeable feeling of corporate responsibility for the work of the court' and no friction between the judges. By strenuous work with full benches, the Chief Justice got rid of conflicting rulings, to the great satisfaction of the bar and the bench and to 'the enhancement of the prestige of the court.' In the process the whole judicial administration received 'the tonic of regular inspection, which had been grievously neglected in the past.'

19

GARDENING IN SOUTH INDIA

When not beset by his administrative and judicial duties, Sidney was able at times to turn to more recreational pursuits. The Wadsworths' first attempt at gardening was 'inspired by the primitive need for food'. At Gudur there were no shops, and fresh garden produce could only be procured from Bangalore, 'whence it arrived tired and unhappy.' They therefore tried to use their 'inexpert hands' to grow plants and, fencing off part of the scrub, 'proceeded to hack up the ground with some ancient battle-axes which were our only tools.' The 'wild man of the woods' who was their waterman then produced a mamooti (mattock) and tackled the digging more successfully. A packet of tomato seeds was sown and, without further preparation of the soil, the seedlings were planted out, which 'the wild man' watered copiously morning and evening. Evidently liking the rough and ready treatment, the seedlings made rampant growth and, following a family council, were pruned 'mercilessly and unskilfully.' Sidney reported that the result was 'a finer crop of tomatoes that I have ever grown since, notwithstanding the acquisition of considerable horticultural lore.' With as many as 100 fine fruits a day, it was possible to send baskets away to friends in Madras, and the deduction was made that 'tomatoes like virgin soil and excessive watering—two things which in an established garden it is often difficult to supply.'

At Madanapalle the Wadsworths had a vegetable garden which supplied nearly all their needs and there was also quite a show of flowering shrubs and creepers. It was a perfect climate and the only problem was shortage of water. However, when the couple were invited to see the beautiful garden of the renowned horticulturist Mrs Louis Wathen in Madras, they began to learn about landscape gardening in earnest. Mrs Wathen in 1928 discovered and successfully cultivated the Scarlet Queen bougainvillea, 'an entirely new and very beautiful variety with a mixture of orange and rose tints' which was propagated by the Madras Agri-Horticultural Society and travelled under her name all over the world. She also taught the gardeners of South India how to make lawns and herbaceous borders, and 'gave the final death-blow to the pot-grown croton,[1] which she aptly described as "the aspidistra of the East".' Mrs. Wathen's garden made an impression on Sidney which proved to have lasting results.

At Chingleput the Wadsworths were handicapped by living on top of a hill with an inadequate water supply, but they acquired a large brandy barrel and a small bullock cart, and by joining the two together managed to get enough water for a pleasant small garden. However, in Madura they were given their first chance to experiment, as the judge's bungalow was entitled for nine months of the year to 'an ample flow of Periyar water twice a week … laden with rich silt which made manuring quite unnecessary.' In fact, with no other fertiliser, they grew zinnias which were larger than any Sidney had seen elsewhere (in particular 'one colossal plant of zinnia grandiflora which grew to a height of six feet and had enormous blooms'), giving a practical demonstration of 'the oft-repeated doctrine that, even in a hot climate, two really good waterings a week are ample for anything with a formed root system.' They also grew a satisfactory lawn, and the total cost of the priceless water which both irrigated and fertilised was the annual water rate of roughly a couple of rupees a year.

When the couple returned to Madras in 1935 they found at Cottingley,[2] the house they occupied for the next twelve years, a garden which was nearly three acres in size with great possibilities and 'nothing but some fine tamarind trees and bamboo clumps on the outer boundary to cramp one's style.' Sidney was by that time a keen member of the Madras Agri-Horticultural Society and determined to establish a show garden which was sufficiently impressive to compete in the annual competition into which gardens were entered as a whole and judged in situ. Starting from scratch on a heavy clay soil and 'with finances which would not stand the strain of extravagant expenditure', this seemed rather ambitious, as the standard was high and was rising every year, 'particularly when the rich Chetties [sic] entered the field with unlimited resources and a very expert nurseryman to back them.' However, the Wadsworths hoped to make up by 'taste, originality and hard work' for what they lacked in wealth. They aspired to the sort of garden which might appear 'round a well-kept English vicarage—nothing apparently formal or expensive, nothing apparently tropical, but a quiet area of peace and restful beauty.'

They succeeded, although it took five years of constant work. First they had to create the effect of space in a limited area, which involved bodily moving a five foot thevetia[3] hedge when the ground was saturated in the monsoon without losing a single plant. The somewhat unsightly back area was then given 'a large curved border, backed by acalypha,[4] bougainvillea, hibiscus and other colourful shrubs, and filled to overflowing with a mixture of annuals and perennials.' It was decided to have lawns on three sides of the house and the existing well was fitted with an electric pump to circulate the water. However, the pump soon exhausted the well and, possibly as a result of over-pumping, its sides caved in, which was a severe blow. They enlisted the help of a water diviner, 'a Brahmin gentleman who had retired from the Public Works Department' but, although his 'contraption' indicated water at two places, at both they failed to find it at a reasonable depth (unlike a friend of the Wadsworths whose water diviner located a strong spring which turned out to be the municipal water main). Sidney was then left to his own devices and, observing the way in which a deep pit at the back of the house filled with water in the monsoon but drained with 'noticeable rapidity', deduced that there was a layer of sand below the pit whereas the rest of the garden was stiff clay. Sand in clay usually indicated water and the Wadsworths set to work to excavate the pit, and a few feet below the surface discovered a 'plentiful' spring.

The next step was to call in the Oddes, 'that remarkable caste of professional earth-workers and well-sinkers', to request a price for sinking, revetting and completing a fourteen-foot well. A few days later there was an invasion of some seventy Oddes, consisting of men, women and children.

In a very short time:

> they had dug down to the water level, the men working at the bottom and the top, while the women and children formed a chain to hand up the baskets of excavated earth. They next step was to make a ring of wood, fourteen feet in diameter, formed by nailing together three thicknesses of roughly curved planks. This ring was wrapped around with straw rope and was to serve as a foundation for the revetment. Curiously enough, wood and straw will last for many years if submerged in water and never exposed to air. This ring was hoisted up with a tackle and lowered to the bottom of the excavation, great care being taken to get it absolutely level. On this foundation a wall of shaped bricks was built, fitted together without any mortar or cement of any kind—obviously a task of great skill, for this wall was to provide the permanent under-water revetment of the well and it had to be absolutely true to allow the water to percolate between the bricks, while providing a firm basis for the cemented revetment which was to go above. Across the top of this uncemented wall planks were laid to serve as a staging. Then half a dozen of the youngest and strongest men got inside the round wall and proceeded to dig the mud into baskets to the chain of women and boys who passed them from hand to hand till they were emptied on the bank and passed down again to be refilled. As the mud was excavated, the ring foundation with the wall built on top of it was gradually sunk, great care being taken to make it sink level. Soon the men at the bottom were hampered by water and a small motor pump was rigged to keep the area moderately dry. Before long every man, woman and child was plastered from head to foot with mud, but this was all part of the job and they seemed to enjoy it.

At noon a halt was called and the whole seventy of them made for the tap behind the house and wallowed in the sump until they were moderately clean. Then they all squatted under a tree in a big circle and several buckets were produced, full of cooked rice. Each of the workers held out two hands 'stretched to their utmost capacity' and these were filled from the bucket, allowing them to gorge themselves until they could eat no more. Then 'they carefully licked their fingers, lay back for a brief rest, or, in the case of the younger women, suckled their babies which had been hanging in a cloth from a tree' and soon they were hard at work again. By the end of the day the staging had been sunk almost to the natural water level and the rest of the job was left to the experts who built up and cemented the upper revetment and parapet wall. In three days the whole well was completed, the ground levelled and the stipulated price paid.

Sadly, the construction proved to be 'a bitter disappointment.' There was plenty of water, but as the hot weather approached it began to grow 'more and more brackish' and too saline even for the grass from the middle of March until the rains came to fill the well with fresh water. However, it did enable the Wadsworths to keep the lawns fresh and green for most of the year. The actual making of the lawns was fairly simple. Labourers were employed 'to collect harialai [cynodon dactylon] grass which grew plentifully near the river and was dug up with a grass-cutter's hoe. This grass was chopped up small. Then a porridge was made of red earth, sand and cow-dung with water and this was spread on the ground which had already been dug up and raked. On top of this porridge the chopped grass was sprinkled and another layer of the porridge was spread on top.' All that then remained to be done was regular watering and in a fortnight or so a lawn began to appear. Unfortunately, there was always a tendency for coarse grass and weeds to drive out the good grass and to keep the lawns in first-class order it was necessary to remake them every three or four years. This was too expensive for the Wadsworths as they had nearly half an acre of lawn and they had to accept the fact that even coarse grass could look presentable if well cut and watered.

One of the difficulties of gardening in South India was 'the Indian passion for symmetry.' In Sidney's view:

> All classes and communities seem to love geometrical patterns, straight lines and matched pairs and, unless carefully controlled, your gardener will give way to his natural instincts. No doubt a formal geometrical garden can be very effective, but it needs to be absolutely flawless. The slightest failure to achieve perfect symmetry hits one in the eye and it is no use explaining that a grub has eaten the missing dahlia.

The Wadsworths decided to have no geometry in their garden, 'no straight lines or stars or triangles.' All their beds were made to curve in an irregular way as if they had just grown and were planted in clumps and masses. The result justified all their hopes, and even their faithful gardener, Doraisamy, who had 'the national hankering for geometry but loved his garden and toiled in it without ceasing', was forced to admit that it was the best solution. However, nothing would grow under the tamarind trees or near the bamboos 'with their greedy roots' and there was a difficulty in taming most of the boundaries. The 'rather laborious but effective' answer was to build up various rockeries and bricked beds above ground level which were emptied every year to get rid of the roots which persisted in making their way upwards. In these beds the Wadsworth planted 'begonias, perennial balsams, ferns, torenias,[5] poinsettias and other plants which give colour even in the shade.'

Gradually 'the garden grew in beauty until the proud moment when it won the cup. Great was the rejoicing in the household. The servants took almost as much pride in the garden as we did and were full of scorn for our competitors.' However, it was one thing to win the cup, keeping it was another. Each year new gardens appeared on the scene, constructed with great skill and much more expenditure than Sidney could afford. The Chettis 'looked upon a successful garden more or less as they looked on a triumphant law-suit or a winning racehorse, as a matter of personal prestige and they grudged no money to win. Some of them displayed considerable taste and one of them, Sir Alagappa Chettiar, was himself a very fine horticulturalist and took immense pains on his lovely garden.' Sidney was personally delighted to see them win and would have happily withdrawn from the contest, but 'to do so would have bitterly disappointed the enthusiastic Doraisamy and all the rest of the household and it would soon have meant the deterioration of our beloved garden.' So every year with a consistently rising standard the Wadsworths were forced to introduce new ideas in the effort to keep their lead. When they failed, it was never by much and they admitted that much fun was had in the effort, while the annual competition proved 'an excellent device for preventing any tendency to sit back and rest on our laurels.'

However, during the war it was increasingly difficult to find the time to keep the garden in first-class order. Not only were there endless committees and other activities connected with the war, but Sidney also became much occupied with other people's gardens. The Madras Agri-Horticultural Society, of which he was chairman, had been founded in 1835 by the East India Company, which at that time was 'beginning to realise its responsibility for the economic welfare of the people over whom it ruled.'[6] Robert Wight, a surgeon in the

Madras Medical Service, was one of the society's founding members, better remembered for his interest in horticulture and his major botanical publications than his medical achievements. At the time of its foundation the society was given 'two magnificent pieces of ground by the Cathedral, one to serve as a botanical and ornamental garden and the other as a nursery and show ground.' In the twentieth century the gardens were used as a route down to the Cooum river by funeral processions, and Lt. Gen. Sir Ernest Bradfield remembered that his children would return from a morning with their ayah reporting on the number of such processions they had seen: 'The Indian corpse, carried on a charpoy (bed) to the burning ghat, surrounded by his friends, often preceded by one with a bell, was completely uncovered, except by flowers. The ayahs, fearful that their charges might see this sight, always pretended that it was a wedding procession, frequently without success'.[7]

With very few breaks the society ran an annual show, and with the development of the government's agricultural department became more horticultural. Except for a small government grant it evolved into an entirely non-official organisation, though still known as the 'Company Garden'. For years it had as its honorary secretary Rao Sahib B. S. Nirody, who had been trained as a professional plant-breeder in America and devoted all his spare time to the society, 'introducing new varieties and experimenting with grafting and other devices to discover ways of making things grow in Madras which would not ordinarily stand up to the climate.' When he retired, a good botanist was found who was young enough to learn the art of gardening and Sidney took on the role of honorary secretary, despite admitting that he had neither the time nor the knowledge to do the work properly.

The post was 'interesting but rather exacting', as the society was not simply devoted to organisation and experimentation. It ran a commercial nursery 'which not only supplied members with their requirements, but also sold plants, trees, seeds, tools, fertilisers, flowers and wreaths to the general public.' It was also responsible for the large ornamental garden which was in effect a public park. With such a wide remit, Sidney found himself 'dealing with angry ladies whose seeds had failed to come up, municipal chairmen who wanted us to train their park superintendents in three months, disappointed mourners whose wreaths were not as florid as those supplied by a private nursery and so on and so forth.' What really interested him was the task of reconstructing the fine old ornamental garden which needed modernising. It contained some magnificent trees, many of them imported in the past from Africa or America, but required the attention of someone with an eye for landscape gardening. There were no lawns, no rock garden and the beds were just as they had been for the last fifty years. It was decided to pull down a derelict palm-house and use the salvage to patch up an equally derelict fernery, then to establish an attractive small lawn backed by a deep mixed border, 'flanked by a lily pond with a colourful rock garden round it.' Although it was impossible for a rock garden in the tropics to grow any of the alpines which were so appealing in Europe, the same effect could be achieved by using the plants which would flourish in the Indian climate, 'such as verbenas, creeping lantanas, commelina, torenia and perennial balsam.' Elsewhere messy little beds of annuals were scrapped and substituted by big, deep, mixed beds some way back from the main drive with lawns in front of them.

However, Sidney admitted that it was 'uphill work' and, unless he controlled matters himself, little progress was made. There seemed to be nobody on the staff who took sufficient pride in the garden to make the improvements when no one was watching, and the funds of the society would not allow for the recruitment of a really well-paid set of gardeners. In fact, competent gardeners were extremely rare in South India; there were 'a few of the old school of professional malis who were quite able within their limitations' but none capable of designing a garden. Not only were they illiterate and in Sidney's view 'quite incapable of learning new ideas', but also most were also 'distinctly idle and disinclined to do the deep digging which is the basis of good gardening.' The best plan was to find an intelligent boy and educate him, but the wages of a gardener compared very unfavourably with those of a mill worker, and unless it was possible to inspire personal loyalty and enthusiasm, there was always a danger of the trained man drifting away to something more lucrative.

When it came to the exhibition ground, Sidney learnt that running a flower show was 'apt to be an education in the tricks of the unscrupulous pot-hunter', and although all the society's exhibits were certified to have been grown by the exhibitor, in fact some of the chief prize-winners 'systematically' bought their exhibits from a local nursery. Sidney recalled how 'One of these gentlemen made a most indignant complaint when his principal rival defeated him by buying his exhibits in Bangalore; and he asked the committee to disqualify any exhibit which was in a dark-coloured pot, the Madras pots being all of light-coloured clay.' However, the society rather shirked the task of acting as censors of the morals of their exhibitors. After some years Sidney's chief challenge became, with the help of several other enthusiasts, to introduce a large display of cut flowers 'more in keeping with modern practice than the old pot-grown exhibits.' It was a great struggle against the climate to maintain a cut flower show for two days, and many of the competitors would not take the trouble to get up at daybreak to send in fresh blooms, but a new layout was contrived for the show to make the whole area look like a beautiful garden. It was hard work but the enthusiasts all thought it 'well worth doing.'

20

MADRAS AT WAR

In September 1939, at the outbreak of the Second World War, the viceroy, Lord Linlithgow, declared India to be alongside Britain at war with Hitler's Germany. Two months later, in protest against this unilateral act, which appeared to Indians as a reassertion of high-handed British imperialism, the Congress ministries in the provinces resigned. In March 1940, taking advantage of what they saw as a fortuitous deliverance from Congress rule, the Muslim League, at its annual meeting in Lahore, enacted the Pakistan Resolution, with its ill-defined demand for independent Muslim states. The stage was set for the crises which were to dominate the decade of the 1940s—the war, the Congress's final movement of non-cooperation, the rise of Muslim nationalism, and finally, in 1947, independence with the devastating partition of the subcontinent into two states.

During the years from 1939 to 1942, the Congress and the British each sought to secure a decisive personal advantage from the wartime crisis. The constant negotiating position of the Congress maintained that India ought to participate in the worldwide struggle for freedom, but could only do so meaningfully if it were itself free. As Britain's military situation became more desperate—from the fall of France in 1940 and the surrender of Singapore and Burma to the Japanese in early 1942—the Congress leaders invested more urgency in their negotiations, while always insisting on a substantial immediate transfer of power. On their part, and with a similar sense of urgency, the British sought Congress support for the war effort. By the time of the flying visit of a leading Labour member of the British War Cabinet, Sir Stafford Cripps, to Delhi in April 1942, the British had stated their willingness to offer India independence at the end of the war, but with the proviso that no unwilling portion of the country should be forced to join the new state. During the war, to aid collaboration, Indians were to be given more seats on the viceroy's executive council, partly to assuage rising anti-colonial sentiment around the world and, above all, at the behest of US President Franklin Roosevelt, who insisted that his country had not joined the war to preserve the British Empire. The Cripps mission was nevertheless doomed. Its proposals did not, as the Congress demanded, transform the viceroy's council into a cabinet responsible to an Indian legislature, and many influential figures, such as the ardent imperialist Winston Churchill, did not want the negotiations to succeed. The failure of the mission made evident the intransigence of the major Indian parties and disillusioned many ICS officers who felt that such political opposition was ill-timed and disloyal.

Confronted with the collapse of discussions, the Congress determined on a massive act of defiance, known as the 'Quit India' movement. Unlike the earlier Gandhian campaigns of 1920–22 and 1930–32, the campaign of August 1942 was not a disciplined movement of civil disobedience. From the start, partly because the Congress leadership had been swiftly jailed, the movement erupted into uncoordinated violence as low-level leaders, students and other activists took matters into their own hands, launching a huge attack on government property and the communications network of the Raj, especially in eastern United Provinces, Bihar and western Bengal. However, despite the passions it unleashed, the 'Quit India' movement did not drive the British from India. Taking advantage of the vast number of troops in the country due to the war, and sustained by the belief that the war justified fierce reprisals against domestic rebels, the British mobilised some fifty battalions and to a large extent crushed the rebellion within little more than six weeks. All Congress leaders were kept in detention for nearly three years until the end of the war.

Although Sidney observed that Madras city was remarkably unscathed by the ramifications of the 'Quit India' movement, Devakottai (a town about sixty miles due east of Madura) was actively associated with Indian independence. There the ICS sub-collector Chakravarthi Vijiaraghava Narasimhan witnessed in his subdivision some of the worst disturbances and violations of the peace during the movement. Sending his wife and daughter to Madras, he left the sub-collector's bungalow and lived for some time in the police station where there was protection on a round-the-clock basis. It was necessary to use armoured police cars to patrol the entire subdivision and he recalled, 'to my great regret, that there were a number of situations where we had to open fire and I saw with my own eyes people being shot and falling down dead. This is an experience which I am not likely to forget.'[1]

For Sidney the initial impact of war had been slight, as at first Madras appeared to be something of a backwater, 'more remote from the great events which were taking place than we were even in 1914.' However, the entry of Japan soon brought the city uncomfortably near the front line. At first local concerns were confined to probable air-raids and, as a precautionary measure, Sidney was authorised to work out an evacuation scheme for use should it be necessary to move the courts away from the coast. This duty was kept highly secret as the authorities did not want to be accused of creating 'despondency and alarm' and he travelled around the area, nominally inspecting courts but in fact to identify centres where there were known to be buildings which 'might at a pinch' be used to accommodate the High Court with its sixteen judges and its hundreds of clerks. Eventually he came to the conclusion that there was no one place in the interior which was fit for the task, and it was decided to prepare a scheme on the basis that, should evacuation become necessary, the court should be divided into two sections: the larger section under the chief justice should go into the Forest College at Coimbatore[2] (about 315 miles to the southwest of Madras city) to serve all the southern and western Tamil-speaking districts; the smaller section under Sidney to go to Anantapur (about two hundred miles to the northwest of Madras and of strategic importance to the British Indian Army) to serve the Telegu districts in the north. Unfortunately, this decision made it necessary to divide all the clerks and records according to language, which complicated matters to a great extent.

Sidney employed an able assistant on special duty to work out the details of the scheme and, while it was desirable to get matters cut and dried as soon as possible, there seemed no immediate likelihood of its being needed. However, early in April 1942 things began to move. The defences of Madras at that time were 'negligible', consisting of the local volunteers, the Madras Guards (in which Sidney had held a commission during the First World War) who had four Bofors guns and a battalion of infantry, which was hardly a substantial force with which to oppose the victorious Japanese should they choose to come to Madras. British anti-aircraft troops were arriving, but were still in the course of building their gun sites. The air force consisted of three old Atalanta passenger planes, each fitted with a Lewis gun 'in the approved 1914 manner.' One of these planes, popularly known as the 'Victory Bus', used to patrol every evening and gave the first air raid warning. She was flying over the sea by moonlight when she encountered three Japanese planes, 'which studied her intently for some time and then, apparently frightened by her four engines and huge size, decided that she was too dangerous to tackle and sheered off, which was a bit of luck for the crew and also for us.' Vizagapatam to the north and Cocanada to the south were then bombed and there were 'very circumstantial, but entirely untrue' reports of other attacks on the coast. As a result, people began to stream out of Madras. Next came 'the formidable raids on Colombo and Trincomalee and it really did look as if the Japs were moving west.'

On Saturday 13 April Sidney led a representative team of managers, clerks and translators from the High Court's office to the General Hospital to help in donating blood. Olive was down at the soldiers' club cooking eggs and bacon for the men working on the new gun sites, as the club servants had fled. A telephone call from Sir Lionel Leach, 'speaking with great earnestness', summoned Sidney to his residence, Brodie Castle,[3] where he was informed by the chief justice that 'a large Japanese fleet with transports had been sighted, heading for the Madras coast, and that it was expected to land somewhere between Madras and the extreme south not later than the following Wednesday morning.' The civil government and the courts were therefore to be evacuated immediately. Sidney was to put his scheme into operation and move everything and everybody out of Madras by the following Tuesday. The summer vacation was to be antedated by a fortnight and was to begin at once.

As the next day was Sunday and the Monday was a public holiday, the first job was to warn the clerks and to inform the other judges. It was not possible to do this over the telephone or wireless until Sir Arthur Hope, the governor, had made an official announcement. Night was beginning to fall and there was a total black-out; however, Sidney managed to get in touch with a sufficient number of people to ensure that the information was passed round to all those concerned. Just after he arrived home, Olive came back from the soldiers' club 'completely exhausted', as 'the catering contractor and all the servants of the club except one chokra had vanished and she and another woman had had to scour Madras for provisions.' They then served about 200 men, 'in a temperature close on 100°, in a tiny blacked-out kitchen with no fan and an open fire.' Unsurprisingly, Olive found it hard to be told to pack up the house in order to depart in about twenty-four hours while Sidney dealt with the High Court.

Nonetheless, everybody knew that if the Japanese did arrive, there was nothing much to stop them and on the information received (which apparently came by wireless from a British Catalina which never returned) the order to depart seemed 'obvious common sense.' On the Sunday morning, while Olive 'mobilised her forces at home', Sidney headed for the High Court and:

> by the time most of the clerks began to trickle in, detailed orders had been duplicated and were handed over to each section and all I had to do was to exercise a general supervision and deal with a few points which had been overlooked. Fortunately we had already sent away all our old records, so that there were only current records to be sorted according to languages, bundled up and labelled. The sorting of the staff was covered by the scheme, as also such things as essential books, stationery and furniture.

The only shortcoming was the transport to the railway, with 'not a lorry to be had for love or money and the humble hand-cart (which ordinarily moves most things in Madras) had ceased to operate for want of coolies. However the registrar rose to the occasion and commandeered some buses and the stuff all got to its destination.'

By midday the organisation was working smoothly and there was little left to do. Meanwhile, Olive had packed up the house and loaded two cars with 'a wonderful collection of necessaries and valuables, after many agonising doubts as to what must be taken and what we could do without.' The two cars were full to overflowing, as the Wadsworths took with them the cook, the butler and the driver, plus three dogs. Mattresses were strapped to the roofs and piled up inside were 'stores, crockery, cooking utensils, clothes, law books, silver, lamps and scores of other things.' The rest of the servants, except the gardener who elected to stay, had been sent off by train on the previous day. The ayah, who had been with the family for more than twenty years, at first refused to go, but when it was explained to her that Sidney and Olive were coming on by road she gave way and departed with the others.

Sidney made first for Chittoor, where he had wired ahead for the use of the district judge's bungalow. He had been told (incorrectly as it turned out) that the main Bangalore road had been closed for troop movements, so the cars struck north and then cut across country by a series of by-roads. Fortunately the banks had opened on the holiday to allow people to draw a reasonable amount of money for travelling expenses. The only excitement on the journey was when the inexpert driver became stuck in a river, forcing the three servants to wade into the river and push. Upon reaching Chittoor it was discovered that the district judge had already left for the hills but they were made welcome by the butler. Since more 'refugees' wanted to stay in the bungalow, it was decided to move on to Madanapalle the next day where further accommodation was available; however, it transpired that the whole place was 'seething with clerks and superintendents', as a department of the Secretariat had been transported to the town and had filled every vacant room. However, two beds were found in the Arcot Mission and the Wadsworths were able to make arrangements to move up to Horsleykonda the next day.

Forgetting that he was twenty years older than when he last climbed Horsleykonda, Sidney announced cheerfully that he would walk up, but had to admit when he arrived 'gasping and exhausted at the top, that climbing mountains in the midday sun was not a suitable form of exercise for a man in his middle fifties.' But the peace and quiet of the forest bungalow was 'like heaven' after the turmoil of the last few days. He had arranged for a daily message giving the wireless news and he was only about sixty miles from his final destination, Anantapur, which at that time of year was like a furnace. Moreover, there was nothing much to do there until the records began to arrive so he and Olive did nothing for a fortnight and thoroughly enjoyed the rest.

During this time Paul Jayarajan, also of the Madras ICS, reported in his memoirs that in Madras, the massive exodus known as the 'flap' (when it was thought that the Japanese would invade the city) never happened. The adviser to the governor, the two secretaries and the two under-secretaries (one of whom was Jayarajan) carried on the government of the entire province, consisting of sixty million people, by themselves for six weeks. They enjoyed the best wines in the club instead of leaving them for consumption by the Japanese and 'The Raja of Chettinad distributed to his friends and myself the contents of his cellar and we poured the surplus down the drain rather than leave it for the Japanese to enjoy.' After six weeks the vanguard of the Secretariat trooped back from Chittoor where they could do no effective work due to the lack of stationery.

According to Jayarajan, British officials felt the loss of prestige very badly, particularly the desertion of Air Raid Precaution and Auxiliary Fire Service Indian personnel which had occurred following the proclamation of the governor of Madras on 12 April advising non-essential citizens to leave the city. Instead of remaining at their posts, wardens had put their possessions in lorries and driven away in panic, some to the hills and others to Hyderabad or Bombay. British wives of Indian Civil Service and other officers were then appointed as drivers of Air Raid Precaution officers, as the British were less inclined to trust Indians, particularly in the light of the activities of the Indian National Army, which had been formed by Indian nationalists in 1942 to secure Indian independence through an alliance with Japan.[4]

By the end of a fortnight it was fairly clear that the invading fleet had gone elsewhere, and it was heard later that it had been deflected to Rangoon, possibly because of the vigorous resistance experienced by the Japanese air force at Colombo and Trincomalee in Ceylon. The Wadsworths then made their way down the hill, loaded up the cars once more and drove back to Madras. Sidney recorded that:

> The city presented a dismal spectacle. Almost all the private houses were shut up, the shops were closed, the offices were nearly all deserted, though most of the European firms had nucleus staffs working in bungalows some miles from the coast. The streets were empty

and except for the police, the A.R.P. and the troops who were now arriving in considerable numbers, the place seemed to be dead.

The Wadsworths went on to Kodaikanal where they were greeted with acclamation as 'the first sign of returning sanity.' Apparently Kodai had suffered a very severe 'flap'. All the Americans and many British visitors had fled for fear of being cut off in the bottleneck of the Palnis by a Japanese advance along the railway. Indeed, had the expected invasion materialised, Kodai would have been a very difficult place to leave, especially for women and children who could not have negotiated the highly demanding tracks leading north to Palni or west to Travancore.

By the time the High Court's vacation was over it had been decided that the Wadsworths were to return to Madras, but the army would not agree to a return to the High Court buildings on the sea front. Accordingly, the court took over an empty girls' school, the Holy Angels' Convent, which was situated in the suburbs. There were enough classrooms to serve as courts and the judges had 'tolerable chambers', but everybody else was extremely congested. Sidney was given a room labelled 'The Immaculate One', but after a few days the label was removed, 'whereupon I threatened the registrar with proceedings for libel, the innuendo obviously being that I had ceased to be immaculate!' The judges rather liked the Holy Angels' Convent as it was much nearer to where most of them lived and had the great advantage of being to the west, 'so that we had the sun behind us both going to court and returning, instead of blazing in our faces both ways as happened when we were in our permanent abode.' However, in due course the authorities were satisfied that the sea front was no longer a place of 'extreme peril' and the judges returned to their accustomed quarters.

By this time:

> Madras was bristling with guns, there was a large dummy fort on the beach for the benefit of Jap bombers, the shore was festooned with barbed wire and the many bridges over the Cooum had been put into a state of defence—not perhaps a very effective measure for the river can be easily fordable anywhere for the greater part of the year. Meanwhile the presence of considerable numbers of troops in and near the city brought obligations. Most people took turns at working in the various voluntary canteens and my wife was put in charge of the hospital welfare work—a job which started as quite a small show, but ended with

> the supervision of the work in twenty three hospitals, with a paid staff of some sixty workers to train and control. It was a busy life, with endless committees and much entertaining of the soldiery, which we thoroughly enjoyed. We were all impressed by the wonderful manners and excellent behaviour of the British troops amongst whom we made many friends.

Gradually, the Indian population of the city returned to their homes, and on all sides there were 'expressions of relief at being back in comfort after months of congested and often unwilling hospitality in the houses of sorely tried relatives.' Many of Sidney's Indian friends informed him that they would rather be bombed in their own homes then live as 'unwelcome guests in the comfortless houses of their country cousins.' However, their troubles were by no means over. In the second week of October 1943 there were heavy rains and the low-lying parts of the city were flooded. Just as these floods were subsiding, both the Cooum and the Adyar rivers began to rise in an alarming manner. There had been a deluge in the Chittoor hills which flooded all the streams so rapidly that scores of irrigation tanks burst their dams and emptied into the two rivers. Throughout the Saturday both rose to unprecedented heights, and late that night they overflowed in all directions. The Cooum flooded the densely populated area of north Madras to a depth of three to six feet, and many thousands of people spent the night on the roofs of their houses. Soldiers encamped on the outskirts took refuge on the hoods of their lorries, and although many people were rescued by boat, there was much loss of life and many narrow escapes.

On Sunday the water was still rising. The 'Mount Road was like a vast canal and the only way of getting to the hotels and clubs was by rickshaw. The Cooum was backing up at each bridge and the water was piling up all the storm drains, until there was hardly any dry land in the centre of the town.' The Wadsworths were fortunate in that, although a quarter of a mile from the river and about twenty-five feet above its level, the water reached their back door and then stopped. But for many people it was a very grim time. There was no electricity, no telephone and no water in the taps, as the mains had been washed away. That evening the water began to recede and by Monday morning it was possible to get to the High Court by a circuitous route. On Monday evening Olive was meeting troops at the Central Station with the mobile canteen and, as the train was delayed, Sidney accompanied her. When it eventually arrived after 11 pm they started to dole out hot tea and buns to some hundreds of very weary sepoys. Sidney recalled that 'There was a brilliant moon, so bright that when a plane flew over at a very low altitude, one could see its shape quite clearly and I remarked that it was a Catalina flying with its floats down which was rather unusual.' They were too busy to pay much attention, and when shortly afterwards there was much gunfire it was suggested that, despite the floods, the army was involved in a gun practice and even a report by a Hindustani picket that it was a 'Japan plane' was dismissed as a joke.

By morning it was discovered that the plane in question was indeed a Japanese seaplane, of a type so similar to the British Catalinas that it had fooled most of the gunners. Owing to the floods, 'the whole system of fire control and air-raid signals was been out of action and there was no firing until the bombs began to fall and machine gun bullets began to fly round the guns.' It was hard to imagine why a bomb had not been dropped on the Central Station; several had been deposited near the fort a quarter of a mile away and also in the harbour premises, but fortunately the plane was flying too low for some of them to explode and the loss of life was small. It was the one and only air-raid that Madras experienced and, admittedly:

> it was rather a flop. Most of the A.R.P. staff slept through it. The gunners were furious because most of them never came into action. The people of Madras were entirely unconcerned, having discovered that air-raids were very small beer in comparison with floods—certainly not a sufficient reason for returning to the discomfort of their relatives' houses.

As the war in the east progressed, Madras was developed as the forward base for the invasion of Malaya. At Avadi, sixteen miles west of Madras, a huge depot was constructed, extending for miles with six loops of railway lines and four large hospitals. It was never really finished and 'seemed altogether too grandiose in conception.' When in 1944 Sidney was consulted, in his capacity as honorary secretary of the horticultural society, about the planting of trees in the Avadi depot, it seemed to him that 'they were preparing for another ten years of war.' As the time approached for the invasion, things started to happen openly. The glacis of the fort, which Sidney passed daily on his way to and from court, was turned into a vast workshop for the final waterproofing of thousands of vehicles and it was 'quite a common thing to see the soldiery doing their shopping in monstrous amphibious vehicles, which caused much merriment by their ridiculous little bulb horns, which were their only means of scaring the jay-walker.'

The whole presidency was seething with troops—Indian, British and African—however 'when everyone was keyed up for D day, which was obviously near at hand, the war suddenly came to an end. Rather than create the confusion which a change of plans would have entailed, the invasion went in as planned, though fortunately without the casualties.' Moreover, hospitals for the wounded and sick were needed and soon pathetic shiploads of rescued prisoners from Singapore were landed at Madras. Olive had to meet all of the ships and at weekends Sidney went with her, declaring that it was:

> a heart-rending experience. So many of the poor fellows were little more than walking skeletons; and of those who looked comparatively well a large proportion were so blind that they could not read the newspapers which we offered them ... But by far the greater number of the ex-prisoners were bright and cheerful and pathetically grateful for any little kindness.

The Wadsworths:

> were struck by the way in which they helped one another and insisted upon sharing everything—even their sorrows. A poor woman while sitting in the hospital train, somehow or other received the news that both her sons had been killed in action. In a minute the news spread round the ward and every woman in it was weeping as if she had lost her own children. They had suffered so much together that they felt like members of a large family. I shall never forget one handsome middle-aged woman, who had somehow managed to make herself look almost smart and was tending with infinite sollicitude [sic] a poor broken old man whose mind had obviously given way under the strain. I suppose he was probably in his fifties, but with skin stretched tight over his bones, white hair and vacant eyes, he looked like a dying octogenarian.

Later on there was one shipload which consisted entirely of mental cases. Sidney supposed that most would recover with kind treatment and good food, but many would never be fit for normal life. In his opinion, thinking of 'the appalling death-roll and the brutal ill-treatment which disgraced nearly all the Japanese prison camps, one cannot help feeling glad that some, at any rate, of the worst of the camp officers, have been made to pay a fitting penalty.'

Outside the narrow window of Madras, as the war drew to a close the British reopened negotiations on India's future. In June 1945 the viceroy Lord Wavell brought Gandhi, Jinnah and the Congress leadership together in the summer capital of Simla. Wavell attempted to resolve the political deadlock by setting up an executive council made up wholly of Indian members (apart from himself and the commander-in-chief) to run an interim government. Although the council was to comprise equal numbers of Hindus and Muslims, thus embracing a key Muslim demand, negotiations collapsed when Jinnah insisted upon the right of the Muslim League to nominate all of its Muslim members. During the months that followed, Britain increasingly lost both the power and the will to control events in India. In July 1945 a Labour ministry under Clement Attlee replaced Churchill's Conservative government, giving the cause of Indian independence, and the Congress in particular, a sympathetic audience. More importantly, although victorious in the war, Britain had suffered immensely in the struggle and did not possess the manpower or the economic resources required to control a subversive India. For the British public, the jobs and housing promised by the new socialist government took precedence over the costly maintenance of the Raj. Moreover, the elite Indian Civil Service, the 'steel frame' of the Raj, had by 1945 become over one-half Indian, and these men began to look ahead to service under a national government.

The opening round in the endgame of the Raj took place with elections held during the winter of 1945–46. These, by sweeping the board of minor parties, reduced the political scene to the Congress and the Muslim League. Unable to secure agreement on any matter from India's two antagonistic political parties, the British authorised a high-level cabinet mission to be sent to India in March 1946. Its proposal for an independent India involved a complex, three-tiered federation, whose central feature was the creation of groups of provinces. Two of these groups would comprise the Muslim-majority provinces of east and west; a third would include the Hindu majority regions of the centre and south. These groups, given responsibility for most of the functions of government, would be subordinated to a union government controlling defence, foreign affairs and communications. The proposal came tantalising close to giving Jinnah what he most wanted, which was not so much an independent state as a 'large' Pakistan of provinces in which he could conciliate provincial leaders afraid of disorder and loss of power. However, although the grouping scheme preserved a united India, Jawaharlal Nehru, now deemed to be Gandhi's successor, increasingly came to the conclusion that under the cabinet mission proposals, the centre would be too weak to achieve the goals of the Congress which saw itself as heir to the Raj. In a provocative speech on 10 July 1946, Nehru repudiated the idea of a compulsory grouping of provinces, effectively extinguishing any hope of a united India.

Backed into a corner and to enforce upon the Congress that he could not be pushed aside in the final settlement, Jinnah turned to 'direct action', precipitating, perhaps unwittingly, the horrors of riot and massacre that were to accompany independence. Thousands of people of both communities were slaughtered in Calcutta, Bihar and the Bengal district of Noakhali during the latter half of 1946, followed by the struggle for control of the Punjab in 1947 in which the province's Sikhs were also involved. As northern and eastern India sank into chaos, Attlee announced the appointment of Lord Mountbatten as the last viceroy, with instructions to transfer power by June 1948, a date soon moved up to 15 August 1947. Under immense time pressure Mountbatten and his staff were forced to decide whether power was to be handed over to two, three or more successor states and where the boundary line between them was to be drawn. In addition, there remained the fate of the princely states, linked only to the Crown and with no recognised place in the Indian constitutional order. Initially Mountbatten had proposed transferring power to the various provinces, which could join India, Pakistan or remain independent. However, Nehru, determined to avoid a fragmentation of India into small states, persuaded the viceroy to agree to hand over power directly, on the basis of the 1935 Act, to two dominions who would remain in the Commonwealth to smooth the transition. At midnight on

15 August 1947, in a dramatic gesture that stirred feelings of pride throughout the land, Jawaharlal Nehru, as the country's first prime minister, stood up in the parliament chamber and announced that India 'would wake to life and freedom'.

21

ENVOI

Sidney recalled that Kipling had referred to India as the 'grim stepmother of our kind' and felt that in a way the writer had been correct as:

> we who have spent our lives working for India, have never been treated quite as members of her family. At the best we have been foster-sons; at the worst nothing more than strangers within the gates. Yet we do not feel like strangers nor are we indifferent to the fate of our stepmother. How can we when our whole life-work has been devoted to the welfare of the people of India, whose happiness was the measure of our success?

By 1947 it was 'futile to discuss what might have been had the process of handing over power been less hurried and more deliberate. For better or for worse, India had been split in order that she might be hustled into independence.' The immediate result had been 'an outbreak of fratricidal strife, such as the world has rarely, if ever, seen elsewhere.' Within a period of three or four months in late 1947 roughly 5 million Hindus and Sikhs moved from West Punjab into India, while 5.5 million Muslims travelled in the opposite direction. A similar but less extensive migration took place between east and west Bengal, although murderous attacks on fleeing refugees with the attendant death toll, were much fewer in the eastern region. Overall, partition displaced some 12.5 million people along religious lines, creating large-scale violence, with estimates of loss of life ranging from several hundred thousand up to a million. In Sidney's view, 'It would indeed be a tragedy if all this bloodshed was but a prelude to future chaos.'

For him, the accusation that Britain often followed the political strategy of 'Divide and Rule' in India, in an attempt to create dissent between the different religious communities, was entirely false, as proved by the events of 1946 and 1947. The truth was rather that British had in the past been 'the chief unifying force in a land whose natural tendency is towards schism; the mere prospect of the removal of this unifying factor was sufficient to bring out into the open the hatreds and suspicions always underlying the divisions into which India has naturally fallen.' Despite his dislike of the word 'fissiparous', Sidney felt that it did accurately describe the social and political structure of India—something which propagates itself by splitting. In his view, 'The joint family, the caste, the village community, the political party, the province and now the great subcontinent, all display the same tendency to copy the bulbs and perpetuate themselves only by a process of division.'[1]

Not long before the partition of India, Sidney was talking to an Indian friend about the future of the country in which they were both deeply interested. Sidney pointed to the danger of civil war following the withdrawal of the British. His friend, who belonged to no particular political party, replied that:

> Of course there will be civil war. But why not? Every country goes through a period of civil war as an inevitable stage in the journey towards freedom. You British did, but so long ago that you have forgotten all about it. France did. America did. And more recently we have seen Russia go through it. Why should India escape the common destiny of nations struggling to be free?

However, Sidney felt that his friend overlooked the fact that:

> India's civil wars, if they come, are likely to be not so much struggles between differing ideologies to settle the form of government, as struggles between different communities to decide which community shall be able to lord it over the others. And there is a very real danger that the weaker of the combatants will call in outside aid, as happened in the days of Clive. If history were to repeat itself to this extent, would not the result to be to substitute for British rule the power of some

other nation, whose yoke would be far less bearable than that which has been removed.

The rule of the British in India, although backed by force, essentially rested on consent. From the time of the Mutiny, it was generally recognised by the vast majority of the governed that 'the British Raj was striving with a considerable measure of success to administer its great charge for the benefit of the people.' When Sidney had first arrived in India:

> the older people remembered the past and were still acutely conscious of the benefits which had flowed from British rule; nor had they the slightest desire to go back to the days when the country languished under the continual threat of famine and the people were ruined by the perpetual strife between Mogul viceroys and robber chieftains. Nor did ordinary people then think of India as a single nation. That is a concept which has slowly gained acceptance as a result of British organisation and British political education; and it is significant that in South Indian vernaculars there is no indigenous name for 'India'. Until the second world war, the average inhabitant of a South Indian village had never seen a British soldier and rarely seen an Indian sepoy. India has never under the British been a military empire. There was no desire to rebel and therefore no necessity for any display of force, except such small concentrations of police as were required to restrain the criminal elements of the population.

Sidney stressed that the number of British members of the Indian Civil Service had never greatly exceeded 1,300, while British officers of the Indian Police were roughly half that number—'not very many to control and administer a vast country with over three hundred million inhabitants.' In his opinion, 'It must surely be obvious that so small a body of men could not have kept such a huge empire in peace and quietness, if their control had not been generally acceptable to the people they had to govern; nor could anything like an adequate standard of good government have been achieved without the loyal cooperation of a multitude of diligent and competent Indian officials.' After retirement many members of the Madras ICS commented that there had been no inhibition or artificial barrier between Indian and European members and when Sidney looked back on his thirty-three years of service he maintained that his happiest memories were of the constant support and help he received from hundreds of Indian assistants and colleagues. From his ignorant early days, when he was 'discreetly and respectfully' taught his work by a succession of loyal subordinates, to his last years when he received continual help and friendliness from his Indian colleagues on the bench, he was always conscious of the great contribution which Indians had made to the success of British administration. He had therefore come to the conclusion that 'It has in fact not been so much a domination of Indians by the British, as a condominium of British and Indians with the common object of giving to India the inestimable blessings of peace, justice, efficiency and public honesty.' Ramaswami Ayyangar Gopalswami, who returned to India from Cambridge in 1927, eventually becoming a sub-collector and joint magistrate in Madras, agreed that the British and Indians within the civil service 'could and did express their views to one another in private, freely and frankly, irrespective of differences in their seniority, when they differed on the merits of official policy relating to current politics.'[2]

With the enormous expansion of education which had been a notable feature of the last forty years, Sidney saw the number of 'really competent' Indians multiplying many times and the necessity for British civil servants in the higher spheres of government became less obvious. To him, 'Technical competence was never our monopoly; in fact there have been in recent years many Indians in every department who were technically the equals, if not the superiors, of their European colleagues.' However, the British had still been able to make a valuable contribution to India in other ways:

> For one thing there was the absolute impartiality which the British officer derived from his nationality and his upbringing—a matter of great importance in a land of warring factions and hostile castes. The Indian official was always suspected of partiality, whatever he did; and the best of them, in their anxiety to be impartial, were often in danger of being unfair to their own communities.

Sidney was convinced that the vast majority of Indian officials with whom he came in contact were 'capable men of good private character, who would not stoop to corruption' but was nevertheless aware of the success of a small number of British officers in wielding a quite disproportionate influence on benchmarks of official morality. The importance of such criteria had increased with the emergence of the 'lowering of standards of probity which inevitably accompanied the assumption of power by a rather mixed company of politicians, most of whom had not been trained in the public service and often had little conception of what a public servant owed to the community.' Sidney also considered that the British contributed 'originality and breadth of view'. Not that they had a monopoly of these qualities, but in his opinion 'originality is not a common quality among Indians and the outlook of most Indians is, by their education and upbringing, extremely circumscribed.'

It was a matter of no personal concern to Sidney, who left India before the transfer of power, but he greatly regretted that 'considerations of amour propre and political expediency' had led the new government of India to get rid of many capable and willing British officers, 'whose cooperation would have been a great help in smoothing over the difficulties of the transition.' He felt that the 'swapping of horses in the middle of the stream had added enormously to the dangers and difficulties of what was inevitably a time of great peril.' C. P. Rajagopalachari had had the wisdom to avoid this error when he established the first Congress government in Madras. Realising that the success of his government would depend largely on the efficiency and loyalty of his Secretariat:

> he combed the whole Presidency for the ablest men he could find and filled the secretariat with officers who might not agree with his politics, but were ready and able to give the utmost support to his administration. Many of them soon became his personal friends and I do not think that he ever regretted the trust which he imposed in the British officers of the Indian Civil Service.

Sidney never failed to be proud of having served, feeling that the 'sneers and unfair criticisms which the Service had to suffer in silence during the last years of British rule, were little more than incidents in a world-wide campaign of anti-British propaganda which displayed a cynical disregard for the truth.' He considered that:

> when the historian of the future comes to study the achievements of British rule in India in an atmosphere purified of the smoke of political warfare, he will regard with unmixed approval the devotion, courage and ability which this small body of men has consistently displayed. Drawn from all classes of society, with a preponderance of the sons of

> country parsons and professional men, they have from their earliest days assumed responsibilities which in most countries are reserved for the last years of a man's working life. This training has produced a degree of self-reliance and initiative which no other system could have engendered. That it occasionally produced a swollen head and an intolerance of control or criticism is no indictment of the system. Such symptoms of youthful exuberance generally disappeared with the passage of time and many a self-sufficient youngster mellowed into a wise and tolerant senior.

Whether or not it was morally acceptable that young people of one race should exercise executive, administrative and judicial power over people of all ages of another race:

> The young ICS man was expected, as soon as he emerged from the chrysalis stage, to give orders, make decision and enforce standards. He was under control, but at very long range and the powers which were delegated to him were extremely wide. Frequent references for orders were viewed with disapproval; and a wise indulgence was always shown to the man who, in an emergency, acted in excess of his powers, provided that he acted with reasonable prudence and foresight. He spent his early days in lonely stations, surrounded by people to whom his word was law. He was conscious of his own importance; but that very consciousness, while it may have given rise to a certain superiority of manner, also led him to put his work first and make it his paramount interest in life. He was well paid, in comparison with other civil servants, but he earned his pay by carrying out with complete integrity and devotion to duty, functions of the highest importance. He was no superman. Intellectually he was on a par with thousands of others who were content to become schoolmasters or lawyers or quill-drivers in Whitehall. The difference lay in the effects of his first five years in India; these years in the vast majority of cases developed in him powers which are allowed to atrophy in those who spend their early manhood in positions of direct subordination.

Looking back after 30 years with the ICS, Sidney's fellow Madras civil servant Henry Downing expressed his amazement at the fact that 'a young man could go out to a distant country and then be vested with authority over thousands of people of a different race and culture and this situation could be accepted and even regarded as normal'. Downing himself felt that 'unacceptable as imperial rule may seem today, I never had the feeling in India of belonging to an oppressing or exploiting class ... The Government of India which we served was an entity of its own and I believed that on the whole it governed India humanely and in the national interest.' At the same time it was obvious to him and to his contemporaries that the days of British rule were numbered and, once the war was over, it was apparent that change could not be long delayed. Although he doubted that independence would necessarily solve the problems of the Indian masses, Downing could sympathise with the feelings of educated Indians that it was 'incompatible with their self respect that authority in their country should rest in alien hands and that they should appear abroad as subordinates of foreign power when far more backward countries had their own flags and diplomatic representatives.' He realised too that 'India's political and economic problems were going to be far too complex to be handled by expatriate rulers lacking mass popular support and by the generalised skills of the district officer.' A benevolent imperial government could do much to build the infrastructure of law, administration and communications on which a modern society could be constructed, but 'the subsequent development for better or worse must be done by the people of the country itself.'[3]

In Sidney's view, in order to bring about the construction of such a modern society it was incorrect to assume that democracy (which appeared to work so well in Great Britain and America) was the only desirable system of government for India, as the evidence in support of this assumption was far from convincing. British policy had attempted to prepare the ground for democracy by 'the gradual introduction of an elaborate system of local self-government.' A complete chain of elected bodies had been established for the management of local affairs of villages, towns, taluks and districts; so long as these bodies had official chairmen and 'a leavening' of nominated official members, they worked 'tolerably well'. However, when they were made entirely elective and given power to appoint their own chairmen:

> a very rapid deterioration set in. The councils became battlefields for the local factions, the administration was stultified by corruption and the people groaned under the oppression and favouritism of their own elected representatives; so much so that it became necessary to abolish the taluk boards, to place the detailed administration of the other bodies in the hands of executive officers appointed by the government and

to stiffen up the central control over the actions of the councils by a system of surcharges and suspensions.

This experience certainly seemed to provide little support for the theory that democratic institutions on the English model were likely to succeed in the larger spheres of provincial and federal government. Sidney feared that, following the first few years of independence when both India and Pakistan had the advantage of effectively single-party governments, the arrival of vigorous opposition parties would challenge the abilities of the legislatures to maintain an adequate standard of administration 'in the heat of party warfare.'

In attempting to visualise the conclusion of the historian on the rule of the British in India, Sidney imagined that criticism would be levelled 'not for our alleged oppressiveness or for our unwillingness to surrender power to Indians, but for the timidity and conservatism of our social and economic policies, for the excessive legalism of our system of justice and our narrow and theoretical approach to the problems of education.' The British would be blamed:

> for bolstering up the medieval anachronisms of the native states, for our reluctance to tackle the social abuses connected with religious customs and institutions, for our slowness in realising that industrial development and a less pennywise attitude towards irrigation were the real cures for India's poverty, for the way in which we have confounded the rule of law with the tyranny of a sterile legalism and for the policy which has raised up an excess of clerks and lawyers instead of a sufficiency of educated merchants, technicians and manufacturers. The historian of the future will make merry over the spasmodic nature of parliament's control over Indian affairs and the a priori dogmatisms of some of our more famous secretaries of state.

However, he might well also praise the loyalty of that 'much-abused person', the district officer, who 'has struggled amidst great difficulties to carry out policies with which he was, more often than not, in complete disagreement.'

And, finally, Sidney questioned the future of the Indians at the base of the social scale, 'the mute illiterate millions who walk behind the plough and pay little regard to what happens outside the confines of their own village.' He asked, 'What is going to happen to them, now that the isolation of the village is breaking down and the stabilising force of caste is beginning to crumble? Are they to remain inarticulate? Will they forever be content to toil from dawn to dusk for a fraction of the produce of the land in order that others may have leisure to play the game of politics and revel in the sport of litigation?' In his view, such tolerance was highly unlikely and already the labour force in the towns was showing signs of political consciousness. A form of communism was recruiting many followers, and it appeared that in India, as in Europe, the future struggle would be between the affluent and the poor. It was only a matter of time before a communist leader gained the support of the agricultural worker by promising the expropriation of 'the idle landowner.' This danger might be forestalled by a bold policy of state-aided purchase of land by the cultivating tenants; but such a policy would not be popular in a legislature packed full of small land-owners. In Sidney's view, the hunger for land was 'the strongest motive for disaffection in a rack-rented farming country. When this is linked with the age-old resentment of the outcaste and untouchable who for generations have suffered the tyranny of the upper castes, forces will be let loose which no one can hold in check.'

However, despite the fact that India had difficult years ahead which would call for 'all the political wisdom and administrative ability of her best brains', the country also had 'great assets':

> a hard-working, frugal and home-loving proletariat, a middle class of considerable ability and fair educational standards and an aristocracy of intellect whose best brains are as good as any in the world. Her people love peace and have high ideals. They are not wanting in administrative capacity and legal acumen. Her soldiers are brave and tenacious. Her leaders have shown themselves capable of great spiritual heights. These are factors which will go a long way to make of India a great nation, if only she can avoid the perils of schism and seek steadfastly for that internal peace which is a real desire of the vast majority of India's millions.

Sidney ends his manuscript by declaring that he, with other British officers 'who have spent the best years of our lives working with Indians for India, will rejoice at every danger past and every step forward towards the goal of the higher *swaraj*.'

NOTES

1. THE HISTORY OF MADRAS

1. The Coromandel Coast, on the eastern side of the South Indian triangle which hangs down from the north of the subcontinent, depends on the rain from the northeast monsoon of the Bay of Bengal; the Malabar Coast on the west enjoys the more bountiful rains of the southwest monsoon from the Arabian Sea.
2. Glyn Barlow, *The Story of Madras* (London: Oxford University Press, 1921), pp. 2–3.
3. Barlow, *The Story of Madras*, p. 12.
4. The Telegu people are a Dravidian ethnic group, the majority of whom reside in what are now the states of Andra Pradesh and Telengana.
5. Barlow, *The Story of Madras*, pp. 18–19.
6. Barlow, *The Story of Madras*, pp. 13–15.
7. Major-General Robert Clive, 1st Baron Clive (also known as Clive of India) established the military and political supremacy of the East India Company in Bengal.
8. Barlow, *The Story of Madras*, pp. 28–32.
9. Elihu Yale (1649–1721) was born in Boston, Massachusetts. In 1652 the Yale family moved back to England and never returned to North America. For twenty years Yale was an employee of the East India Company and became the second governor of the settlement at Madras in 1687. Yale amassed a substantial fortune in his lifetime, largely through secret contacts with Madras merchants, contrary to the East India Company's directive. His repeated flouting of East India Company regulations and the growing embarrassment at his illegal profiteering resulted in his removal from the post of governor. Upon his return to London, Yale was contacted for funds to provide a new building in New Haven for the Collegiate School of Connecticut. He dispatched a

carton of goods which was subsequently sold by the school for £800, a substantial sum in the early eighteenth century, and in gratitude in 1718 the building was named after him.

10. Barlow, *The Story of Madras*, pp. 35, 37, 65.
11. Ibid, pp. 66, 67. In Sir Sidney's day a sum of Rs 1,50,000 per annum was spent annually in pensions for the prince and some of his relatives. He lived in a house called the Amir Mahal, which was given to him by the government.
12. Julian Spilsbury, *The Indian Mutiny* (London: Weidenfeld and Nicholson, 2007), p. 6. The soldiers in these areas were particularly irate when asked to bite off the paper cartridges, which they believed were greased with beef and pork fat, against the religious beliefs of Hindus and Muslims respectively.
13. William Pitt's India Act of 1784 established a Board of Control in England both to supervise the East India Company's affairs and to prevent the Company's shareholders from interfering in the governance of India. The presidencies of Madras, Bombay and Bengal (the three principal factory locations of the East India Company which had developed into the centres of British military and political control during the eighteenth and nineteenth centuries) were increasingly broken up into different provinces after Company powers were transferred to the Crown in 1858. Thereafter, the head of the area was styled 'Governor' rather than 'President' and became subordinate to the Governor-General in Calcutta.
14. The India Office, over-lorded by the Secretary of State, was the only civil service department devoted to the affairs of one imperial member, demonstrating the subcontinent's importance to Great Britain.
15. David Gilmour, *The Ruling Caste: Imperial Lives in the Victorian Raj* (London: John Murray, 2005), p. 90.
16. There was a distinct difference between an assistant or sub-collector and a deputy collector. The former was a member of the Indian Civil Service (Indian or British) while the latter was appointed from the ranks of the civil service of the Madras Presidency, i.e. the local service, members of which were not transferable to other provinces. Both wielded the same powers and authority, yet it was noticeable that if there was higher land within a district, it would normally be found in the division of the sub-collector, the theory being that the temperature would be more suitable for a British officer, who would work harder as a result. John Coldwell Griffiths, *Memoirs 1937–82*, Mss Eur D1111 26(a), Asian and African Studies, British Library, p. 24.
17. Gilmour, *The Ruling Caste*, pp. 90–91.
18. During the latter half of the nineteenth century Madras was devastated by two great famines, first in 1876–78 and later in 1896–97.

The population of the presidency fell from 31.2 million in 1871 to 30.8 million in 1881 as a result of the 1876–78 famine.

19. In an average year about 200 candidates competed for some forty places in the ICS, and if successful they then had to spend a year on probation, requiring them to pass a riding test, study Indian history and law and receive a grounding in the language of the province to which they had been assigned.

2. MADRAS 1913

1. W. O. Horne, *Work and Sport in the Old ICS* (London: Blackwood, 1928).
2. Giles Tillotson considers that the term Indo-Saracenic was poorly chosen, as the Islamic element in Indian buildings was not strictly Saracenic. India's Muslim conquerors were not Arabs, but Afghans and Central Asians, who drew many of their cultural ideas from Persia. However, given the nineteenth-century association of Islamic with Saracenic, the term was clear, if inexact, in its application to the architecture of the Mughals and their predecessors. G. H. R. Tillotson, T*he Tradition of Indian Architecture: Continuity, Controversy and Change since 1850* (New Haven and London: Yale University Press, 1989), p. 46. See also Tillotson, 'Orientalizing the Raj: Indo-Saracenic Fantasies' in Christopher W. London (ed), *Architecture in Victorian and Edwardian India* (Bombay: South Asia Books, 1994), pp. 15–34.
3. Gilmour, *The Ruling Caste*, pp. 57–8.
4. Philip Woodruff (Mason), *The Men Who Ruled India, Vol II The Guardians* (London: Cape, 1971), p. 116.
5. John Coldwell Griffiths, *Memoirs 1937–82*, Mss Eur D1111 26(a), AAS BL, p. 22.
6. Sir Christopher Hughes Masterman, Mss Eur C319, AAS BL, p. 2.
7. Humphrey Trevelyan, *The India We Left* (London: Macmillan, 1972), p. 139.
8. Ewing Papers, Cambridge Centre for South Asian Studies, B. W. Day, No. 26.
9. Brian Stoddart, *A People's Collector in the British Raj: Arthur Galletti* (New Delhi: Readworthy, 2011), p. 23. Also Sir Edward Blunt, *The ICS—the Indian Civil Service* (London: Faber, 1937).
10. Ewing Papers, CCSAS, B. W. Day, No. 26.
11. 61,000 soldiers, about 10,000 women and children, and some 5,000 officers commanding both the British regiments and the 120,000 Indian troops known as sepoys. Gilmour, *The Ruling Caste*, p. 11.
12. Originally the British living in India were known as Anglo-Indians

while people of British-Indian descent were called Eurasians. The terminology changed and Sidney would probably have known the latter group as Anglo-Indians.

13. A. J. Platt, *Indian Civil Service Memoir (Madras 1932–47)*, Mss Eur F180/57, AAS BL, p. 5.
14. Geoffrey Lamarque, *Memories of India 1937–47*, Mss Eur F180/54, AAS BL, p. 8.
15. Mount Road is an arterial road in Chennai, almost 400 years old and has its origins in a cart track which was used by the European employees of the East India Company to travel from the factory at Fort St George to São Tomé (now San Thome). With the construction of the Marmalong Bridge in 1724 the road began to gain prominence and in the following years became part of the city's central business district which originally covered only Georgetown. The road's proximity to Government House and the palaces of the Nawabs of Arcot resulted in the appearance of several shops selling cars and other luxury goods.
16. Hilton Brown, *Dictators Limited. A novel without incident* (London: Allen and Unwin, 1923), p. 23.
17. Sir Joseph Herbert Thompson, *Icarus Went East*, Mss Eur F226/29, AAS BL, p. 59.
18. The word 'coolie', used freely in a colonial context for an unskilled Asian labourer, is now viewed as offensive.
19. A river island created in the northern part of the city in the early nineteenth century by merging the Cooum and Elambore rivers. An equestrian statue of Sir Thomas Munro, Governor of Madras from 1814 to 1827, popularly known as 'His Stirrupless Majesty', is located on the island.
20. Reservoirs, or artificial ponds or lakes, made either by excavation or by damming.
21. Alfred Lyall, the distinguished Indian Civil Servant, nearly drowned before reaching Calcutta in 1856 for his first posting. After going ashore at the harbourless Madras, a vast wave swamped or capsized the boats returning passengers to their ship and three people died. Gilmour, *The Ruling Caste*, p. 84.
22. John Edward Maher, Mss Eur F180/55, AAS BL, p. 1.
23. Although the army presence in Madras was negligible and there was little social interaction with the ICS.
24. Geoffrey Lamarque, *Memories of India 1937–47*, Mss Eur F180/54, AAS BL, p. 8. It seems that the 'heaven-born' members of the ICS were inclined to view themselves as such. There is a memorial plaque to the service in the cloisters of Westminster Abbey, bearing the quotation from Chapter VI of the Book of Micah, 'what does the Lord

require of thee but to do justly and to love mercy?' The verse goes on, 'and to walk humbly with thy God', but a proposal to include these words was apparently turned down flatly by the chairman of the Memorial Committee, Lord Hailey, with the remark, 'Who ever saw, who ever even heard of any member of the civil service walking humbly with anyone?' Paper read to a Wimbledon society in February 1963 by Arthur Beatson Reid (ICS 1888–1965), F173/247, AAS BL.

25. Boxwallahs were small-scale travelling merchant peddlers in India, so called because of the large boxes in which they carried their merchandise. The title was later applied to Europeans involved in business activities as opposed to civil servants.
26. Members of the priestly caste.
27. William Whiteley (1831–1907) was an English entrepreneur of the late nineteenth and early twentieth centuries. He was the founder in London of the Whiteley's department store in Westbourne Grove in Bayswater.
28. Spring was the first person in Madras to own a registered automobile and Sidney recalled that, armed with registration number MC1, he was prone to 'hurtle' down the Mount Road at 18 miles an hour.
29. The area in the vicinity of the Thousand Lights mosque, one of the largest mosques in the country. It was said that 1,000 lamps were needed to illuminate the assembly hall and that the lights were provided by the Indian National Congress to mark their first visit to the city of Madras.
30. From 1899 the rupee had stabilised at one shilling and fourpence, or fifteen rupees to the pound. Gilmour, *The Ruling Caste*, p. xxi.
31. 'Madras: Clive kissed me on the mouth and eyes and brow, Wonderful kisses, so that I became Crowned above Queens—a withered beldame now, Brooding on ancient fame'. *The Song of the Cities, Collected Verse of Rudyard Kipling* (New York: Doubleday, Page & Co, 1907), p. 90.

3. VELLORE 1913–14

1. Tipu Sultan, the 'Tiger of Mysore', ruled the kingdom from 1782 to 1799. In the Third Anglo-Mysore War he was forced into a humiliating treaty, losing a number of previously conquered territories, including Malabar and Mangalore. In the Fourth Anglo-Mysore War, the combined forces of the Company and the Nizam of Hyderabad defeated Tipu and he was killed on 4 May 1799 while defending his fort of Srirangapatna.
2. For a full account of the Vellore mutiny, see Ferdinand Mount, *The Tears of the Rajas* (London: Simon and Schuster, 2015), pp. 41–73.
3. The system of temporary land settlement in India was introduced in

1892 with a view to fixing land revenue for a period, subject to change at the time of the next settlement. Ordinarily, the interval between two settlements was 25 to 30 years. Land settlement work involved a continually repetitive process of surveying and measuring plots, assessing their quality, and recording landed rights, and constituted a large proportion of the work of Indian Civil Service officers working for the government.

4. The Theosophical Society, founded in New York City in 1875, incorporated aspects of Buddhism and Brahmanism, especially the belief in reincarnation and spiritual evolution. One of the founders of the society, Helena Blavatsky, moved to India and established the international headquarters in 1882 at Adyar in Madras. The theosophy movement was linked to Indian nationalism via Annie Besant, a prominent British women's rights activist, writer and orator, who met Blavatsky in 1890 and became herself a highly successful lecturer in theosophy and President of the Theosophical Society in 1907. Besant became involved in politics in India, joining the Indian National Congress and helping to launch the Home Rule League in 1916 to campaign for democracy in India and dominion status within the Empire.
5. H. J. Downing, Mss Eur F180/50, AAS BL, p. 12.
6. Bradfield Papers, CCSAS, *Unimportant Story*, p. 34.
7. See Chapter 6 re: the Montagu Chelmsford reforms.
8. In the early nineteenth century the kingdom of Travancore, located at the southern tip of the Indian subcontinent (covering most of modern-day central and southern Kerala), became a princely state of the British Empire and the king was accorded a 19-gun salute. It became highly prosperous, with a Communist Party functioning under democratic conditions, producing major achievements in education, political administration, public work and social reforms.
9. The cavalry sport of removing wooden tent pegs from the ground from the back of a galloping horse, using a sword or lance.
10. *The Administrative Origins of the Friends of Vellore*, Mss Eur C545, AAS BL, p. 3.
11. John Edward Maher, Mss Eur F180/55, AAS BL, p. 1.

4. GUDUR 1916–17

1. Sir Robert Clegg was educated at Manchester Grammar School and Balliol, Oxford, and entered the Indian Civil Service in 1882. He served in Madras as Assistant Collector and Magistrate; Special Assistant Agent to the Governor (Godaveri); Sub-Collector and Joint Magistrate; Collector and District Magistrate; and, at the end of his Indian career,

First Member of the Board of Revenue, Madras and Additional Member of the Council of the Governor. He was knighted in the 1917 New Year's Honours.

2. H. J. Downing, Mss Eur F180/50, AAS BL, p. 11.
3. The Vijayanagara Empire was based in South India in the Deccan Plateau region. It was established in 1336 and rose to prominence as a culmination of efforts by southern Hindu states to ward off Islamic invasions. The empire lasted until 1646, although its power declined after a major military defeat in 1565 by the Deccan sultanates.
4. For most of the sixteenth and seventeenth centuries Europeans on the Coromandel Coast were extensively involved in the trading, brokering and shipment of slaves from India to Ceylon and the West Indies. Between 1621 and 1665 alone, 131 Dutch ships were used to transport 38,441 Indian slaves obtained mostly from Pulicat brokers. Domestic slavery was officially recognised by the British at Madras and run mainly by the Dutch at Pulicat.
5. Sriharikota today houses the Satish Dhawan Space Centre, one of the two satellite launch centres in India used by the Indian Space Research Organisation.
6. Casuarina, although profitable and quick growing, is dangerous when dry and old. The army used much of this timber for temporary huts in 1944–45 in preparation for the invasion of Malaya, and a large shed housing West African troops in Madras crumpled up in the middle of the night with serious results.
7. Ewing Papers, CCSAS, B. W. Day, No. 26.
8. Geoffrey Lamarque, *Memories of India 1937–47*, Mss Eur F180/54, AAS BL, p. 12.
9. In 1947 Venkatagiri became part of the newly independent Indian Republic and the kingdom was dissolved. The Velugoti family still commands great respect and influence in the region, and the thirty-second Raja of Venkatagiri died in 2010.
10. A loose long-sleeved outer silk or cotton robe. Historically, richly adorned khilats were used as honorific rewards, but by the nineteenth century in British India the word 'khilat' had come to mean any gift of money or goods awarded by the government of India in return for service from tributary princes and tribal leaders.
11. Sir Henry Cotton had a long career in the Indian Civil Service, during which he was sympathetic to Indian nationalism. In 1904, he served as president of the Indian National Congress, one of the few non-Indians in that role. As president he led the opposition to Curzon's invasion of Tibet and partition of Bengal. See Sir Henry Cotton, *Indian and Home Memories* (London: T. Fisher Unwin, 1911).

12. Under the Raj the town of Bobbili was within the Vizagapatam district of Madras, and the title of maharaja was conferred on the raja in 1900. The town was famous for the attack on the fort by the French under Bussy in 1756. When Bussy entered the fort, he found every man of the garrison dead or mortally wounded. During the attack, in order to save the women and children from violation by the enemy, the living quarters of the fort were set alight and those who attempted to escape were stabbed. Ramakrishna Ranga Rao, the son of Venkata Sweta Chalapati, the Maharaja of Bobbili who officiated at the installation of the Raja of Venkatagiri, served as the Chief Minister of Madras during the 1930s and was 'blatantly pro-British and disliked the idea of an independent India ... especially if the new India was to be governed by Brahmans as he feared'. Masterman Papers, CCSAS, 'Letter to Miss Thatcher', 8 May 1974. In the Second World War a large air force station was constructed in his territory, being completed just as the war was drawing to a close and never occupied.
13. 'Mansabdar' literally means rank-holder. Under the Mansabdari system of the Mughal Empire, introduced by Akbar in 1571 AD, every civil and military officer was given a mansab, and different numbers which could be divided by ten were used for ranking purposes. Those who commanded 1,000 or below were called Amir. Those who commanded above 1,000 were called Amir-al Kabir (Great Amir) and some Great Amirs who commanded above 5,000 were given the title of Amir-al Umara (Amir of Amirs).
14. Velama or Velama Doralu is a social group found mainly today in Andhra Pradesh. The historical military exploits of Velamas form an important part of Telegu tradition, history and folklore.
15. Most notably, in the nineteenth century, Sir Henry Marion Durand (1812–71), Lieutenant-Governor of the Punjab, who while making a tour of his province visited the town of Tank. His howdah was crushed against the ceiling of a gateway and he was thrown to the ground, dying the following day.
16. Over 460,000 of the Yanadi tribe still live in the southeastern Indian state of Andhra Pradesh. A significant number used to be concentrated on Sriharikota Island, mentioned earlier in the chapter, where they were repeatedly visited by anthropologists. In 1970–71 the entire population of the island was removed so that India could develop its space rocket launching facility. Over half the Yanadis still live in the Nellore district, but they also live in rural areas and the margins of towns such as Chittoor, Kadapa and Visakhapatnam. While many are now labourers, a 1995 sample of 320 people showed that nearly one third still chose to hunt, gather, fish, trap and dig roots for their subsistence.

17. The colonial debate about hook-swinging existed from the 1830s onwards and was part of the larger discourse about religious reform in colonial India, triggered by the prohibition of sati in 1829 as a symbol of the backwardness of Indian civilisation. Despite the policy of non-interference in religious affairs which was adopted after the 1857 Mutiny, measures were put in place to suppress the practice of hook-swinging, although an outright ban was avoided. Instead the colonial administration concentrated on exerting its influence over local elites so that they would renounce their support for the hook-swinging festivals. The elimination of the practice through discouragement was only partly successful and the matter was taken up by the House of Commons, resulting in the 1894 ban. See Nicholas B. Dirks, 'The Policing of Tradition: Colonialism and Anthropology in Southern India', *Comparative Studies in Society and History*, Vol. 39, No. 1, January 1977, pp. 182–212; and Ulrike Schroder, 'Hook-Swinging in South India: Negotiating the Subaltern Space within a Colonial Society', in *Negotiating Rites*, eds Ute Husken and Frank Neubert (New York: Oxford University Press, 2012), pp. 215–36.
18. A kedda is a structure built of very strong poles in the shape of a 'V' into which elephants are driven, trapping the animals with a gate lowered behind them.
19. Sir Herbert Thompson, *Icarus Went East*, Mss Eur F226/29, AAS BL, p. 71.

5. THE SECRETARIAT 1918–19

1. Becoming a Member was a career aspiration for most ICS officers due to the fact that salaries, prestige and influence were significant.
2. Geoffrey Lamarque, *Memories of India 1937–47*, Mss Eur F180/54, AAS BL, p. 13.
3. Yvonne Fitzroy (1891–1971), a privileged socialite and actress, served on the battlefields of Russia and Romania between 1916 and 1917 as a nursing orderly with the Scottish Women's Hospitals.
4. Yvonne Fitzroy, Mss Eur E312/10–11a, AAS BL, diary entry 31 May 1926.
5. Gently undulating hills in the proximity of Ootacamund, often compared with the Yorkshire Dales.
6. Trevelyan, *The India We Left*, pp. 120–21.
7. Ewing Papers, CCSAS, B. W. Day, No. 26.
8. Cochin was a late medieval Hindu kingdom and subsequently a princely state on the Malabar Coast, the narrow coastal plain between the Western Ghats range and the Arabian sea.

9. The need for a modern port on the southern part of the west coast of India was identified first by Lord Willingdon during his governorship of Madras province. In 1920 Willingdon appointed Sir Robert Bristow, a leading British harbour engineer with extensive experience in the maintenance of the Suez Canal, to oversee the project. By relocating a formidable ridge of heavy and densely packed sand, Willingdon Island was artificially created to house Cochin Port and other trade-related establishments.

6. TWO INTERLUDES 1920–21

1. The Marquess of Willingdon (1866–1941) was a British Liberal politician and administrator who served as Governor-General of Canada (1926–31) and Viceroy of India (1931–36). Upon returning to England at the end of his tenure as Governor of Madras, Willingdon was elevated to the status of viscount in June 1924.
2. The Moplah Rebellion began as a reaction by Mappila Muslims against a heavy-handed British crackdown on the pan-Islamic Khilafat movement, which wanted the British government to maintain the Ottoman emperor's status as caliph. The Mappilas attacked and took control of police stations, British government offices, courts and government treasuries, and the rebellion, which began as a fight against the British, ended up as a large-scale massacre and persecution of Hindus. For six months from August 1921, the rebellion extended over 2,000 square miles of the South Malabar region of the Madras Presidency. An estimated 10,000 people lost their lives and many Hindus were forcibly converted.
3. Barbara Groseclose, *British Sculpture and the Company Raj* (Delaware: University of Delaware Press, 1995), p. 34. The Banqueting Hall is now known as Rajaji Hall and used for public social functions.
4. Known as Mauve Mary, because of her penchant for purple.
5. Sir Herbert Thompson, *Icarus Went East*, Mss Eur F226/29, AAS BL, p. 61. Lord Willingdon also tried to get Indians admitted to British clubs in Bombay and Madras, but not even the initiative of a popular governor (not otherwise suspected of liberal tendencies) could change old practices, and he was only able to break new ground by founding new clubs in Delhi and Bombay. Trevelyan, *The India We Left*, pp. 112–13.
6. The title 'Seven Pagodas' refers to a myth that has circulated for over twelve centuries. Mahabalipuram's Shore Temple, built in the eighth century, stands on the shore of the Bay of Bengal and it is said that six other temples once stood with it. Before the tsunami of 26 December

2004, evidence for the existence of these temples was largely anecdotal. However, when the ocean water of Mahabalipuram's coast receded approximately 500 metres from the beach, tourists and residents who witnessed the event recalled seeing a long, straight row of rocks which, when the water rushed back, were covered again. Although this sighting does not necessarily correspond to the seven pagodas of myth, it does indicate that a large complex of temples did exist in that part of the coast and has stimulated archaeological research.

7. The title of Duke of Connaught and Strathearn was granted by Queen Victoria to her third son, Prince Arthur. He was appointed as Governor-General of Canada in 1911 by his nephew, King George V, and occupied the post until 1916.

7. MADANAPALLE 1921–24

1. H. H. Carleston, *Recollections of South India 1927–47*, Mss Eur F180/49a, AAS BL, p. 23.
2. R. C. C. Hunt considered that tahsildars were the backbone of the administrative system in Madras and, in most cases 'men of intelligence, initiative and often considerable personal courage'. Hunt Papers, CCSAS, *Innocents in India*, p. 20.
3. Masterman Papers, CCSAS, Answers to questionnaire set out by Dr. Christopher Bayly, July 1973.
4. Alan Westlake, *A Kaleidoscope for Krishnan*, Mss Eur C353, AAS BL, pp. 7–8.
5. Nancy Dearmer, Mss Eur C326, AAS BL, Letter dated 9 Dec. 1916.
6. Alan Westlake, *A Kaleidoscope for Krishnan*, Mss Eur C353, AAS BL, pp. 7–8. The historian Nicholas Dirks has argued that before colonialism caste affiliation was quite loose, but the British constructed a significantly more rigid hierarchy than had existed previously, with some castes being criminalised and others being given preferential treatment. Nicholas Dirks, *Castes of Mind; Colonialism and the Making of New India* (Princeton: Princeton University Press, 2001), p. 181; and *The Scandal of Empire: India and the Creation of Imperial Britain* (Cambridge: Harvard University Press, 2006), p. 27.
7. Geoffrey Lamarque, *Memories of India 1937–47*, Mss Eur F180/54, AAS BL, p. 18.
8. His formidable wife, Margaret, who was an accomplished concert pianist and social activist with a strong interest in women's rights, was appointed as British India's first woman magistrate then, bizarrely, went to prison herself for supporting Gandhi in the early 1930s.
9. During 1919 the Nobel laureate Rabindranath Tagore accepted an

invitation from Cousins to spend a few days at the theosophical college in Madanapalle where Tagore sang his composition 'Jana Gana Mana' in Bengali. When the college authorities selected it as their prayer song, Tagore translated the song into English, entitled 'The Morning Song of India', after which it was adopted by the Congress and the first stanza subsequently became the national anthem of India.

10. H. J. Downing, Mss Eur F180/50, AAS BL, p. 12–13.
11. Sir Herbert Thompson, *Icarus Went East*, Mss Eur F226/29, AAS BL, p. 70.
12. A taluk is an administrative area for taxation purposes, typically comprising a number of villages. In British India an average district had 6–8 taluks.
13. Sidney William Cecil Dunlop, Mss Eur F180/51, AAS BL, pp. 5, 10.
14. The Gurrumkonda fort was constructed 500 years ago under the Vijayanagara kingdom. Originally of mud and rock, the Golconda sultans later strengthened the fortifications with substantial solid rock walls. The fort was later taken over by the Marathas, the Cuddapah Nawabs, the Mysorean rulers Hyder Ali and Tipu Sultan, and eventually the British.
15. Major-General Sir Thomas Munro (1761–1827) was a Scottish soldier and colonial administrator, appointed governor of Madras in 1820, where he introduced systems of revenue assessment and general administration which survived into the twentieth century, in particular the ryotwari system, whereby the land revenue was imposed directly on the ryots (individual cultivators) who worked the land, at times causing them great hardship.
16. The Deccan plateau is located between the ranges of the Western and Eastern Ghats and makes up most of the southern part of the subcontinent.
17. The Arakan Campaign of 1942–43 was the first tentative Allied attack into Burma following the Japanese conquest of the country earlier in 1942.
18. Initially warriors, Reddys later became feudal overlords and peasant proprietors, who were appointed by the British as zamindars and tax collectors. They were also enlisted into the British army.

8. POLITICAL WARFARE: GODAVERI 1921

1. However, following a number of violent outbreaks and the murder of 22 or 23 police officers at Chauri Chaura in the United Provinces in February 1922, Gandhi himself called off the movement.
2. The Northern Circars (or provincial areas) made up a narrow strip of

territory lying along the western side of the Bay of Bengal. The British annexation of the Northern Circars deprived the princely state of Hyderabad of the considerable coastline it formerly possessed, leaving it landlocked and bounded on all sides by British India.

3. As a result of the non-cooperation movement the Prince of Wales processed through streets that were empty and silent as the boycott took effect.
4. A good description of the area is the entry on Godaveri by Arthur Galletti in *The Imperial Gazetteer of India, Madras Vol. I* (Calcutta: Government of India Press, 1908), pp. 268–98.
5. Rajamundry is acclaimed as the birthplace of the Telegu language, its grammar and script evolving from the work of the city-born poet, Nannayya, who translated the Sanskrit version of the *Mahabharata* into Telegu. The city acted as a base for many key leaders of the Indian independence movement between 1885 and 1905.
6. Later Sir Geoffrey Bracken KCIE, Chief Secretary to the Government of Madras.
7. The Dowleishwaram Barrage is an irrigation structure built on the lower stretch of the Godavari river before it empties into the Bay of Bengal. It was built by the British irrigation engineer Sir Arthur Thomas Cotton, whose many projects averted famines and stimulated the economy of southern India. The barrage is 3.5 km long, with 175 crest gates to allow flood passage, and its construction was completed in 1850.
8. The Sri Lakshmi Narasimha Swamy temple constructed in the eighteenth century.
9. Stoddart, *A People's Collector in the British Raj*, p. 38.
10. Ibid, p. 45.
11. See Arudra Burra, 'The ICS and the nationalist movement: neutrality, politics and continuity', *Commonwealth and Comparative Politics*, Vol. 48, No. 4, November 2010, p. 407.
12. One lakh equals one hundred thousand, written as 1,00,000 in the Indian convention of digit grouping.
13. It was reported that British district officers in Guntur could not get their clothes washed, their hair cut, buy food, find accommodation when away from home, or receive service in post offices. Protest flags, chants and posters supporting non-cooperation confronted them, cars were stoned and in some areas there was danger of physical assault. As a result, British troops en route to Lahore were briefly diverted to make an appearance in what were deemed to be the most disaffected villages. Stoddart, *A People's Collector in the British Raj*, p. 150.

9. THE BOARD 1924

1. See C. T. Buckland, *Sketches of Social Life in India* (London: W. H. Allan, 1884), pp. 131–3.
2. In the early 1670s a garden space was carved out of the Guindy Forest and a residence called Guindy Lodge was built by Governor William Langhorne. The remainder of the forest area was owned by a British citizen, Gilbert Rodericks, from whom it was purchased by the government in 1821, and the original area of 505 hectares was established as a reserve in 1910.
3. When the kingdom of the of Carnatic was abolished in 1855 as a result of the British adoption of the Doctrine of Lapse (allowing the annexation of a princely state if the ruler was manifestly incompetent or died without a male heir), the Chepauk Palace was brought to auction to pay off the Nawab of Arcot's debts and was eventually purchased by the Madras government (see Chapter 1). In 1871 Robert Chisholm built a new records office and a revenue board building in the Indo-Saracenic style of architecture.
4. South Kanara, a coastal area on the west flank of the Madras Presidency, was annexed by the British East India Company following the defeat of Tipu Sultan in the Forth Mysore War of 1799.
5. The princely state of Coorg on the eastern slopes of the Western Ghats was annexed in 1834 by the Madras Presidency, and established as Coorg district following the accusation that the ruler, Chikka Vira Raja, was conspiring against the British.
6. Later Diwan Bahadur Appadurai Pillai, Companion of the Order of the Indian Empire.
7. Stoddart, *A People's Collector in the British Raj*, p. 43.
8. From the 1920s there was a history of attempts at church union among the churches of South India, involving negotiations between the Anglican church, the South India United church and the South India Provincial Synod of the Wesleyan Methodist church. It took about twenty years to reach an agreement, and the Church of South India was inaugurated on 27 September 1947.
9. In 1901 Bellary was the seventh largest city in the Madras Presidency and one of the chief military stations in South India, garrisoned by British and native Indian troops. The industries in the city included a small distillery and two steam cotton-presses.
10. Kollengode was a division of the Palakkhad region of the Malabar District of the Madras Presidency. Along with other rulers of the Malabar area, the rajas of Kollengode ceded their right to rule to the British around 1792 and thereafter became a large landowning fam-

ily. The raja in Sidney's time was nominated to the Madras Legislative Council in 1906.

11. Ewing Papers, CCSAS, Ann Ewing, p. 5.

10. BELOW THE LIGHTHOUSE 1925

1. The High Court building, a fine example of Indo-Saracenic architecture, was built in 1892 under the guidance of the renowned architect Henry Irwin. It was damaged in the shelling of Madras by the SMS Emden on 22 September 1914. There are several features of architectural interest in the building, including the painted ceilings and the stained glass doors. It was reported in 2015 that the old lighthouse of the city, which functioned from the tallest dome of the High Court and below which Sidney worked, had been poorly maintained and was in disrepair.
2. Spencer's son, Bernard, who was a fellow poet of W. H. Auden, Stephen Spender and Louis MacNeice, recalled little of imperial India, having been sent back to England at the age of eighteen months and, in his own words, 'farmed-out to the families of rectors and vicars'. Adrian Caesar, *Dividing Lines: Poetry, Class and Ideology in the 1930s* (New York: Manchester University Press, 1991), p. 123.
3. A firman at the constitutional level was a royal mandate or decree issued by a ruler in certain historical Islamic contexts, such as the Ottoman Empire, the Mughal Empire, the state of Hyderabad and Iran under the shah.
4. Sir Theodore James Tasker (1884–1981) was in the Madras ICS from 1908 to 1944, and seconded to the government of the nizam of Hyderabad from 1927 to 1942. See Tasker Papers, Mss Eur D798, AAS BL.
5. A study of 1954 stated that almost two thirds of the Malabar Hindus were members of castes 'polluted' by birth or occupation, and high among these and larger than any other Hindu caste (about 35 per cent of the total) were the matrilineal Tiyyans of North Malabar and the patrilineal Tiyyans of South Malabar and Cochin. Some were small tenant cultivators and many were labourers. Eric J. Miller, 'Caste and Territory in Malabar', *American Anthropologist*, Vol. 56, 1954.
6. V. V. Srinivasa Iyengar, born on 19 March 1871, was enrolled as an advocate in 1898 and had 56 years of practice at the Bar, editing the *Law Weekly* in Madras from 1936 to 1954.
7. Sir Chettur Sankaran Nair prided himself upon speaking his mind to Europeans. When he berated Sir Michael O'Dwyer for his part in the Jallianwala Bagh affair in a book entitled *Gandhi and Anarchy*, 'O'Dwyer

sued for libel and the case was heard in 1924 in London. Sankaran Nair was found guilty and O'Dwyer awarded £500 damages and costs. *The Hindu* newspaper at the time thundered, "The case has only served to demonstrate once again that when there is the lightest touch of politics involved for an Indian, justice cannot be expected in an English court and from an English jury".' S. Muthiah, 'Madras Miscellany', *The Hindu*, 6 Feb. 2012, available at https://www.thehindu.com/features/metroplus/madras-miscellany/article2860453.ece.

8. Diwan Bahadur Sir Mannath Krishnan Nair KCIE (1870–1938) was a politician of the Indian National Congress, and later the Justice Party, who served as a member of the Madras Legislative Council before joining the executive council of the governor of Madras. He also served as the diwan of the princely state of Travancore in southwest India from 1914 to 1920.
9. The Administrator-General's Department protected the interests of minors, beneficiaries and creditors of estates.
10. Sir d'Arcy retired prematurely from the Madras High Court for reasons of health, but was later appointed Chief Justice of Mysore.
11. The Guindy Race Course was set up in Madras in 1777. It is the oldest racecourse in India and hosts events in the winter season. The course was brought to a temporary halt by World War I until Lord Willingdon revived it in 1919. In 1920 a stand was constructed with funds provided by the Maharajas of Bobbili and Venkatagiri.
12. S. Varadachari's grandson remembered his grandparents' 'huge' house in Mylapore along the banks of the Buckingham Canal where he watched sailing boats steered by men with long poles to gain momentum.
13. Norton was elected to the Imperial Legislative Council in India in 1894 but was forced to resign within a month due to an adultery suit against him.
14. Bradlaugh, the Member for Northampton, was the first atheist to become an MP and his act of 1888 established the legal right to affirm the Parliamentary oath rather than swearing the oath on the Bible. He was unofficially known as the MP for India due to his support of Indian self-government.
15. On the night of 15 October 1919 at Newington House, a school which educated the sons of petty rajas and zamindars of the presidency, de la Haye was shot dead in his bed with a 12-bore gun. Various motives were assigned to the murder. The much circulated theory was that, with Clement preoccupied with cricket, his young wife could well have sought entertainment elsewhere and seduced some of the boys. In addition, according to eyewitnesses, the boys in

the school were frequently offended by de la Haye's racist remarks. Eventually the main suspect was acquitted and the case remained unsolved.

16. A guardian ad litem is appointed to prosecute or defend a suit on behalf of a party who is legally incapable of doing so, such as an infant or an insane person.

11. CHINGLEPUT 1926–28

1. The area of Chingleput was annexed by the Mughals in 1687 and was later conquered by the Nawab of the Carnatic, who ceded it to the East India Company in 1763. It was one of the sites of the Carnatic Wars and was from time to time under the control of Tipu Sultan during the final years of the eighteenth century. In 1801 the Nawab of the Carnatic relinquished complete sovereignty over the region to the Company.
2. Jiddu Krishnamurti was 'discovered' on the private beach attached to the headquarters of the Theosophical Society at Adyar. The boy was groomed extensively for his expected role as the future 'World Teacher' following in the footsteps of Moses, Buddha, Zoroaster, Jesus Christ and Mohammed. During the late 1920s, Krishnamurti renounced this role, disassociated himself from the Society and its doctrines, and over the next six decades became known as an authoritative speaker on philosophical and religious subjects.
3. Leadbeater was originally a priest in the Church of England whose interest in spiritualism resulted in his joining the Theosophical Society, where he became an associate of its leader, Annie Besant, and a high-ranking officer of the society, from which he resigned in 1906 under charges of misconduct. His prolific writings include works on clairvoyance, the sacraments and Christian esotericism.
4. Under the British, the city of Tirupati was administered under the North Arcot district of the Madras Presidency. It is one of the most sacred Hindu pilgrimage sites due to its temple complex, including the Tirumala Venkateswara Temple, which is believed to be the most-visited holy place in the world. In 2016 it was reported that 27.3 million pilgrims visited the temple.
5. The Kalahasti estate was one of the ancient territories belonging to an aristocratic landowner, or zamindar, in the presidency and was distributed among the three districts of Nellore, Chittoor and Chingleput. In 1915 it was said to be heavily encumbered and for some time under the management of the Court of Wards.
6. Courts of Judicial Magistrate of First Class are at the second-lowest level of the Criminal Court structure in India. The ranking consists of

the Supreme Court at the head, followed by the High Courts, the District Courts, Judicial Magistrate of First Class and Judicial Magistrate of Second Class.

7. The District Munsiff Court is the court of the lowest order handling civil matters in India.
8. Katherine Mayo was born in Ridgway, Pennsylvania, in 1867. Her polemical book *Mother India* (1927) alluded to the treatment of India's women, the Dalits (members of the 'untouchable' caste), animals, dirt and the character of India's nationalist politicians. Mayo singled out the allegedly rampant sexuality of Indian males to be at the core of all problems, leading to masturbation, rape, homosexuality, prostitution, venereal diseases and, most importantly, to too early sexual intercourse and premature maternity. Critics of Mayo accused her of being racist, pro-imperialist, and Indophobic, but British Indian authorities supported her claims as a countermeasure to growing sympathies for the Indian independence movement.

12. SCOUTING

1. Vice-Admiral Bertram S. Thesiger was Commander-in-Chief of the East Indies Station, a squadron of the Royal Navy which covered the Indian Ocean (excluding the waters around the Dutch East Indies, South Africa and Australia, but including the Persian Gulf and Red Sea), from 1927 to 1929.
2. The kingdom of Pudukkottai was founded in about 1680. One of the staunch allies of the East India Company in the Carnatic and Anglo-Mysore Wars, the kingdom was brought under Company protection in 1800 and placed under the control of the Madras Presidency.
3. One of the most important events that led to temple entry was the satyagraha (non-violent resistance movement) which took place in the town of Vaikom in the princely state of Travancore in the southwest of the Madras Presidency in 1924 and received national attention when Mahatma Gandhi visited Vaikom to meet the leaders of the movement. Gandhi also met the regent maharani of Travancore and the twelve-year-old minor Maharaja Sree Chithira Thirunal, who throughout his reign proved to be highly supportive of social equality and religious tolerance. As a result, the roads to the Vaikom Madadeva temple were opened for the use of Dalits (untouchables) and in 1936 the Temple Entry Proclamation abolished the ban preventing low castes from entering Hindu temples in Travancore.

13. MADURA 1929–33

1. Masterman Papers, CCSAS, Letter to Miss Thatcher, 8 May 1974.
2. Chakravarti Rajagopalachari was an Indian politician, independence activist, lawyer, writer and statesman. When the Indian National Congress came to power in the Madras Presidency in the elections of 1937, he served as premier but resigned in 1940 due to Britain's declaration of war on Germany. Rajagopalachari served as Governor-General of India from June 1948 until January 1950 and was not only the last Governor-General of India but also the only Indian national ever to hold the office.
3. According to the 2011 census, the city had a population of 1,017,865.
4. The temple is dedicated to Meenakshi (or Parvati), the Hindu goddess of love, fertility and devotion, and her consort, Shiva. The present structure was built between 1623 and 1655, housing 14 gopurams (gateway towers) ranging from 45 to 50m in height and contains an estimated 33,000 sculptures. The annual 10-day Meenakshi Tirukalyanam festival in April celebrates the wedding of the divine couple and currently attracts over 1 million visitors.
5. Geoffrey Lamarque, *Memories of India 1937–47*, F180/54, AAS BL, p. 10.
6. Yvonne Fitzroy, Mss Eur E312/10–11a, AAS BL, diary entry July 25 1926.
7. The Naicks ruled the former Madura kingdom from 1545 to the 1740s, and Tirumal Naick (1623–59) was one of their greatest kings. During the seventeenth century the kingdom accommodated Portuguese, Dutch and other European traders, missionaries and visiting travellers.
8. See Sir Philip Hutchins, *An Indian Career, 1858–1908* (private publication, 1927); and Gilmour, *The Ruling Caste*, p. 276.
9. The Ancient Monuments Preservation Act 1904 was passed by the Indian government under the viceroyalty of Lord Curzon to provide for the preservation of ancient monuments (such as the Taj Mahal), for the exercise of control over traffic in antiquities and over-excavation in some places, and for the protection and acquisition in certain cases of ancient monuments and objects of archaeological, historical or artistic interest.
10. The estate of Ramnad was one of the largest and most populous zamindari holdings in the Madras Presidency.
11. The Mariamman Teppakulam, built by Tirumal Naick in 1645 and connected to the river Vaigai through underground channels.
12. A mantapam in Indian architecture is a pillared outdoor hall or pavilion for public rituals.

13. Humphrey Trevelyan has a less happy account of the story. In his version, the god Alagar was on his way to visit Meenakshi in the great Madura temple and, arriving at the river, learnt to his fury and dismay that the Brahmins had married her to Shiva. He refused to go further and stayed for a few days in the dry riverbed before returning to the hills. To Trevelyan, the ceremony could be seen as reflecting the impact of Aryan Brahminism on the Dravidian religions of the south. Trevelyan, *The India We Left*, pp. 147–8.
14. Trevelyan, *The India We Left*, p. 150.
15. The town of Salem is situated about 200 miles southwest of Madras city. It was occupied by Robert Clive, remaining a military station until 1861.
16. The first steps towards self-government in British India were taken in the late nineteenth century with the appointment of Indian counsellors to advise the British viceroy, and the establishment of provincial councils with Indian members; the British subsequently widened participation in legislative councils with the Indian Councils Act of 1892. Municipal Corporations and District Boards were created for local administration, which included elected Indian members.
17. Although equally at home with the Brahmin and the Catholic priest, Ffoulkes admitted to 'finding the English and American missionary trying'. Yvonne Fitzroy, Mss Eur E312/10–11a, AAS BL, diary entry 19 July 1926.
18. Humphrey Trevelyan recalled how Ffoulkes played a significant part in the Chittrai festival, owning one of the pavilions on the festival path. He invited Trevelyan to 'meet' the god Alagar, 'a little figure riding a horse, with ruby and gold stirrups … and a ruby and gold belt given by Ffoulkes'. Trevelyan, *The India We Left*, p. 147.

14. SOME CRIMINALS

1. The Palni Hills are an eastward extension of the Western Ghats range.
2. The Maravar, with the Kallar and Akamudayar, are three related castes of southern India which constitute the Mukkulathor social group. Although their locations and heritages are wholly separate, they share a common myth of origin (being the offspring of the god Indra and a celestial woman) and claim to have been members of various ancient South Indian dynasties.

15. THIEVES, USURERS AND SNAKE-CATCHERS

1. The state of Pudokkottai was bounded by Trichinopoly district to the west, Tanjore district to the east and southeast, and Madura district to

the south. Ruled by the Tondaiman dynasty until just after independence in 1948, it was entitled to a seventeen-gun salute.

2. Geoffrey Lamarque, *Memories of India 1937–47*, Mss Eur F180/54, AAS BL, p. 15.
3. Yvonne Fitzroy, Mss Eur E312/10–11a, AAS BL, diary entry 27 July 1926.
4. The rivalry between French and British interests in southern India gave Robert Clive the opportunity for fame and fortune. In 1751 he offered to lead an expedition to relieve Trichinopoly where Mohammed Ali, the British candidate for Nawab of Arcot, was besieged by Chanda Sahib, the French candidate. With only 200 European and 300 Indian troops, Clive seized Arcot, Chanda Sahib's capital, thereby diverting 10,000 of Chanda Sahib's men from Trichinopoly. Clive withstood a fifty-day siege in Arcot and, when he received reinforcements, began guerrilla warfare against the French. The siege of Trichinopoly was finally lifted and a truce in 1754 recognised Mohammed Ali as nawab. This was confirmed by the Treaty of Paris in 1763, and in 1765 the Mughal emperor recognised British hegemony in southern India.
5. Yvonne Fitzroy recalled a 'delicious' party given by Bertie Ffoulkes where Kallar Boy Scouts and Girl Guides performed against a background of tall palms, declaring that they delivered 'as spirited a piece of comedy as I have seen on any stage'. Yvonne Fitzroy, Mss Eur E312/10–11a, AAS BL, diary entry 26 July 1926.
6. Yvonne Fitzroy, Mss Eur E312/10–11a, AAS BL, diary entry 27 July 1926.
7. The Nagarathar or Nattukottai Chettiar Tamil community follows the religious traditions of Hinduism that focus on the deity Shiva. The Brahmins consider the community as a Vaishya (mercantile) caste. Historically itinerant, they claim Chettinad as their traditional home, consisting of adjacent parts of the ancient states of Pudukkottai, Ramnad and Sivigangai. In the nineteenth century some members of the community wielded considerable influence in the affairs of zamindars, as landowners increasingly needed to borrow money in order to fight legal battles designed to retain their property and powers.

16. KODAIKANAL

1. Ghat roads are access routes into the mountainous Western and Eastern Ghats mountain ranges to connect to hill stations.
2. The Cauvery is one of the major rivers in South India, flowing from its source in the Western Ghats through a series of great falls in the Eastern Ghats before emptying into the Bay of Bengal. The river is cel-

ebrated for its scenery and sanctity in Tamil literature, and its entire course is considered holy ground. It was said that after various ineffective attempts to build a bridge over the turbulent water, a local maharaja dreamt that the god Shiva had shown him a curvaceous snake and told him to copy it. He did so, and 'the bridge, looking like a 400 yard corkscrew, survived the annual floods of the two monsoons for more than a century'. Below the bridge, the Cauvery cascades down the famous Sivasamudrum falls, 250 feet high. In the 1890s the administrators of Mysore state trapped the flow with a hydro-electric dam to power not only Mysore's greatest source of wealth, the Kolar gold fields, but also the cities of Bangalore and Mysore. Sir Herbert Thompson, *Icarus Went East*, Mss Eur F226/29, AAS BL, p. 74.

3. Formed by the northern bifurcation of the Cauvery.
4. Yvonne Fitzroy had a less convincing picture of the Raja of Ramnad, declaring that he was 'almost bankrupt, quite unscrupulous' but nevertheless enjoyed a fine dinner in his 'delightful house overlooking the Teppakulam tank'. Yvonne Fitzroy, Mss Eur E312/10–11a, AAS BL, diary entry 26 July 1926.
5. Chief Sec. Govt. Madras to Sec. GoI, FD, 6 August 1897, R/2/892/271, AAS BL. See Caroline Keen, *Princely India and the British: Political Development and the Operation of Empire* (London: I. B. Tauris, 2012), pp. 92–3. Martanda Bhairava Tondaiman's liking for European culture and manners resulted in his marriage to an Australian socialite and giving up his claim to the throne of Pudukkottai in 1921.
6. Geoffrey Lamarque, *Memories of India 1937–47*, Mss Eur F180/54, AAS BL, p. 15. The maharaja of Nabha was forced to relinquish control of his state to a British administrator in 1923 after he was suspected of kidnapping and attempted murder through poisoning. He was formally deposed for sedition in 1928 and exiled to Kodaikanal.

17. CHITTOOR AND BANGALORE 1934–35

1. The judicial commissioner was the chief judge of appeal and his court was the final appellate court.
2. Lieutenant Colonel Charles Terence Chichele Plowden (1883–1956) was appointed as political agent to the Baluchistan States in 1920 and Resident in Mysore from 1933–37. At the end of the Second World War he served as a Press Reader in the British Embassy in Moscow. Every Plowden in India was a descendant of Richard Plowden, who had joined the East India Company as a 'writer' in the 1770s, and the family belonged to 'the closest thing that Anglo-India had to an aristocracy, based partly on class but principally on Indian service'. Charles Allen, *Kipling Sahib* (London: Abacus, 2007), p. 84.

3. Whiteside's unofficial hobby was woodcarving and he employed several first-class native workmen to carry out his beautiful designs in St Luke's Church, Chittoor, where the lectern and the font were 'striking works of art both in design and execution'. The Rev. Frank Penny, *The Church in Madras* (London: Smith, Elder, 1904), p. 43.
4. Sir Christopher Hughes Masterman, Mss Eur C319, AAS BL, p. 3.
5. Trevelyan, *The India We Left*, pp. 120–1.
6. Ibid, p. 113.
7. Citing maladministration, the British took direct control of Mysore in 1831, and for the next fifty years the state was ruled by a succession of British commissioners, the most notable of whom was Sir Mark Cubbon, who served from 1834 until 1861 and put into place an efficient and successful administrative system. In 1881 Maharaja Chamaraja X, educated by the British, assumed the rule of the state following the success of a lobby set up by the Wodeyar dynasty, who were in favour of rendition. A resident British officer was appointed at the Mysore court with a diwan to handle the administration, and the Wodeyars continued their rule until Indian independence in 1947.
8. Trevelyan, *The India We Left*, pp. 196–7.

18. THE HONOURABLE MR JUSTICE 1935–47

1. Literally the upper civil court. The British established Sudder Dewani Adaulats to hear civil disputes in matters arising in the districts under their control.
2. Ewing Papers, CCSAS, F. W. A. Morris, No. 41.
3. In the last quarter of 1906, Madras was hit by the worst financial crisis in its history. Arbuthnot and Co., a mercantile bank established in 1810, was the city's strongest commercial organisation in the city. Prior to its collapse, it employed between 11,000 and 12,000 people, had 7,000 creditors and £1,000,000 in liabilities. The bank entered into an arrangement with a businessman, Patrick Macfadyen, who effectively operated Arbuthnot's London branch. Macfadyen engaged in speculation, in the process losing huge amounts of the firm's money, and subsequently committed suicide. The senior partner of the bank, Sir George Arbuthnot, was tried for fraudulent activity and received a sentence of eighteen months' imprisonment.
4. Raja Sir Annamalai Chettiar was also an educationalist and philanthropist who is largely remembered for his social works and endowments in Tamil Nadu. He also served a term as a member of the Council of State, the upper house of the legislature for British India.
5. In 1947 Sastri was made a judge of the Federal Court, which

subsequently became the Supreme Court. Following the unexpected death of Chief Justice Sir Harilal Kania in 1951, Sastri was appointed Chief Justice of India until he reached retirement age in 1954.

6. Shortly afterwards, shattered by the death of his son, S. Doraiswami Iyer created a sensation by 'suddenly abandoning his very lucrative practice and retiring to an ashram in Pondicherry … to live the life of a religious recluse' which was a great loss to the Madras bar.
7. A region comprising the southern third of current Vietnam in which the principal city is Ho Chi Minh City.
8. Sir Lionel served as Chief Justice of the Madras High Court from 1937 to 1947 and was a member of the Judicial Committee of the Privy Council in London from 1949 to 1960.
9. *The Times*, 16 April 1938.
10. Masterman Papers, CCSAS, Answers to questionnaire set out by Dr. Christopher Bayly, July 1973.

19. GARDENING IN SOUTH INDIA

1. Croton is an extensive flowering plant genus of the spurge family, Euphorbiaceae, which grows to a height of six to eight feet.
2. Cottingley at 24 Anderson Road in the inner suburb of Nunqambakkam stands on land which was once part of the 110-acre orchards and gardens created by Dr James Anderson while he was surgeon-general and later physician-general in Madras from 1781. The house in which the Wadsworths lived was built in about 1912 and is still one of the best remaining 'garden houses' (bungalow plans with villa elevations) in Chennai, with ornamental iron gates which had formerly stood at Cochin Palace, the Maharaja of Travancore's Madras residence. It is currently the residence for the British deputy high commissioner in southern India.
3. Thevetia peruviana, also called Yellow Oleander, is a large shrub or small tree up to ten to twenty feet tall.
4. A common herb with catkin inflorescence.
5. Also called the wishbone flower or bluewings.
6. Sugar cane was brought in from Mauritius by the society for research purposes in order to understand its potential for growth in the climate of southern India.
7. Bradfield Papers, CCSAS, *Unimportant Story*, p. 50.

20. MADRAS AT WAR

1. C. V. Narasimham, *Memoirs of District Officers of the Indian Civil Service 1930–47*, Mss Eur F180/56, AAS BL, p. 7.

2. The Madras Forest College, a fine redbrick Indo-Saracenic building with a campus of about 195 acres, was inaugurated by Lord Pentland, Governor of Madras, in 1915.
3. Brodie Castle on the banks of the Adyar is one of the historic homes of Chennai, with two castellated turrets, built by James Brodie of the firm Jarvis and Brodie in 1796. The house is said to have brought ill luck to several of its residents. Brodie himself drowned in the Adyar and, one afternoon in October 1943, the Adyar burst its banks and destroyed many of Sir Lionel Leach's possessions. Lawyers had a good time imagining the dour judge sitting in his high-backed chair and futilely commanding the river to rise no further. *The Hindu*, 2 May 2013.
4. Paul Jayarajan, *Facets of My Life under the British Raj*, Mss Eur C509, AAS BL, p. 55.

21. ENVOI

1. As early as 1920 Maulana Shaukat Ali, an Indian Muslim leader of the Khilafat Movement, declared to a British officer that 'it's you British who do the ruling, but it's we, Muslims and Hindus, who do the dividing'. Paper read to a Wimbledon society in February 1963 by Arthur Beatson Reid (ICS 1888–1965), F173/247, AAS BL, p. 23.
2. Ramaswami Ayyangar Gopalswami, *Administration in India, Section II*, Mss Eur D1064, AAS, BL.
3. H. J. Downing, Mss Eur F180/50, AAS BL, pp. 28–9.

BIBLIOGRAPHY

Secondary sources

Allen, Charles, *Kipling Sahib* (London: Abacus, 2007).

Baker, C. J., *The Politics of South India, 1919–1939* (Cambridge: Cambridge University Press, 1976).

Barlow, Glyn, *The Story of Madras* (London: Oxford University Press, 1921).

Beals, Alan R., *Gopalpur: A South Indian Village* (New York: Rinehart and Winston, 1962).

Besant, Annie, *How India Wrought for Freedom* (Madras: Theosophical Publishing House, 1915).

Beteille, Andre, *Studies in Agrarian Social Structure* (Delhi: Oxford University Press, 1974).

Bhattacharya, S., *Southern Indian Economy: Agrarian Change, Industrial Structure and Social Stratification* (London: Asia Publishing House, 1969).

Blunt, Sir Edward, *The ICS—the Indian Civil Service* (London: Faber, 1937).

Braibanti, Ralph and Joseph J. Spengler, *Administration and Economic Development in India* (Durham: Duke University Press, 1963).

Brown, Hilton, *Dictators Limited. A novel without incident* (London: Allen and Unwin, 1923).

Brown, Judith M., *Gandhi and Civil Disobedience: the Mahatma in Indian Politics* (Cambridge: Cambridge University Press, 2008).

Burra, Arudra, 'The ICS and the nationalist movement: neutrality, politics and continuity', *Commonwealth and Comparative Politics*, Vol. 48, No. 4, November 2010.

Caesar, Adrian, *Dividing Lines: Poetry, Class and Ideology in the 1930s* (New York: Manchester University Press, 1991).

Chettur, S. K., *The Steel Frame and I: Life in the ICS* (Bombay: Asia Publishing House, 1962).

Chirol, Valentine, *India Old and New* (London: Macmillan, 1921).

'Civilian' (J. C. Molony), *The Civilian's South India* (London: John Lane, 1921).

Cohn. Bernard S., 'Society and social change under the Raj', *Indo-British Review*, Vol. III, No. 3 (January–March 1971).

Cotton, Sir Henry, *Indian and Home Memories* (London: T. Fisher Unwin, 1911).

Coupland, R., *The Constitutional Problem in India* (London: Oxford University Press, 1943).

Dewey, Clive, *Anglo-Indian Attitudes: the Mind of the Indian Civil Service* (London: Hambledon, 1993).

Dirks, Nicholas, *Castes of Mind; Colonialism and the Making of New India* (Princeton: Princeton University Press, 2001).

———, *Scandal of Empire: India and the Creation of Imperial Britain* (Cambridge: Harvard University Press, 2006).

———, 'The Policing of Tradition: Colonialism and Anthropology in Southern India', *Comparative Studies in Society and History*, Vol. 39, No. 1, January 1997.

Dutt, R. C., *Land Problems in India* (Madras: G. A. Nateson, 1903).

Gallagher, John, Gordon Johnson and Anil Seal (eds), *Locality, Province and Nation: Essays on Indian Politics, 1870–1940* (Cambridge: Cambridge University Press, 1973).

Gilmour, David, *The Ruling Caste: Imperial Lives in the Victorian Raj* (London: John Murray, 2005).

Gopal, Ram, *British Rule in India, an Assessment* (New York: Asia Publishing House, 1963).

Groseclose, Barbara, *British Sculpture and the Company Raj* (Delaware: University of Delaware Press, 1995).

Guha, Ranajit, *Subaltern Studies: Writings on South Asian History and Society* (Delhi: Oxford University Press, 1982).

Horne, W. O., *Work and Sport in the Old ICS* (London: Blackwood, 1928).

Hunt, Roland and John Harrison, *The District Officer in India, 1935–1947* (London: Scolar Press, 1985).

Hutchins, Sir Philip, *An Indian Career, 1858–1908* (private publication, 1926).

Judd, Denis, *The Lion and the Tiger: the Rise and Fall of the British Raj 1600–1947* (Oxford: Oxford University Press, 2004).

———, *Empire: the British Imperial Experience from 1765 to the Present* (London: Harper Collins, 1996).

Keay, John, *A History of India* (London: Harper Collins, 2000).

Keen, Caroline, *Princely India and the British: Political Development and the Operation of Empire* (London: I. B. Tauris, 2012).

Kipling, Rudyard, *The Song of the Cities, Collected Verse of Rudyard Kipling* (New York: Doubleday, Page, 1907).

Lawson, Sir Charles, *Memories of Madras* (London: Swan Sonnenschein, 1905).

Low. D. A., *Congress and the Raj: Facets of the Indian Struggle, 1917–1947* (London: Heinemann, 1977).

Machonochie, Evan, *Life in the Indian Civil Service* (London: Chapman and Hall, 1926).

Macleod, R. D., *Impressions of an Indian Civil Servant* (London: Witherby, 1938).

Metcalf, Barbara D. and Thomas R. Metcalf, *A Concise History of Modern India* (Cambridge: Cambridge University Press, 2006).

Metcalf, Thomas R., *Ideologies of the Raj* (Cambridge: Cambridge University Press, 1995).

Misra, B. B., *The Administrative History of India, 1834–1947* (Delhi: Oxford University Press, 1991).

Moon, Penderel, *Divide and Quit* (London: Chatto and Windus, 1962).

Moore, R. J., *The Crisis of Indian Unity, 1917–1940* (Oxford: Oxford University Press, 1974).

Mount, Ferdinand, *The Tears of the Rajas* (London: Simon and Schuster, 2015).

Muthiah, S., *Madras Rediscovered* (Chennai: East West Books, 2008).

Nair, Sir C. Sankaran, *Gandhi and Anarchy* (Madras: Tagore, 1922)

O'Malley, L. S. S., *The Indian Civil Service* (London: Frank Cass, 1965).

Penny, Fanny, *Fort St George, Madras* (London: Swan Sonnenschein, 1900).

Penny, the Rev. Frank, *The Church in Madras* (London: Smith, Elder, 1904).

Pillai, G. Paramaswarah, *Representative Men of Southern India* (London: W. H. Allen, 1889).

Rao, K. Sreerajjani Subba, *Struggle for Freedom: Case Study of the East Godaveri District, 1905–1947* (New Delhi: Mittal Publications, 1989).

Rice, Henry, *Native Life in India* (Oakland, CA: Pacific Press Publishing, 1891).

Robb, Peter and David Taylor, *Rule, Protest, Identity: Aspects of Modern South Asia* (London: Curzon Press, 1978).

Schroder, Ulrike, 'Hook-Swinging in South India: Negotiating the Subaltern Space within a Colonial Society', in *Negotiating Rites*, Ute Husken and Frank Neubert (eds) (New York: Oxford University Press, 2012).

Sharp, Sir Henry, *Goodbye India* (London: Oxford University Press, 1946).

Spangenberg, Bradford, *British Bureaucracy in India* (Columbia, MO: South Asia Books, 1976).

Spilsbury, Julian, *The Indian Mutiny* (London: Weidenfeld and Nicholson, 2007).

Srinivasachari, C. S., *History of the City of Madras* (Madras: P. Varadachari, 1939).

Stoddart, Brian, *A People's Collector in the British Raj: Arthur Galletti* (New Delhi: Readworthy, 2011).

The Imperial Gazetteer of India, Madras Vol. I (Calcutta: Government of India Press, 1908).

Tillotson, G.H.R., *The Tradition of Indian Architecture: Continuity, Controversy and Change since 1850* (New Haven and London: Yale University Press, 1989).

———, 'Orientalizing the Raj: Indo-Saracenic Fantasies' in Christopher W. London (ed), *Architecture in Victorian and Edwardian India* (Bombay: South Asia Books, 1994).

Trevelyan, Humphrey, *The India We Left* (London: Macmillan, 1972).

Vadivelu, A., *The Aristocracy of Southern India* (Madras: Vest, 1903).

Washbrook, D. A., *The Emergence of Provincial Politics: The Madras Presidency, 1870–1920* (Cambridge: Cambridge University Press, 1976).

Washbrook, D. A. and C. J. Baker, *South India: Political Institutions and Political Change, 1880–1940* (Delhi: Macmillan, 1975).

Woodruff (Mason), Philip, *The Men Who Ruled India, Vol II The Guardians* (London: Cape, 1971).

Primary sources

British Library: Asian and African Studies (AAS BL) Private Papers

Indian Civil Service Memoirs Madras 1930–47 F 180/49–57
H. H. Carleston F180/49
H. J. Downing F180/50
S. W. C. Dunlop F180/51
W. W. Georgeson F180/52
R. C. Hope F180/53
W. G. Lamarque F180/54
J. E. Maher F180/55
C. V. Narasimhan F180/56
A. J. Platt F180/57

F525 Arthur Reginald Brand
F487 C. Eileen Butterfield
C326 Nancy Dearmer
D1039 Sidney William Cecil Dunlop
D596 Lord Erskine
E312 Yvonne Fitzroy
MSS Eur Photo 112 James Thomas Gillespie
D1064 Ramaswami Ayyangar Gopalaswami
C429 George Goschen
D1111 John Coldwell Griffiths
C363 William Francis Alfred Hamilton
F241 Margaret Hunt
C509 Paul Marcus Jayarajan, Facets of My Life under the British Raj
E353 John Edward Maher

C319 Sir Christopher Hughes Masterman
D832/1 and D832/2 Arthur James Platt
F472 Capt. Melville Portal
F173/247 Arthur Beatson Reid, The Indian Civil Service in Historical Perspective
F304 Euphemia Stokes
F226/29 Sir (Joseph) Herbert Thompson
C353 Alan Robert Cecil Westlake
C796 James Williams
C545 Oliver Hugh Wooller, The Administrative Origins of the Friends of Vellore
C413 Women's Christian Colleges in Madras

Cambridge Centre of South Asian Studies (CCSAS) Private Papers

J. M. Bourne
Sir Ernest Bradfield

Ewing Papers Answers: to ICS Questionnaire
6 W. W. Georgeson
8 J. P. L. Gwynn
17 C. F. V. Williams
26 & 27 B. W. Day
30 R. Galletti
41 F. W. A. Morris
42 A. J. Platt
47 A. R. C. Westlake

R. C. C. Hunt
A. Innes Cox
T. I. S. Mackay
Sir Christopher Masterman
A. J. Platt
Sir Richard Tottenham

INDEX